BLACK WOMEN IN
UNITED STATES HISTORY

Editor

DARLENE CLARK HINE

Associate Editors

ELSA BARKLEY BROWN

TIFFANY R.L. PATTERSON

LILLIAN S. WILLIAMS

Research Assistant

EARNESTINE JENKINS

A CARLSON PUBLISHING SERIES

See the end of this volume for a comprehensive
guide to this sixteen-volume set.

Ida B. Wells-Barnett

AN EXPLORATORY STUDY OF AN AMERICAN BLACK WOMAN, 1893-1930

Mildred I. Thompson

CARLSON
Publishing Inc

BROOKLYN, NEW YORK, 1990

See the end of this volume for a comprehensive guide to the sixteen-volume set of which this is Volume Fifteen.

Library of Congress Cataloging-in-Publication Data

Thompson, Mildred I., 1929-
    Ida B. Wells-Barnett : an exploratory study of an American Black
woman, 1893-1930 / Mildred I. Thompson.
        p.   cm. — (Black women in United States history ; v. 15)
    Includes bibliographical references.
    ISBN 0-926019-21-X
    1. Wells-Barnett, Ida B., 1862-1931. 2. Afro-Americans–
–Biography. 3. Civil rights workers—United States—Biography.
4. Lynching—United States—History. 5. Afro-Americans—Civil
rights. 6. United States—Race relations. I. Title II. Series.
E185.86.B543 vol. 15
[E185.97.W55]
973'.0496073 s—dc20
[973'.049607302]
[B]   90-1399

Typographic design: Julian Waters

Typeface: Bitstream ITC Galliard

The index to this book was created using NL Cindex, a scholarly indexing program from the Newberry Library.

This book was originally written as a Ph.D. dissertation in 1979 at George Washington University. It has been edited for publication. Ida B. Wells-Barnett's *Selected Essays* are gathered together here for the first time.

Printed on acid-free, 250-year-life paper.

Manufactured in the United States of America.

Contents

List of Illustrations xi
Preface—1990 xiii
I.   Introduction 1
II.   Beginnings in the South 11
III.   The Beginning of the Anti-Lynching Crusade 25
IV.   Introduction to Chicago 41
V.   The Second British Tour 51
VI.   White Racism and Black Organizational Response 67
VII.   Social and Civic Activity in Chicago 85
VIII.   Politics and Legal Action in Illinois 107
IX.   Conclusion: A Brand-New Thing 127
Notes 131
Bibliography 149

IDA B. WELLS: SELECTED ESSAYS

Publisher's Note 163
1. Afro-Americans and Africa 165
2. Lynch Law in All Its Phases 171
3. The Reason Why
        Chapter IV. Lynch Law, by Ida B. Wells 195
        Chapter VI. The Reason Why, by F. L. Barnett 209
4. Two Christmas Days: A Holiday Story 225
5. Lynch Law in America 235
6. The Negro's Case in Equity 245
7. Lynching and the Excuse for It 249
8. Booker T. Washington and His Critics 255
9. Lynching, Our National Crime 261
10. How Enfranchisement Stops Lynching 267
11. Our Country's Lynching Record 277
Index 281

Guide to the Series . . . . follows index

List of Illustrations

All illustrations are courtesy of the Department of Special Collections, The Joseph Regenstein Library, The University of Chicago, unless otherwise indicated.

1. Ida B. Wells in the 1890s . . . . frontispiece
    (Courtesy of the Schomburg Center, NYPL)
2. Ida B. Wells (ca. 1887). From I. Garland Penn,
    The Afro-American Press and Its Editors,
    Springfield, Mass., Wiley and Co., 1891. 21
    (Courtesy of the Schomburg Center, NYPL)
3. Ida B. Wells, Maureen Moss, Betty Moss,
    Tom Moss, Jr. (ca. 1893) 31
4. Ida B. Wells-Barnett and Charles Aked Barnett
    (ca. Oct. 1896) 73
5. Ida B. Wells-Barnett, with Charles A. Barnett, 14,
    Herman K. Barnett, 12, Ida B. Barnett, Jr., 8,
    and Alfreda M. Barnett, 5. (1909) 95
6. Ida B. Wells-Barnett, with Ida B. Barnett, Jr.,
    and Alfreda M. Barnett. (ca. 1914) 103
7. The Barnett family in 1917 111
8. Ida B. Wells-Barnett wearing her controversial button:
    "In Memorial MARTYRED NEGRO SOLDIERS" after the
    execution of the soldiers following the incident in
    Brownsville, Texas. (December 1917) 121
9. Posed scene by a traveling photographer at a
    lynching in Clanton, Alabama. (August 1891) 205
10. Back of photograph, with inscription 206

Preface
1990

When I began this study in 1975, I had just noted the name of Ida B. Wells in a list of three examples of nineteenth-century black feminists. Recognizing the other two, I wondered why I knew nothing of Wells. I was then teaching at Rosary College in River Forest, Illinois, and a quick check in *Notable American Women* provided information that directed me to her daughter, Alfreda Duster in nearby Chicago.

My first weeks of research were done at the Duster home, before the Ida B. Wells Papers were deposited at the Department of Special Collections, The Joseph Regenstein Library, The University of Chicago. Duster had edited and published her mother's autobiography five years earlier. She became a great source of information and encouragement to me.

The questions I hoped to answer in my study were: 1. Why had I not encountered Wells in the texts and lectures that were part of the black American history courses I had taken? 2. Would the public record show her to be the civil rights activist she claimed to be in her autobiography? 3. How were her last years spent? Digging through the newspaper records, the old histories and the public documents related to Wells's civil rights activities was a tedious but inspiring challenge.

Here was a women whose life exemplified concepts that seemed to be opposites, concepts that can be inclusive. She was an integrationist, aspiring to participate in the general society with the privileges of first class citizenship. On the other hand, having learned resourcefulness and independence at an early age, she was unwilling to wait for others to hand her rights she considered hers in the first place. There is no doubt that Wells-Barnett was an aggressive woman. It is fair to say that she was an angry woman. Motivated as she was, however, she researched, wrote, lectured and acted in the interest of equal opportunities and equal treatment for black men and women in American society and politics.

At the time I wrote my dissertation, Chicago had named a housing project in honor of Ida B. Wells, and the home in which she lived was designated a National Historical Landmark. Recognition of her place in the nation's history is today much more widespread through the National Educational Television program about her and through the United States Postal Service issuance of a stamp in her honor as part of the Negro Heritage Series.

It is particularly gratifying to have my work included in the Carlson Publishing series, *Black Women in United States History*. My continued thanks go to Clarence C. Mondale, who directed my dissertation at The George Washington University, and to the other scholarly readers for their helpful comments. I am grateful, also, for the confidence and support assured me by my religious congregation, the Dominican Sisters of Sinsinawa, Wisconsin, and to the members of my family in Mobile and in San Antonio.

Mildred Thompson
January 25, 1990

Ida B. Wells-Barnett

ONE

Introduction

T. Thomas Fortune wrote in 1893 of Ida B. Wells, "No history of the Afro-American of the future will be complete in which this woman's work has not a place." This statement was no small compliment, coming from the New York editor whom John Hope Franklin describes as "preeminent among the secular black leaders of his time." It was prompted by the young black woman's journalistic success and her daring in having confronted racists in the South on three occasions. She had been the loser in each instance, but she had brought attention to the black American's unwillingness to accept less than the equal treatment provided by the law. With almost prophetic insight, Fortune mused on her place in history:

> There is scarcely any reason why this woman, young in years and old in experience, shall not be found in the forefront of the great intellectual fight in which the race is now engaged for absolute right and justice under the Constitution. No other woman of the race occupies today a better position to do good work, or is more generously endowed to perform it. Strong in her devotion to race, strong in the affections of her people, and strong in the estimation of influential men, co-workers with her in the cause, with all the future hers, if she fails to impress her personality upon the time in which she lives, whose fault will it be?[1]

The question was well placed, for Ida Wells's activity in the civil rights movement has until recently been lost to the collective memory of the race and the nation. During the last year of her life, she brooded over the fact that the founder of the Association for the Study of Negro Life and History had not recognized her anti-lynching effort in his highly regarded and much used volume *The Negro in Our History*.[2]

An article by Pauli Murray, black feminist, attorney, educator, activist and later Episcopalian priest, indicated that the omission of Wells-Barnett from the Woodson treatise was not exceptional. Using the Association's official publication, *The Journal of Negro History*, as a basis for her study, Dr. Murray states that even in this day when the black male is finally finding a place in American history, the black woman remains the neglected entity.

Of the many books published on the Negro experience and the Black Revolution in recent times, to date not one has concerned itself with the struggles of black women and their contributions to history. Of approximately 800 full-length articles published in *The Journal of Negro History* since its inception in 1916, only six have dealt directly with the Negro woman.[3]

At the time Fortune wrote, professional black men acknowledged black women as equals. Fortune wrote about Miss Wells, "She handles her subjects more as a man than as a woman; indeed she has so long had the management of a large home and business interests that the sharpness of wit and self-possession which characterize men of affairs are hers in large measure."[4] In 1894, her "forcible pen" and "her caustic oddness" were noted by Monroe A. Majors for having "disarmed the disputing South as to women's ability and set up a sign post portraying her power with the pen."[5] The author Lucy Wilmot Smith indicated in 1889 that there were several proven black women journalists, and she observed that unlike their white American sisters, black women who had been educated were invited to participate in the professions with their brothers.[6] But they have not been remembered. In 1971, Roland E. Wolseley, in his study of the black press, acknowledges: "The women editors and writers of the nineteenth century have been ignored as journalists by almost all who have written on black journalism. Possibly the one woman journalist of the nineteenth century remembered in this century was Mrs. Ida B. Wells-Barnett."[7]

Various scholars have studied the sociological changes in the position of black women. It is in the context of these changes that the neglect of Ida Wells-Barnett can be understood. Dr. Murray states that during the period of slavery black women learned independence and self-reliance for survival. She quotes Dr. E. Franklin Frazier, who says that these characteristics in the black woman "provided generally a pattern of equalitarian relationship between men and women in America." The sociologist explains, "Neither economic necessity nor tradition has instilled in her the spirit of subordination to masculine authority. Emancipation only tended to confirm in many cases the spirit of self-sufficiency which slavery had wrought." Murray notes that apart from the family's need for her support partially or entirely, there was the black community's need to draw on all its resources.[8]

Many of the post-Reconstruction black leaders in the North, however, were descendants of free blacks of the South and those closely associated with the plantation families, who patterned their social ideas and behavior on the patriarchal household. In explaining male ascendancy, Dr. Frazier indicates that black men, free before the Civil War, gained a dominant role in their families through the acquisition of property and the economic subordination of women. These men, he contends, were responsible for giving black family life its institutional character. In some financially secure families, the wife generally depended on her husband's support, and her leisure was considered a sign of superior social class. Black emulation of white society was transferred to the lower classes through the middle class.[9] Dr. Murray, referring to the superior attitude of black men toward women, observes, "While Blacks generally have recognized the fusion of white supremacy and male dominance . . . male spokesmen for Negro rights have sometimes pandered to sexism in their fight against racism."[10]

In the civil rights struggle, effective race leadership became a masculine prerogative. St. Clair Drake and Horace Cayton indicate that whether or not male race leaders lived up to the community's expectations of sincerity and constancy, they were respected for their race pride. These writers go so far as to say that in reality the motives of race leaders were often suspect. Race men were regarded no less as leaders, however, when their plans and procedures for community welfare worked to their personal advantage. On the other hand, race women were expected to be honest, but little faith was put in their ability to be effective. The authors of *Black Metropolis* quote a businessman: "A Race Woman is sincere; she can't capitalize on her activities like a Race Man." She was described as a forceful, fearless, outspoken champion of rights, idealized as a fighter, but associated with uplift. She was not taken seriously as an agent of change in the general society. The cynical recognized her intelligence and forcefulness but belittled her influence as slight among whites.[11]

In view of black women's treatment by historians, black or white, Ida B. Wells-Barnett fares no better and no worse than most. Fortune's question about her, nonetheless, is not easily dismissed: "If she fails to impress her personality upon the time in which she lives, whose fault will it be?"[12] Ida B. Wells was not simply neglected by historians and cynics. She was forgotten and sometimes shunned by some of her notable contemporaries engaged in the struggle for civic and social progress for black Americans.

In 1951, Herbert Aptheker attested to the fact that Wells-Barnett's contributions were worthy of recognition: "This woman whose career has been sorely neglected had more to do with originating and carrying forward the anti-lynching crusade than any other single person."[13] Yet almost twenty

3

years later, Alfreda Duster, the daughter of Wells-Barnett and editor of her autobiography, emphasized the isolation in which her mother worked and again called attention to the scholarly neglect of her achievements.

> The most remarkable thing about Ida B. Wells-Barnett is not that she fought lynching and other forms of barbarism. It is rather that she fought a lonely and almost single-handed fight, with the single-mindedness of a crusader, long before men or women of any race entered the arena; and the measure of success she achieved goes far beyond the credit she has been given in the history of the country.[14]

Despite an awakening of interest in this black woman, no extensive study of her activities is available beyond her autobiography, written almost entirely from memory.[15] In 1941, a master's thesis entitled "Ida B. Wells-Barnett: Her Contribution to the Field of Social Welfare" was completed by Eunice Rivers Walker. It quotes copiously from interviews, but follows closely the material in Mrs. Barnett's manuscript. Two unpublished papers on the effects in America of Ida B. Wells's European tours were delivered by Lloyd W. Crawford at meetings of the Association for the Study of Negro Life and History in 1958 and 1962. Albert Kreiling's 1973 dissertation, "The Making of Racial Identities in the Black Press: A Cultural Analysis of Race Journalism in Chicago, 1878-1929," deals with F. L. and Ida Barnett as journalists and Afro-American agitators. A study concentrating on the rhetorical form of Wells's anti-lynching lectures during 1892-95 was done as a doctoral dissertation by Mary Hutton in 1975. Several biographical anthologies contain sketches of the life of Wells-Barnett, and a number of documentary studies include portions of her speeches or writings. The most substantial research has been done on her anti-lynching crusade and her place among journalists.

The purpose of this study is to supply data on Wells-Barnett not brought together before and to explore her various contributions to black civic and social progress. This project began as an attempt to authenticate the story of Ida Wells-Barnett's life and achievements as she recorded them. Since she saw herself as an effective anti-lynching agitator and civil rights worker, neglected by a noted black historian and ignored by her contemporaries, my task was to find evidence to support or deny her assessments of her achievements and to explain to some extent her failure to be recognized.

The research involved gathering fragments of data from scattered sources. The collection of Ida B. Wells Papers, contributed to the University of

Chicago by Alfreda Duster, is limited in content and scope, but it contains valuable materials. Among these are the original manuscript of Wells-Barnett's autobiography and two diaries, one covering 1886-87 and another 1930, which give useful insights into the personality of their author. Other valuable items in the collection are the pamphlet *The Reason Why the Colored American Is Not in the World's Columbian Exposition*, by Frederick Douglass, I. Garland Penn, and Ferdinand L. Barnett with Ida B. Wells, and *A History of the Club Movement among Colored Women of the United States of America*, composed of the minutes of the 1895 and 1896 meetings held in Boston and Washington, respectively. Only one letter written by Barnett to her family remains among her papers to reveal her maternal sentiments. In a number of personal interviews, Alfreda Duster filled in much helpful information on the Barnett family and the Chicago in which they lived.

Ida B. Wells published three pamphlets on the problem of lynching: *Southern Horrors*, *A Red Record*, and *Mob Rule in New Orleans*. A number of her articles on race appeared in such liberal magazines as the *Arena*, the *Independent*, and *Survey*. Her anti-lynching publications are significant for their presentation of statistics and detailed descriptions of lynchings as they were given in the white press. They contain Wells's arguments against the current rationalizations for the practice and her vitriolic protest against the inaction of the federal government as well as the credulity of influential national leaders in accepting the South's rape myth. The chief sources of data on her activities are black newspapers, which carried articles by and about her. The column "Ida B. Wells Abroad," which ran in the *Chicago Inter-Ocean*, a white paper, during her European anti-lynching crusade is useful. Several articles that appeared in the Memphis press show that city's reaction to her protest campaign, while a limited number of news items in *The New York Times* and the *Chicago Tribune* indicate the national attention her activities gained at various times. Scattered among the papers of such persons as Frederick Douglass, Albion Tourgee, Joel Spingarn, and Mary Church Terrell are letters that shed light on her relations with these people and on organizations and activities in which she was involved. Although few in number, the public documents that bear on her projects in Illinois supplement with precise information her own record of events in the state. These are housed at the State Archives at Springfield. Folders and files held by the Chicago Historical Society and the University of Illinois, Chicago Circle, contain material on her participation in women's organizations and in the women's suffrage movement. Among the Claude A. Barnett Papers and the Municipal Court Papers at the Chicago Historical Society, there are several items related to her Republican Party activities.

These documents testify that Wells-Barnett continued her anti-lynching protest while she was involved with women's clubs, the women's suffrage movement, and a settlement house for downtrodden black men in Chicago. In her effort to interest a group of young black men and women in the less fortunate newcomers to Chicago, she set up with them a shelter and reading room for homeless men. Her salary as a politically appointed probation officer enabled her to maintain the facility, which did not receive the community support she had anticipated. Unlike many other prominent black woman of her time in Chicago, she was politically aware and active. Not only did she encourage black voters to use their vote effectively, she also used her influence among them to campaign for politicians amenable to black progress. She supported her husband's political bid for a judgeship and ran for a state senate seat. For a time she relinquished the more strenuous aspects of civic and social work in order to assume more fully the responsibilities she felt toward her prominent lawyer-husband, her two stepsons, and the four children of her marriage. This lull in activity ended when racial tensions and attempts at subverting the civil rights laws of Illinois called her into action. The relationships between this outspoken woman and other social and civic leaders were often very uneasy, frequently resulting in disregard for her and her efforts.

Once the questions of Mrs. Barnett's place in her community and her contributions had been researched, there remained the problem of her decline in popularity after her initial triumphs and her failure to be taken seriously by prominent blacks during the last years of her still-active life. This question seemed to be best approached from the point of view of developments in the black community. For the purpose of exploring her relationships in the society in which she lived and operated, a number of sociological studies were used. Most helpful were E. Franklin Frazier's *Black Bourgeoisie* and *The Negro Family in the United States*, Allan Spear's *Black Chicago*, St. Clair Drake and Horace Cayton's *Black Metropolis*, and Harold Gosnell's *Negro Politicians*. Two recent works add new insights to these studies. Albert Kreiling's cultural interpretation brings attention to characteristics of the Afro-American agitators, who the author contends have been overlooked in the emphasis of historians on the Washington-Du Bois dispute. Charles Branham's "Black Chicago: Accommodationist Politics before the Great Migration," a chapter in *The Ethnic Frontier*, edited by Melvin Holli and

Peter d'A. Jones, gives a succinct analysis of the history of the black politicians' link with the Chicago political machine.

Ida B. Wells retained throughout her life a spirit of independence and self-reliance reinforced by her early successes as an aggressive and outspoken agitator for racial justice. Her family background might have prepared her for greater compliance with the social expectations for women of her professional class, but adverse circumstances interfered. While her parents were slaves, her father was the son of his master and belonged to that favored class whose close association with the ruling families allowed them to imbibe the patterns of thought and behavior of the white society. He had lived under the protection of his father and had been trained as a skilled artisan. As a family man, he assumed the leading role as provider and head of his household.[16] This early experience of well-regulated family life with father and mother playing distinct roles came abruptly to an end, however, when Ida was sixteen. The result was that she, in a real sense, assumed the roles of provider and manager of the household, taking the place of both her father and mother, as head of the family.

By profession, marriage, and association, Ida Wells-Barnett was a member of the black social elite of Chicago. Unlike others of this middle-class group, she maintained a bond with the black masses and was inclined to be critical of those whose social position and ambition removed them from the needs of the lower class. It is of interest that Frazier points out the tendency of the black bourgeoisie, in its struggle for acceptance by whites, to neglect its responsibility to the black community. He also observes, "Many individuals among the first generation of educated Negroes, who were the products of missionary education, had a sense of responsibility toward the Negro masses and identified themselves with the struggles of the masses to overcome ignorance and poverty."[17]

Ida Wells was the product of a Freedman's school. Her appreciation of the fact was demonstrated in a denunciation of Booker T. Washington's emphasis on industrial education. Her appraisal of the Northern teachers who were the first to give the freedmen the opportunity to learn as "intellect and ambition craved" was one of the most generous expressions of gratitude that her writings revealed. She wrote that their students "cherish most tender memories of the northern teachers who endured ostracism, insult and martyrdom to bring the spelling book and the Bible to educate those who had been slaves." She stressed that the essence of their work was the education of the lower classes, noting that they had sacrificed "to the end

7

that they brought the light of knowledge, the strength of manhood and the example of Christian culture to those who would otherwise have been without."[18] These were elements she found lacking in the ambitious middle-class blacks of her day.

Wells's adult experiences in the South had given her confidence and a sense of success. In 1889, she had enthusiastically endorsed the ideals enunciated by Fortune for his Afro-American League and had already exemplified the mission of the Afro-American agitator "to force the concession to him of absolute justice under State and Federal Constitutions."[19] She had managed to produce a self-sustaining newspaper that educated Southern blacks about their rights and pointed out when they were being infringed. In 1892, the lynching of her friends, members of the growing middle class in Memphis, changed the course of her life. She had already shown tendencies to be a radical race woman, but that event, her subsequent protest, and exile from the South gave her a sense of prophetic mission to crusade against lynching. Her fervor was reinforced by public acclaim and denunciation, indicating that she was being heard. The determination with which she carried on her anti-lynching crusade was transferred to every area of civil rights reform in which she was involved. Her single-minded persistence and aggressiveness lost their force, however, as leaders and organizational patterns changed.

In 1895, the year that Ida B. Wells took up residency in Chicago as the wife of Ferdinand Barnett, Frederick Douglass died. The elder statesman of the civil rights movement had been a strong supporter of the young woman propagandist. During Douglass's declining years, one of the strongest black protest voices was Well's benefactor, T. Thomas Fortune. The year of Douglass's death, however, witnessed the sudden rise of Booker T. Washington and a movement that had no place for radicals.[20]

It required eight years for W. E. B. Du Bois to take a stand against Washington, although it was his name that would be used to identify the opposition. By that time Ida Wells-Barnett and William Monroe Trotter, the radical editor of the *Boston Guardian*, had already denounced the accommodationist. Francis Broderick, the biographer of Du Bois, points out the "extravagant claims made by him and for him," and notes, "It is important to remember that Du Bois's position was less that of a pioneer than that of the first among equals: Trotter preceded him in fighting Washington, as did Ida Wells-Barnett; the Association [NAACP] brought Negroes and whites together in an entente in which Du Bois shared influence with others, first with Villard and Spingarn, later with Johnson and White."[21]

Mrs. Barnett congratulated Du Bois cordially when he published his opposition to Washington in *The Souls of Black Folk*. She could not be said, however, to have been his follower. Her assessment of him was that he was exclusive. She resented his indicating that nothing more than membership was expected of her in the NAACP, and this determined her decision not to "bother much with the Chicago branch."[22]

Conflict with Du Bois was inevitable. Barnett's need to dominate was as great as his arrogance appeared to her. She was a strong advocate of unity and solidarity, a founding spirit in organizational efforts, but she was temperamentally unsuited for mere participation. She expected to be a leader. Her frustration at seeing liberal whites at the head of civil rights endeavors and her tendency to voice her dissatisfaction, with blacks and whites, made her difficult and a center of conflict, better ignored than opposed. She distrusted the overarching mechanisms for uplift represented by the Urban League, which commanded the funds of white philanthropy influenced by Tuskegee, and which was detrimental to the survival of smaller enterprises like her own Negro Fellowship League.[23]

Although Mrs. Barnett shared her husband's political ambition, she was not disposed to placate community powers in the interest of his advancement. Her own political interest and activity extended beyond that of any other black woman in Chicago. The evidence indicates, however, that the Barnetts' loyalty to the Deneen faction of the Republican Party allowed other more pragmatic politicians to replace them as influential figures on the Chicago scene.[24]

This study of Ida Wells-Barnett reveals the complexity of a woman who was not merely engaged in almost constant civil rights activity, but who initiated many of these reform efforts. It points out some of the factors that motivated her daring and steadfastness in a climate of blatant racial prejudice, national indifference, and changing black ideologies. It also shows the relationship between her declining influence and the increasing significance of organizational powers in the black community. Ida Wells-Barnett was a militant civil rights activist during most of her adult life, but in her mature years she was out of step with her time, attuned to a drummer whom she had heard earlier, a drummer whose beat would not be heard again for another generation.

TWO

Beginnings
in the South

The Emancipation Proclamation was issued when Ida B. Wells was an infant. Her memory did not go back to actual bondage, but she knew of its harshness from the glimpses given by her parents, who lived in slavery until the close of the war. Born in Tippah County, Mississippi, her father, Jim Wells, was the son of his master and a slave woman, Peggy. He was spared some of the cruelties of the slave system; he was neither whipped nor sold. His father, who had no children by his wife, saw to it that the boy was trained as a carpenter and apprenticed him to a contractor, Mr. Bolling, in Holly Springs. Despite these concessions, Jim harbored the memory of his mother's being stripped and whipped at the command of the widowed Mrs. Wells the day after his father's death.

Lizzie Warrenton Wells, Ida B. Wells's mother, was born in Virginia. Her life had not been as protected as that of her husband. She had experienced the auction block, separation from family, beatings, and other miseries of slave life. In Holly Springs she was the cook at the Bolling place. Jim and she were married there as slaves and again as free persons. Their first child, Ida, was born on July 16, 1862.[1]

According to one account, the political scene in the Mississippi town at that time was tolerable. There was neither evidence of great corruption in the Republicans in power nor violent expressions of white outrage at the new order. Some of the leading residents joined the Republican Party, and relations between the two political organizations were generally considered decent. Two former slaves even gained some political prestige. One, Henry House, founded the Negro Democratic Club, which gathered enough black votes to warrant his being rewarded with a house. The other, James Hill, a Republican, was elected Mississippi secretary of state. The first two black senators to the United States Congress represented Mississippi, and one, Hiram Rhodes Revels, chose to live in Holly Springs in 1875. The relative peace among factions did not preclude some troublesome activity, however.

11

A black political society called the Loyal League held incendiary meetings with fiery rituals, which the Ku Klux Klan matched with its own brand of intimidation, vote-stealing, and tampering with elections.[2]

It was Jim Wells's first venture at exercising his right to vote that freed him from the ties of his apprenticeship. Refusing to cast his ballot for the Democratic ticket, as Bolling had advised him, he found himself locked out of his shop. Without troubling anyone, he rented a house some distance from the Bolling property for his family. He bought a set of tools and set up his own business.

He was a good provider, politically aware and active, and a trustee on the board of Shaw University, established by the Freedman's Aid. His children all went to school. Their mother attended class with them until she had learned to read the Bible. Thereafter she visited their classes. Discipline in the Wells home was guided by Lizzie, a religious woman. She saw to it that the children were regular in performance of housework, schoolwork, and religious service.[3]

By 1878, eight children had been born to the Wellses. That year a yellow fever epidemic decimated the population of Holly Springs. Jim, Lizzie, and their nine-month-old son, Stanley, were among its victims. Another son, Eddie, had died several years before. Sixteen-year-old Ida was staying in the country with her maternal grandmother, Peggy, when the news came that her parents had died. Because passenger trains had stopped running to the disease-ridden area, the oldest Wells offspring had to ride in the caboose of a freight train to return home. Neither the difficulty of travel nor the warnings about the danger deterred her, however, from going to care for the other five survivors. A physician who had high regard for Jim Wells was regularly visiting and providing nursing care for the children when Ida arrived. Once the epidemic had passed, the problem of finding homes for them was assumed by a Masonic group to which Jim had belonged. Their decision to send the children to different homes met with obstinate resistance from Ida. She insisted that she was old enough to be a provider. Their father had bought the house in which they lived; they had a home. She refused to have the family separated. The men scoffed at her determination, but were relieved of the responsibility and allowed her to have her way.[4]

When the disaster that had put her in charge of the household occurred, Ida was a student beginning the collegiate level of work at Shaw University. The school had been established in 1866 by a Northern Methodist missionary for the Freedman's Aid Society. In 1870, it was taken over by the

Mississippi Conference of the Methodist Church, which was dominated by Northern interests. (Later it was renamed Rust University.) At the time Ida was in school, Shaw University encompassed all levels of education.[5] Even though she did not graduate from the college course, the academic environment had a sturdy effect on her enthusiasm for learning. She later took private lessons in elocution and dramatics and spent several summers studying at Fisk University in Nashville, Tennessee.

With the knowledge she had acquired at Shaw, she passed the examination required for country schoolteachers. She used money left by her father to take care of brothers and sisters until school began. Ida was assigned to a school six miles from home. Her grandmother helped by coming to stay with the children during the week. After a year, she was invited by an aunt to bring the children to Memphis. She secured a teaching job in Woodstock in Shelby County. Here her salary was higher, and she prepared to take the city schoolteacher examination. It was here also that she had her first experience of jim crowism and began her career of protest.[6]

In May 1884, the young black teacher took a train from Memphis to Woodstock. When the conductor approached her, he informed her that he could not take her ticket where she sat. Finding her still in the ladies' car on his return, he told her that she would have to move to the other car. She refused, saying that the other car was the smoker and that she had bought a first-class ticket. When he attempted to remove her physically, she stubbornly resisted, biting his hand. Urged on by the white passengers, the conductor brought in the baggageman to assist him in dragging her off the coach. Since the train had stopped, she got off. In Memphis, she hired the only black lawyer, T. F. Cassells, and brought suit against the Chesapeake, Ohio and Southwestern Railroad.

Cassells was bought off by the railroad. Later, Wells wrote in her diary, "A tried friend of mine has unfolded a conspiracy to me that is on foot to quash the case. It is a painful fact that white men choose men of the race to accomplish the ruin of any young girl but that one would deliberately ask a man of reputation for the sake of gain is a startling commentary on the estimation in which our race is held."[7] Wells hired Judge Greer, a white associate of the black attorney, who won the suit before the Circuit Court. Judge J. O. Pierce ruled that the railroad company had failed to comply with two statutes, one of 1881 forbidding the railroads to charge black passengers first-class rates while providing second-class accommodations, and another of 1882 providing that blacks be given accommodations equal to those in first-class cars. The railroad was judged to have used a pretense at compliance by placing black passengers in a coach of the same construction as the first-class coach, which was reduced to second-class standard by the smoking and drunkenness permitted in it.

In awarding Wells damages, Pierce stated that the railroad had a right to use separate cars, but the grievance of the plaintiff was that she had not been offered equal accommodations. For this offense she was awarded $300. Because, in addition, she had been forcibly ejected from the coach, the judgment for the plaintiff was $500.[8]

When the railroad company appealed this decision before the Supreme Court of the state, Greer again represented Wells. The circumstances leading to the suit against the railroad, as reported at the time of the first court decision and as recorded by Wells, were reconstructed at the time of the appeal. The railroad asserted that Wells, who was designated a mulatto, had been halted before entering the rear car and had refused to submit her ticket except for a seat in that car, which was reserved for white ladies and their gentlemen attendants. A witness had indicated that there was no smoking in the forward car. The conductor was said to have threatened to put her off the train, but when it stopped some 400 feet on, "she was politely assisted from the car by a colored porter."

The Supreme Court ruled:

> The conduct of the plaintiff below was upon an idea without the slightest reason. Having offered as the statute provides, "accommodations equal in all respects in comfort and convenience to the first class cars on the train and subject to the rules governing other first class cars," the company had done all that could rightfully be demanded.
>
> We think it is evident that the purpose of the defendant in error was to harass with a view to this suit, and that her persistence was not in good faith to obtain a comfortable seat for the short ride.[9]

Judge Greer notified his client of the decision, indicating that four of the judges had decided, contrary to all the evidence, that "the smoking car was the first class coach for colored people and provided for by that statute that calls for separate coaches but first class, for the races."[10]

Wells initiated her suit against the railroad one year after the 1883 repeal of the Civil Rights Act. In spite of regained states' rights and the ferment among whites in the South reestablishing rules of white supremacy, she was disappointed that the first decision in her favor was overturned. In her autobiography many years later, she wrote, "There were no jim crow cars then."[11] Ever concerned with defending her rights, she was not one to tolerate a personal indignity nor to allow an unjust practice to go unchallenged. Even as the appeal was being decided, she continued to agitate against discrimination on the railroad. She noted in her diary in June 1886 that on a trip to Holly Springs, she and several friends refused the accommodations offered them and succeeded in getting first class seats.[12]

She lamented, "I had hoped such great things from my suit for my people generally. I have firmly believed all along that the law was on our side and would, when we appealed to it, give us justice."[13] Her disappointment was increased by the fact that she felt that the black people of Memphis were oblivious of the step she had taken and of its ramifications for them. She found some consolation in the fact that men like the young, scholarly minister Benjamin Imes and the elderly political activist Ed Shaw attempted to inspire blacks to an awareness of themselves and to motivate them to action. Her concern was that blacks begin to think for themselves and realize that their strength was in their unity.[14]

Wells's account of the 1884 railroad suit in the religious weekly *Living Way* ushered her into the field of journalism. She had in the course of the suit secured a teaching job in Memphis. Preparation for her classes occupied much of her time, but she continued to be an avid reader of classic and current literature. She had joined a lyceum in which teachers formed the majority of the membership. To her participation in its dramatic exercises, she added elocution lessons. By 1887, she was considered one of the most prominent members in the literary circle of the black community.[15] As a member of the lyceum she was elected to edit the *Evening Star*, a popular compilation of various types of literary compositions that the editor prepared and read at the Friday evening meetings. At one of these sessions she was asked by the pastor of the Baptist church that published *Living Way* to write for the paper. The readership of this weekly was composed of rural people of limited education and Wells tailored her articles to meet their needs. She chose to be identified as "Iola."[16]

Memphis offered a wide range of activities which, out of curiosity or genuine interest, she included in her schedule. She made critical comments on these cultural and civic affairs in her diary, and on occasion these events became the subjects of published articles. In December 1886, she attended a lecture at a Knights of Labor meeting. Earlier, she had been present at a Moody-Sankey revival meeting. In an article for the *Watchman*, another Memphis journal, she compared the two experiences. She wrote of the

Knights' meeting, "It was the first assembly of the sort in this town where color was not the criterion to recognition as ladies and gentlemen. Seeing this I could listen to their enunciation of principles of truth and justice and accept them with better grace than all the sounding brass and tinkling cymbals of a Moody or Sam Jones, even though expounded in a consecrated house and over the word of God."[17]

The articles of "Iola" appeared in a number of periodicals during the late 1880s, and reprints of them were often carried by the black newspapers. She contributed to the *New York Freeman*, later called the *Age*, and was invited to write for the *Indianapolis World* and the *Chicago Conservator*. Although she maintained her position in the Memphis school system, teaching was for her a source neither of satisfaction nor delight. It was a stable means of livelihood, but one that taxed her irascible nature. The proper education of black children was, however, an issue about which she came to be concerned as she worked in the schools.[18] She had her first distasteful experience of a black community's self-segregation in a school situation.

At the request of the aunt who continued to care for her younger sisters, Wells obtained a teaching position in Visalia, California. She felt conscience-bound to show her gratitude to her aunt by staying at least a year. But, this resolve was destroyed when Wells discovered that the black residents of the little community had requested the separate school in which she was to teach. Comparing the one-room facility for the black pupils with the large building that accommodated all other children, she decided that she could not perpetuate this self-imposed segregation. Despite her aunt's protests, she resigned and left town, taking one of her sisters with her.[19]

Later the *New York Freeman* quoted "Iola" from an article she had written for the *American Baptist*. In this discussion of the manner in which blacks reinforced discrimination, one of her examples was the Visalia two-school system. "There was not a separate school in the State of California until the colored people asked for it. To say that we want to be to ourselves is a tacit acknowledgement of the inferiority that they take for granted anyway."[20]

During this period of her life, Wells seemed not to have had any particular rationale guiding her choice of journalism as a career or the subjects on which she wrote. She was uncertain about the prudence of her protest articles, but she concluded after publishing her outrage at the lynching of a black woman accused of poisoning a white woman, "It may be unwise to express myself so strongly but I cannot help it."[21] She gained the attention of black editors by her forthright style, and she continued to vent her indignation at any breach of justice toward blacks and at any lack of integrity among them. Her vehement reactions were as quickly directed at the dishonesty, tepidity, or immorality of other blacks as against whites. She was a severe critic of Southern black men. She despised the man who curried favor from whites, and she censured the "leader" who forgot the poverty and deprivation of the masses.[22] She was condemnatory and abrasive, a fact that was the subject of her own introspection. She resolved to curb her temper and to pray about the matter, but she did not lower her expectations.

Several unpleasant experiences of black men's disparaging attitudes regarding the morality of Southern black women, her own included, caused "iron to enter my soul."[23] In the Christmas 1885 edition of the *New York Freeman*, she published an essay called "Woman's Mission," an adulatory piece that pointed out the influence and contributions of women to the history of mankind. She praised women of the Judeo-Christian tradition but expressed some disappointment that "masses of the women of our race have not awakened to a true sense of the responsibilities that devolve on them, of the influence they exert." A year later, on New Year's Day, the *Freeman* carried her article entitled "Our Women," in which she said that one of the disheartening aspects of the Negro's life in the South was the "wholesale contemptuous defamation of their women." She referred to accusations of worthlessness and immorality, when no opportunity was given to refute the charges. Describing the typical black woman of the South as true, noble, and of refined qualities, she added, "Our race is no exception to the rest of humanity. We have weaknesses, but we would like to be given credit for our strengths, too."[24] She described the "The Model Woman":

> As a miser hoards and guards his gold, so does she guard her virtue and good name. For the sake of the noble womanhood to which she aspires, and the race whose name bears the stigma of immorality—her soul scorns each temptation to sin and guilt. She knows that our people, as a whole, are charged with immorality and vice; that it depends largely on the woman of today to refute such charges by her stainless life.[25]

In her relationships with men, "She strives to encourage in them all things honest, noble and manly," and added that she honors honest toil in both sexes.[26]

On one occasion, Ida Wells indicated the harshness with which she viewed the double standard of morality. A young man having boasted of an affair with a married woman was shot by the woman's brother. In her diary, Wells wrote, "It seemed awful to take human life but hardly more so than to take a woman's reputation and make it the jest and byword of the street; in view of these things, if he really did them, one is strongly tempted to say his killing was justifiable."[27]

Wells alienated her male teaching colleagues. Feeling that she was the object of unkind and unjustified reports, she conferred with a man whom she respected. Being admonished that it was foolish to swim against the tide, she wrote, "I already know of the enmity of the men in societies against me for expressing my honest convictions. God help me to be on the watch and to do the right; to harm no man but do my duty ever!"[28]

Wells was not averse to the companionship of men and when her aloofness isolated her from them, she felt pangs of loneliness. It was a dilemma for her to maintain their friendship while spurning their romantic notions and offers of marriage. She was involved in activities that challenged her, and despite the fact that discouraged young men described her as a "heartless flirt," she had not met anyone to satisfy her ideal of manliness. In a moment of frustration, she wrote, "I feel so disappointed in them all."[29]

By the summer of 1887, the notoriety she was receiving from the black newspaper world absorbed her attention. In August, she represented the *Little Rock Sun* at the National Colored Press Association's convention and had the distinction of being the only woman participating. It was her first opportunity to meet many veteran newsmen. They elected her first assistant secretary of the conference.[30]

The following summer she met the editor T. Thomas Fortune, for whom she had great esteem and to whom she had submitted articles for his *New York Age*. Fortune was impressed with the young woman he met at the Indianapolis Conference for Colored Democrats. He expressed disdain for "colored conventions, conferences and the like," at which persons deliberately harangued in order to get newspaper notoriety and that ended having accomplished nothing. "Iola's" presence was for him a refreshing change. After the convention, he wrote a complimentary description of the "girlish looking" teacher, noting that, "She stuck to the conference through all the row and the gas, and seemed to enjoy the experience largely." He hypothesized, "If Iola was a man she would be a humming independent in politics. She has plenty of nerve; she is as smart as a steel trap, and she has no sympathy with humbug."[31]

In 1889, she bought one-third interest in the *Free Speech and Headlight* in Memphis. Reverend F. Nightingale and J. L. Fleming had been the owners when "Iola" was taken in as a third partner. The paper was published in Nightingale's Beale Street church. It had a militant stance for which the minister was censured by the white press. As Wells continued to teach, she had become more aware of the poor conditions of the schools for black children and the low mental and moral character of some of the teachers who she said had been hired because of their relations with members of the school board. When she decided to articulate this criticism in the press, she knew that her teaching position would be jeopardized. She asked Nightingale to sign the piece, but he could not be persuaded to accept responsibility for it. Since it was already in type, she removed his name and let it run. The result was that she was not appointed to a school the next year. Although she had a lawyer look into the reason for the school board's action, she did not mind giving up teaching and did not fight the decision. Her own assessment of the situation was that she had conscientiously done her job. But she had not been promoted above the fourth grade and as a result, "The confinement and monotony of the primary work began to grow distasteful. The correspondence I had built up in the newspaper work gave me an outlet through which to express the real 'me' and I enjoyed my work to the utmost." As in the railroad affair, her disappointment was related to the ignorance of blacks. The people whose children were the victims of the school board's negligence and chicanery did not understand her risking her job to make the situation known.[32]

Without a teaching appointment, Wells was determined to make the newspaper business a paying proposition. During the summer she spent her vacation in the Mississippi Valley getting subscribers. Using passes available to the press, she went into the larger towns of the Delta region, seeking correspondents as well as subscribers. In many rural homes she had seen copies of current magazines distributed by white agents and vendors. She followed their example and advocated that other black publishers do the same. As a woman agent and editor of a newspaper she was a novelty, and she was warmly received into homes and meetinghouses. The result of her travels and contacts was enough subscriptions to make the paper self-sustaining and provide her with a salary comparable to the one she earned teaching.[33]

When Wells joined the editorial staff of the militant *Free Speech*, she had already tried her hand at articles on various subjects of national import. She had sparred with Fortune early on, who delighted in her editorial reactions. In response to an article which he wrote on "Mr. Cleveland and the Colored

People," she penned an analysis of freedom of political action, which Fortune printed and entitled "A Woman's Magnificent Definition of the Political Situation." In that letter to the editor, she wrote, "If you are a man worthy of the name, you should not become a scoundrel, a 'time-server' in my estimation because you differ from me in politics or otherwise—for intelligent reasons. I can respect your views without endorsing them and still believe you to be honest, nor will I stop my paper on that account." Of greater significance, at the end of that response, Wells challenged Fortune, himself a native Southerner, asking whether he really believed as he had indicated that "if appealed to in honesty the white people of the South could not nor would not refuse us justice"? For herself she answered, "I don't believe it."[34]

In 1887, Fortune called for the organization of a National Afro-American League. "There is no dodging the issue; we have got to take hold of the problem ourselves, and make so much noise that all the world shall know the wrongs we suffer and our determination to right the wrongs."[35] The grievances about which the League would agitate were centered in the South. There were six in particular: suppression of voting rights, lynch law, unequal distribution of school funds, the convict lease system, discrimination on railroads, and the denial of such public accommodations as hotels and theaters.[36]

Local leagues preceded the formation of the national organization. Two years after the original call, Fortune issued a circular letter to which Ida B. Wells gave an enthusiastic response. In the *Detroit Plaindealer*, for which she was a regular correspondent, she expressed her wholehearted belief in the Afro-American League, but she warned that its beginning would be delayed by endless discussion and dissension. As for herself, she stated, "I am ready to cooperate with anything that is not wrong, to establish the League—only let it be established." She considered the organization a lever for the protection and the development of the race. Urging Fortune on, she wrote, "Do not let it die. Agitate and act until *something* is done."[37]

The term "Afro-American agitator" had been coined by Henry Grady of the *Atlanta Constitution*. Fortune picked it up and identified the new aggressive black with the League. He exulted in the strident qualities of the militant black, that "brand new thing," a black who "looks like a man," bearing "no resemblance to a slave, or a coward, or an ignoramus," and demanding that he be given his Constitutional rights.[38] Wells had been compared with Fortune as a brilliant journalist. She was now caricatured with the radical New York editor as an agitator. The *Indianapolis Freeman* ran a

Ida B. Wells in the 1890s
From I. Garland Penn, *The Afro-American Press and Its Editors*,
Springfield, Mass., Wiley and Co., 1891.

cartoon depicting "Fortune and his 'Echo.' " The caption under the drawing of two barking dogs read, "There is a species of the canine tribe known as fice—and one well developed characteristic is their propensity to bark. There is no remedy yet known to prevent their yelping at unseemly hours and humanity is thus forced to grin and bear it."[39] That a woman should be included in such a lampooning was a matter of discussion, but the *Freeman* replied that if "Iola" expected a place with journalists, "in a journalistic sense, she must take a man's fare."[40]

Wells had decided what her portion would be. After she bought into *Free Speech* enterprise as editor, with Fleming as business manager and Nightingale as sales manager,[41] the newspaper continued to print scathing attacks on the unjust practices of the South and uncompromising criticisms of the foibles and weaknesses of blacks. Copies of *Free Speech* no longer exist, but reprints of its articles were preserved in some Northern black newspapers. In a short comment on the fact that blacks were sent to prison for stealing five cents while whites were honored for absconding with thousand of dollars, the editor's advice for the black thief was, "Let him steal big." Blacks who took advantage of other members of the race in order to gain favor with whites were written off as the despised "good niggers." There was a relentless war on black leaders who defended the federal government's position that it could do nothing to protect blacks in the Southern states. "A few big offices and the control of a little Federal patronage is not sufficient recompense for the lives lost, the blood shed and the rights denied the race." With fury, one exclaimed, "Many of our contemporaries locate hell in the South. We protest that it is a reflection on hell. Only those upon whom judgement is passed, are sent to hell for punishment. Here we are punished and murdered without judgement."[42]

Fortune came under censure by the *Indianapolis Freeman* in September 1891 for approving the *Free Speech* attacks on ex-Senator Blanche K. Bruce. The old politician was accused by the Memphis paper of speaking no word of protest, nor of arousing any public sentiment against Southern atrocities, nor of exerting any effort for his people "save when he wanted votes to save his job."[43] But Fortune went along with the accusations because his League had gotten no support from the nationally known political figures, whose leadership Wells had questioned from her earliest days as a journalist.[44]

Some of the daring protest editorials of *Free Speech* were reprinted in Southern white papers. The kind of militance that they projected came under close scrutiny and was hardly to be tolerated in the growing atmosphere of racial hostility. *Free Speech* served notice that the black man of that day was not the cringing figure of thirty years before who accepted the subjugated role imposed on him by the white man. It applauded retaliatory violence on the part of blacks in Georgetown, Kentucky, after a lynching, stating, "Of one thing we may be assured, so long as we permit ourselves to be trampled upon, so long we will have to endure it. Not until the Negro rises in his might and takes a hand in resenting such cold-blooded murders, if he has to burn up whole towns, will a halt be called in wholesale lynching." The response in the white press to this inflammatory rhetoric was a rejoinder directed to Nightingale, who was held responsible for the Wells and Fleming articles. Lynching, it said, was justified by the higher law that a "rapist" must pay for his crime with his life.

The city authorities, assuming that the minister was the guiding spirit of the newspaper printed in his Baptist church building, determined to rid Memphis of the incendiary agitation of *Free Speech* by destroying the clergyman's influence. When a breach between ousted members of his congregation and Nightingale resulted in a charge of assault and battery against him, he was convicted and sentenced to eighty days in the workhouse. He managed to flee to Oklahoma. The militancy of the black paper was not affected, however, since the remaining owners continued to wield their pens as before.[45]

Wells then acquired Nightingale's share of the weekly. Fortune congratulated her on the acquisition: "The *Free Speech* is a mighty bright newspaper and Miss Wells furnishes the light of it." He criticized her, however, for giving no explanation for the organization of the Southern Press Association, which had recently come into being in Memphis. Wells was an active member of the National Press Association, having been elected secretary of the convention in Washington in 1889. In January 1892, she met with twenty Southern journalists and gave her support to a new association. Fortune showed his distaste for the proliferation of organizations, commenting, "It appears to us as if the brethren and sisters have proceeded upon the maxim that divided we stand, united we fall.[46]

After the 1884 railroad suit, Ida B. Wells continuously moved in the direction of protest. She was equipped with the ability to articulate grievances and the passion to persist in a cause. These assets brought her satisfaction and earned the attention of other professionals. She had learned through the reversal of a court decision in her favor the black person's pitiful disadvantage before the Southern judicial system. She knew what it was to be a member of a despised race and a defamed sex. Experience taught her that blacks could be as despicable in their obsequiousness as whites were ruthless in their vindictiveness. If she was aware of the peculiar plight of blacks in the post-Reconstruction South, there were others who forgot it in their personal ambition and comfortable situations. She was impatient with the excess of talk and the lack of action among conventioneers, but she recognized the necessity that blacks be conscious that what affected one had ramifications for others, and that concerted resistance was the only recourse against the advancing threat of renewed white domination.

The call of the Afro-American League founder to "Agitate, agitate, agitate" was a refrain to which she could respond. She was a radical race woman, who had risked alienation among blacks and stirred up sentiments of outrage among whites. She was not a new black woman; she was a militant black agitator. Until the spring of 1892, however, she had not found the focus that would channel her bristling energies.

THREE

The Beginning
of the
Anti-Lynching Crusade

After the 1883 Supreme Court decision to repeal the Civil Rights Act of 1875, contempt for black Americans was epitomized by lynchings that increased in number and violence. August Meier estimates that this form of brutality in the United States reached a peak average of 150 a year during the 1880s and the 1890s, excluding the exceptional year 1892 when 235 lynchings took place. Most of these incidents occurred in the rural South.[1]

In 1905, James Cutler made an intensive study of the history of lynch law. He defined lynching as it was carried out in his time as "the practice whereby mobs capture individuals suspected of crime or take them from the officers of the law or break open jails and hang convicted criminals with impunity." Even though the most frequently publicized reason for lynchings was a community's outrage at the commission of some dastardly crime that it felt the lawful authorities too slow or otherwise inefficient in prosecuting and vindicating, the most frequently recognized reason was a community's racial or ethnic differences and tensions. Lynching was considered "our country's national crime." Cutler referred to lynch law as an institution "peculiar to the United States," and expressed the concern of other scholars of the American scene: "The frequency and impunity of lynchings in the United States is justly regarded as a serious and disquieting symptom of American society."[2]

William Graham Sumner expressed his outrage at the multiplicity and brutality of lynchings during the decade preceding 1905: "It is a disgrace to our civilization that men can be put to death by painful methods, which our laws have discarded as never suitable, and without the proofs of guilt which our laws call for in any case whatsoever."[3] Writing more than a half century later, historian John Walton Caughey described the uncivilized character of lynching: "To gang up and discipline an alleged wrong-doer is an ancient and deep-seated impulse. It runs counter to a principle on which all government insists, that trial and punishment for crime are the business of the state and solely of the state." He pointed out that whether the term used was lynch law, vigilantism, or mobocracy, the essential element was the substitution of group action for the regular dispensation of justice.[4]

Cutler noted, "There is a readiness on the part of the people of the United States to take the law into their own hands which is not found in other countries, and consequent immunity from punishment which is generally accorded to lynchers renders an American mob exceedingly open to the suggestion of lynching." To this he added that lynching was commonly approved by the American public. "Indeed, it is not too much to say that popular justification is the *sine qua non* of lynching."[5]

Both Cutler and Caughey describe mob action as habit-forming and contagious. Every community had its expendables, according to Caughey, and they became the victims of the mob's urge to avenge itself for some alleged crime. A mob had no intention of reestablishing order; its object was retaliation and intimidation.[6] At the time that lynchings were at their peak in number and viciousness, the Southern blacks were at the lowest level of society and were the chief victims.

By the early 1880s, public attention was being drawn to the lynching phenomenon as the number of incidents rose and the tortures reached shocking proportions. On January 1, 1883, the *Chicago Tribune* published a list of the lynchings of the preceding year. This was the beginning of twenty-one such annual reports. The *Tribune* derived its statistics from accounts of lynchings in its own columns. The figures were accompanied by the names of victims, their races, the crimes of which they were accused, and the places where they were lynched. Individuals and groups involved in social protest found the *Tribune* records a valuable source of statistics; historian Carter G. Woodson considered them important in anti-lynching reform.[7]

Although lynching was thought by American blacks to be the greatest deterrent to their progress during the post-Reconstruction era, anti-lynching protest was usually only one among many points to which organizations gave attention and addressed resolutions. Much of the protest rhetoric condemning various forms of oppression was directed to black audiences only. Northern whites had lost interest in the grievances of the black population during the murky years after 1883. While lynching was an acknowledged blight on the national scene, the prevalent view among the white population was that lynching was a necessary measure for keeping the criminally inclined black in line. The Southern proponents of lynch law had successfully propagated the myth of the black man's lust and criminality.[8]

As late as 1909, Quincy Ewing conjectured that the average American white, including the professional, explained the "race problem" by describing black Americans pejoratively in this way:

> The Negroes, as a rule, are very ignorant, are very lazy, are very brutal, are very criminal. But a little way removed from savagery, they are incapable of adopting the white man's moral ideals. They are creatures of brutal untamed instincts, and uncontrollable feral passions which give frequent expression of themselves in crimes of horrible ferocity. They are, in brief, an uncivilized, semi-savage people, living in a civilization to which they are unequal.[9]

Ewing's contention was that the real race problem was the Southerner's struggle to keep blacks at the inferior level of this degrading description.[10] The commonly held notion was that the host of discriminatory practices, were necessary to deal with a severely limited people who frequently manifested bestial proclivities. The propagation of this belief was an essential part of the Southern machinery of exploitation and control of the black man.

When the last of the federal troops were withdrawn from the South in 1876, the region went about regaining its losses, not the least of which was its political and economic control of the black population. The most effective device for controlling and later taking the black's vote, for keeping him economically dependent and disadvantaged, was the terror of the lynch mob. The immediate purpose of lynching was intimidation. Since the real reason for the upsurge in lynchings was not admissible, the complex mythology of the black man's lust for white women and children was contrived to justify the practice.[11]

The myth was strongly entrenched in the public mind and no notable challenge to its justification came forth until 1892, when the black population of Memphis, Tennessee, was shaken by the lynching of three of its men who were capable, responsible, and successful managers of a grocery business. Thomas Moss, Calvin McDowell, and Henry Steward were joint operators of the People's Grocery, a cooperative endeavor, in a heavily populated black section just outside the city. Their competitor was a white grocer, W. H. Barrett. The location of the grocery stores, called the "Curve,"[12] was the place at which the streetcar line turned. The black business prospered there. Friction developed between the managers of the People's Grocery and Barrett, who had established his grocery first. In an account derived from several newspapers, David M. Tucker indicates that Barrett had instigated several incidents of violence against the rival enterprise. On one occasion he called for a grand jury indictment against the People's Grocery for maintaining a public nuisance. The black community was outraged, and a meeting was called at which fiery threats against the white man were voiced. Barrett used this response from associates of the black grocers to bring charges of conspiracy. After obtaining warrants for the arrest of two of the men involved, Barrett set about aggravating the situation. He warned the People's Grocery that a white mob was preparing an assault on the store. The blacks, who were outside the jurisdiction of the Memphis police, prepared to defend themselves. The result was that when a group of the sheriff's deputies approached, dressed as civilians, the black men fired into the group, wounding three officers. Why nine deputies unrecognizable as officers of the law were needed to serve two warrants was not explained; nevertheless, when their identities were made known, the blacks in the grocery surrendered to them. Thirty blacks, including Moss, McDowell, and Steward, were eventually arrested and jailed. The judge who had issued the warrants of arrest at the insistence of Barrett, now ordered all the blacks of Memphis disarmed and illegally had the weapons of the black militia confiscated from the armory. Four days after the shooting at the "Curve," Moss, McDowell, and Steward, who were named ringleaders of the supposed conspiracy, were moved from the county jail during the night by men who were apparently the sheriff's deputies. They were taken on a switch engine to a place about a mile from the prison and shot to death.[13]

Ida B. Wells, editor of the local black newspaper, *Free Speech*, was in Natchez, Mississippi, when these events occurred. On her return she expressed her consternation at this calamity in the city that had seemed devoid of the lynching mentality. In an editorial, she lamented:

> The city of Memphis has demonstrated that neither character nor standing avails the Negro if he dares to protect himself against the white man or become his rival. There is nothing we can do about the lynching now, as we are outnumbered and without arms. The white mob could help itself to ammunition without pay, but the order was rigidly enforced against the selling of guns to Negroes. There is therefore only one thing left that we can do; save our money and leave a town which will neither protect our lives and property, nor give us a fair trial in the courts, when accused by white persons.[14]

The advice to the black people to move out of Memphis was based on the report of one who was evidently a spectator at the murder. Thomas Moss was said to have cried out before he was shot, "Tell my people to go West—there is no justice for them here."[15] Ida Wells went to Oklahoma herself to investigate the opportunities available to blacks in the West. At the request of I. F. Norris, a former state legislator who planned to take his family from Memphis, she used a railroad pass to go to Kansas City, Missouri, and into parts of Oklahoma then being opened to settlers. Convinced of the possibilities for black development in the new territory, she wrote letters encouraging migration westward. She proposed on her return to Memphis that *Free Speech* be moved to Oklahoma, but her partner and business manager J. L. Fleming did not agree.[16] She stayed in Memphis, but her editorials repeatedly harked back to the tragedy. During the weeks following the "Curve" lynching, she began to look more closely at the rationalization for lynchings that was voiced abroad by the South and to make her own investigations.

At one time, Wells believed, as did many others, that cases of rape were frequently the reason for the lynchers' fury. The men brutally murdered in Memphis, however, had been accused of no such crime. This fact led her to look into the cases in which the lynch victims were accused of rape. She began to suspect that lynchings were a device for eliminating blacks who were becoming prosperous. From March until May, she investigated every lynch case reported to be the consequence of rape. She contended that in every instance the rape story was an invention to gain public sympathy with the lynchers. The cry of rape, she said, was a solution to the problem of some white women who were willingly involved with black men but were fearful about their reputations.[17] It was a solution also for the families and neighbors of women in this predicament. With this in mind, Wells penned the editorial that infuriated the white community of Memphis and became the excuse for an assault on the office of *Free Speech*.

> Eight Negroes lynched since last issue of the *Free Speech*. Three were charged with killing white men and five with raping white women. Nobody in this section believes the old thread-bare lie that Negro men assault white women. If Southern men are not careful they will over-reach themselves and a conclusion will be reached which will be very damaging to the moral reputation of their women.[18]

At the time she made this statement, the mere possibility that a white woman, despite her low station, could be attracted to a black man was incredible and outrageous slander to the white mind. To imply as much required an intolerable audacity that infuriated the white community to the point of threats of emasculation and lynching of the supposed black male writer.[19] Five years earlier, J. C. Duke, the editor of the *Montgomery Herald*, made the suggestion that "a growing appreciation of white Juliets for colored Romeos" might explain what seemed to be the sudden attraction of black men for white women. Despite a disclaimer that he had no libelous intent, Duke was forced to leave Montgomery.[20]

Fortunately, when her editorial appeared, Ida B. Wells had started for Philadelphia to attend the African Methodist Episcopal (A.M.E.) General Church Conference. J. L. Fleming, the business manager of *Free Speech*, had been warned in sufficient time to leave Memphis before an outraged "committee" descended upon the office of the newspaper to silence its protest. The type and the furnishings of the *Free Speech* office were destroyed. The response of white newspapers indicated hostility toward a male writer, and Fleming was generally believed to be the author of the infuriating article. Wells, however, claimed to have written the editorial before her trip north. She indicated later that Fleming bitterly criticized her for the incendiary piece that resulted in the destruction of their newspaper. Neither returned to Memphis. Fleming made his way to Chicago, where he was encouraged to start *Free Speech* anew in that city. Wells went to New York and joined the staff of the *New York Age*. With the support of the coeditors, T. Thomas Fortune and Jerome B. Peterson, she continued her expose of the lynching facts and the rape myth.[21]

In the June 25 issue of the *Age*, she told the story of her exile from Memphis. Even though 10,000 copies of that edition were distributed, requests were made for Wells's article, entitled "Exiled," in pamphlet form. The interest of the Northern blacks in the facts that she presented about the March 9 lynching, and her interpretation of lynch law and the rape myth of the South, seem to have given her a sense of prophetic calling. She felt that she had been chosen by circumstances to demonstrate the evils of lynching and to make known the false reasoning given by Southerners for continuing the practice. In the preface of the pamphlet, which she published in October of 1892, she wrote, "Somebody must show that the Afro-American race is more sinned against than sinning, and it seems to have fallen upon me to do so."[22]

Ida B. Wells with the family of her lynched friend Tom Moss.
Maureen Moss, Betty Moss, and Tom Moss, Jr. (ca. 1893)

With this motivation, Ida B. Wells began her crusade against lynching, and initiated the anti-lynching movement that would eventually involve blacks and whites in organized effort. As a journalist and a single-minded agitator for the black American's rights, she had been recognized and honored in the black community. As an anti-lynching crusader, she moved into a position in which her almost single-handed efforts would be variously approved, rewarded, and condemned by blacks and whites in the United States and Europe.

Many Northern blacks were aware of the evils of lynching but they had become imbued with the belief that lynch victims belonged to a criminal type and deserved what they got. Wells claimed that she presented facts contradicting the common contention that the growing number of lynchings was directly related to a growing licentiousness among black men. Frederick Douglass was one who admitted that for lack of contrary evidence, he had been inclined to believe the rape myth.[23]

Two black club women were impressed with the story of the Memphis exile. Victoria Earle Matthews of New York and Maritcha Lyons of Brooklyn, representing the Women's Loyal Union of New York and Brooklyn, decided to have a testimonial fund-raiser to assist Wells in reestablishing *Free Speech*. Held at New York's Lyric Hall on October 5, the fund-raiser was a resounding success. In the audience that night were prominent black women from Boston, Philadelphia, New York, and Brooklyn. Wells gave an account of her experiences, during which she was overcome with emotion. She thought she had failed her listeners, but the contrary was true. The sympathy aroused and the interest generated by this first speech set the Southern journalist on a course of lecturing in Boston, New Bedford, Providence, Newport, New Haven, Philadelphia, Wilmington, and Washington, D.C. Rather than trying to reestablish *Free Speech*, she used the testimonial gift to publish the pamphlet *Southern Horrors*, which was substantially a reproduction of "Exiled."[24]

Frederick Douglass had praised the article and Wells wrote to him about the pamphlet:

> I take the liberty of addressing you to ask if you will be so kind as to put in writing the encomiums you were pleased to lavish on my article on Lynch Law published in the June issue of the *Age*. I am revising the matter for a pamphlet and would feel highly honored if you would send me a letter with your opinion of it, which I could use as an introduction.[25]

Douglass obliged, thanking Wells for her "faithful paper on the lynch abomination now generally practiced against colored people in the South." He added, "There has been no work equal to it in convincing power. I have spoken, but my word is feeble in comparison. You give us what you know and testify from actual knowledge."[26]

In *Southern Horrors* she directed arguments against the common Southern defense that lynching was the only method of protecting white women and children who were beleaguered by bestial black males. She proposed that the white men of the South were not willing to allow their women the same liberties with black men that they themselves had traditionally taken with black women. In this first pamphlet, she reinforced the statement that had cost her *Free Speech* in Memphis.

> There are many white women in the South who would marry colored men if such an act would not place them at once beyond the pale of society and within the clutches of the law. The miscegenation laws of the South only operate against the legitimate union of the races; they leave the white man free to seduce all the colored girls he can, but it is death to the colored man who yields to the force and advances of a similar attraction in white women.[27]

Wells had looked into a number of cases reported by Southern newspapers recording illicit affairs between white women and black men. In various ways several of the men involved had escaped death, but public disdain for the women or spurious defenses of their positions accompanied the disclosures. Not so fortunate were other black men such as Frank Weems, who was lynched with letters of his white paramour in his pocket, and Ed Coy, who was made a human torch lighted by the woman with whom he had been romantically involved. Judge Albion Tourgee, who wrote a column for the *Chicago Inter-Ocean*, investigated the Coy affair and his conclusion coincided with the generalization made by Wells. He wrote, "The woman was a willing partner in the victim's guilt."[28]

Using the *Chicago Tribune* statistics of January 1, 1892, Wells showed that of the 728 blacks lynched within the past eight years, only one-third were accused of sexual assault. Allowing for the Southern mentality out of which these charges were made, she suggested that perhaps only one-third of those accused were guilty. The "better class of Afro-Americans" were inclined to believe that the problems of racial injustice were suffered by the entire race for the foibles of a certain low type of black. They believed that lynchings and other forms of oppression would be overcome by the accumulation of educational and financial achievements among a greater number of blacks. What Wells had come to believe was that there was a conscious effort on the part of the Southern white to keep the black subjugated, and that the blacks' acquisition of education and wealth increased the whites' need to suppress them. The consequence of this was that every black lived under the threat of lynching since the political and economic domination of all black Americans was the object of whites in the South. With these conjectures in mind she reiterated the falsity of the rape myth and condemned the blindness of status-seeking blacks who kept silent about lynching because they were repelled by the crime it presupposed. She pointed out that there was little to prevent any black man from being accused of assault on a white woman in light of the growing conviction that all blacks were tainted with inferior appetites and perverted lusts. She argued further that to justify the illegal killing of any man for a particular crime was to justify the illegal killing of any man for any crime.[29]

After the lynchings in Memphis, Ida Wells bought a pistol for her own protection. Her feeling was, "If I could take one lyncher with me that would even up the score a little bit."[30] She had reason to believe that the only cases in which lynchers had been diverted from their intentions were those in which the would-be victims had armed themselves. This, she said, had happened in 1892 in Jacksonville, Florida, and in Paducah, Kentucky. There was an object lesson in these incidents, which she passed on, indicating that a Winchester rifle was a good investment for every black home.[31]

In a 1973 study, Albert Kreiling shows Ida B. Wells to be representative of a definite type of Afro-American militant. In his cultural interpretation of the black press in Chicago, Kreiling states, "Most existing literature has failed to delineate the distinctive style of the Afro-American Agitators."[32] He places Wells preeminently among the Afro-American agitators. Her advocacy of retaliatory violence illuminates the character of these militants in forcing attention on the problems of the South. Violence was not the chief element of her program for securing justice for blacks; nonetheless, it was not entirely absent from her rhetoric, particularly at the time of her most intense anti-lynching activity. Wells urged with greater energy three other means of protest: the economic boycott, emigration from Southern towns, and investigations into lynchings by the black press. As a journalist, her emphasis was on factual reporting, so that the American public could take informed action against lynching.[33]

In her lectures, the points were the same.[34] She expressed conviction that the nation's indifference and apathy about the primitive practice of shooting, hanging, and burning persons without recourse to law were due to ignorance of mob action in the South. She explained that she had assumed the task of crusader against lynching not because she had a natural inclination to recite its horrors, but because she had witnessed society's need to be informed about it. Again she pointed out that charges of ignorance, immorality, worthlessness, and criminality among blacks were excuses for taking away their rights and their lives. Wells admitted that she, like many other aspiring black Americans, had given credence to the notion that the lowly condition of the masses of blacks was the real basis for the humiliating and inhibiting circumstances that all black Americans were forced to endure. She had believed that when education, wealth, and moral rectitude were more general among blacks, justice and equality would follow. Recalling, however, the lynching of the three men in Memphis, she reiterated that she had experienced a conversion in her thinking. Mob law had worked as viciously in a city where the black community had raised itself educationally, economically, and morally as it would in an area of the deepest intellectual, financial, and ethical poverty.

The chief lesson that she sought to teach her listeners was that where white supremacy was the basis of the law, the lynch mob could exist without reprisal. Blacks had no recourse in the courts. There was no thought of punishing the lynchers. Newspaper reports were biased. Since professional whites participated in lynchings, Wells felt certain that in some instances published accounts were written by members of the mob. There was hardly a ripple of concern about a lynching in the white community generally, because it was a foregone conclusion among the white population that black lynch victims were brutes of less than human nature.[35]

To contrast this lack of concern and action when blacks were lynched, Wells reviewed the case of eleven Italians lynched in New Orleans for the shooting of a police chief. All Europe, she said, was amazed, and retribution was required by the Italian government. The State of Louisiana used its right to investigate the case and claimed the usual "Death at the hands of parties unknown." The United States, nevertheless, paid $25,000 to the Italian king. No such indemnity could be claimed by black Americans.[36]

Likening the threat under which blacks lived to a new slavery, Wells emphasized the vindictiveness and bitterness of the South, which in 1876 accomplished its purpose "to rule the black man and to dictate to the

National Government." Referring to disfranchisement and other discriminatory practices against the Southern black, she said, "Having destroyed the
citizenship of the man, they are now trying to destroy the manhood of the
citizen."[37]

Leniency on the part of the national government, indifference in the pulpit
and in the press, abandonment of its principles by the Republican Party were
all blamed by Wells for their part in the prevailing rule of the mob. She
proposed universal condemnation of the practice and discarded as pretense
the Southern governors' offers of rewards that they did not expect to be
collected for the apprehension of lynchers. She advocated a sincere effort to
arouse public indignation at the crime, calling for: "Public sentiment that
shall denounce these crimes in season and out; public sentiment which turns
capital and immigration from a section given over to lawlessness; public
sentiment which insists on the punishment of criminals and lynchers by
law."[38]

She had an advantage from her position in the North. Her audiences were
predominantly black, but there were whites, too, disposed to be receptive to
her message. What she said and wrote was also observed in the South.
Within days of the publication of "Exiled" in the *New York Age*, there was
a comment of some length in the *Memphis Appeal-Avalanche*, a white news
organ. The article, entitled "Decent Colored Folk Protest," noted that the
Age, for which Ida Wells regularly wrote, was being circulated in Memphis.
That decent blacks in the Southern city disapproved of Wells's statements
was the message of the article. Reverend B. A. Imes, whose stand for racial
justice Wells had found comforting in the 1880s, was said now to have
voiced before an integrated audience his dissatisfaction with her manner of
protest. The *Appeal-Avalanche* pointed out that the speech of Reverend
Imes had been ignored by the *Age*, but the Memphis paper quoted the letter
addressed to its editor by the minister and his committee. Their objection was
to "the course pursued by Miss Ida Wells through the medium of the *New
York Age*, in stirring up from week to week, this community and wherever
that paper goes, the spirit of strife over the unhappy question at issue."[39]

Besides attempting to discredit Wells by showing that she did not
represent respectable blacks, the Memphis press waged a campaign to defame
her character. Early in 1893 she asked the opinion of Judge Albion Tourgee
on the possibility of vindicating her reputation by suing the *Memphis
Commercial*, which had printed libelous allegations against her. She also
sought assurance of his support in his "Bystander" column in the *Chicago*

Inter-Ocean. In her correspondence with Tourgee, Wells explained her seeking counsel from him rather than a black lawyer. She was deliberately choosing "one who was not a member of the race" for consultation, because, "The manhood of my race as lawyers is too partisan to give cool unbiased counsel."[40]

Wells had come to distrust the integrity of two black attorneys in Memphis. She expressed her belief that they were "doing everything they can to hurt me it seems and curry favor with white people."[41] She had had prior dealings with both men; one had initially represented her in the suit against the Chesapeake and Ohio Railroad. She explained, "Both are sycophants and do not half defend their clients and the *Free Speech* with more zeal than discretion chided them for it. I do not like to expose the weaknesses of my race but I do wish a clear impartial opinion as to the prospects of winning the suit I have in contemplation."[42]

At the same time that Wells was making inquiries of Judge Tourgee, she had engaged two black attorneys in Chicago to look into the suit against the *Commercial*. These men, Ferdinand L. Barnett and S. Laing Williams, also consulted Tourgee on the feasibility of the suit. Barnett had secured the testimony of persons in Memphis regarding the character of Wells and was convinced of the falsity of the newspaper charges. His chief concern was that his client should win the case, if there should be a trial.[43]

The character assault by the white press enhanced Wells's position and publicity among blacks. In the black press, there were frequent items on her activities and editorials written in her defense. Eventually, the editors, who continuously sparred among themselves, began quarreling about the exaggerated publicity and praise given their journalistic colleague. In the spring of 1893, both Wells's thoughts about a lawsuit against the *Commercial* and the black editors' bickering gave way to the fact that she had been invited by a distinguished Englishwoman, Catherine Impey, editor of *Anti-Caste*, to go to Britain to help organize an "Emancipation League," the object of which would be "the removal of all disabilities (or inequalities) on the ground of race anywhere."[44]

In November of 1892, Ida Wells had been in Philadelphia to give a lecture. She was a guest in the home of William Still, former director of the Underground Railroad and its recorder. At the same time, Catherine Impey was visiting relatives in the Quaker city. Impey, who was interested in the colored peoples of the world, had made several visits and gained a number of prominent black friends in the United States. On this occasion she made arrangements to interview Ida Wells at Still's home. She registered shock at the atrocities that Wells had recited and at the indifference that she herself had witnessed among whites in the United States.[45] In April 1893, Wells published in *New York Age* a letter from Catherine Impey dated March 19, requesting her presence in England to organize an anti-slavery movement. The letter stated that recent lynchings in Texas had been reported by the English press and had caused concern in Britain. Although the problems in India and South America were serious, the proposed organization would concentrate its first efforts on the United States. Wells was assured that all her expenses would be paid, although she could not be promised remuneration for her time and effort. Asking an immediate reply, Impey urged, "We are very anxious to have you here before folks go to the World's Fair."[46] This invitation reached Wells while she was visiting the home of Frederick Douglass, who had invited her for a second lecture before a Washington audience. He urged her to accept the invitation from England. Except for one meagerly attended lecture in Boston, she had not been able to deliver her message to a white audience. Neither had she secured white press coverage. The opportunity to speak to English assemblies was an unexpected means to reach the white American public.

On April 5, before news of this venture reached the public, Ida B. Wells was on her way to England, although she was disappointed at having to put aside the publication of a pamphlet for distribution at the World's Columbian Exposition and by the impossibility of speaking before the Southern governors at a meeting in Richmond shortly after her departure.[47] She began her lecture tour in Aberdeen, Scotland, the home of Isabelle Fyvie Mayo, who was widely known under the pen name of Edward Garrett. It was she who had initiated the idea of having an American lecturer come to Britain to explain the reason for lynchings in the American Southern states. Mayo, like Impey, was committed to aiding oppressed peoples. Her home had been opened to a number of East Indians in need of asylum.[48]

With the assistance of these prestigious women, Wells was introduced to reform groups in the large cities of Scotland and England. She was cordially received by people and press. Almost immediately, her message resulted in the founding of the Society for the Recognition of the Brotherhood of Man. The purpose of this body was to oppose separatism, which was regarded as the chief cause of discrimination, "of lynching and other forms of brutal injustice inflicted on the weaker communities of the world." It required its members to extricate themselves from involvement in any system of racial segregation. Those who joined pledged "to help in securing to every member of the human family, *Freedom*, *Equal Opportunity* and *Brotherly Consideration*."[49]

The question of the value of English protest against an American practice was presented by a city councillor at Birmingham. Wells's response enabled her to express in print her purpose and the grievances she hoped to alleviate. She answered that the American public could not afford to ignore the religious and moral sentiment of a nation of superior civilization. "The moral agencies at work in Great Britain did much for the final overthrow of chattel slavery. They can in like manner pray, write, preach, talk and act against civil and industrial slavery, against the hanging, shooting and burning of a powerless race."[50]

The lecture tour had the desired effect. The enthusiasm of the British for the anti-lynching efforts of the black American lecturer caught the attention of the Southern press. While its journalists showed intense hostility to her, they could not ignore her message. After her return in June 1893, she commented that evidence of the usefulness of her time spent in Britain was the abuse poured out on her by the *Memphis Appeal-Avalanche*, the *Atlanta Constitution*, the *Macon Telegraph*, and the *Washington City Post*.[51]

In October 1893, however, Bishop Atticus G. Haygood published an article giving evidence of how deeply entrenched were the ideas of Southerners on the criminality of American blacks. Haygood was a Southern Methodist Episcopalian, the general agent for the John Slater Fund, and a recognized advocate of black progress.[52] He had been asked to explain the lynchings that had aroused the interest of the English people. In so doing, Bishop Haygood expressed his own objection to the practice, which he identified as a "crime against society." He termed the tortures inflicted in the slow burning of victims a horror. He admitted that lynchings had become so common that they no longer surprised the public. On the other hand, he reverted to the stock answer given to explain lynchings: "Unless assaults by Negroes on white women and little girls come to an end, there will most probably be still further displays of vengeance that will shock the world." He reasoned that the men who inflicted the "monstrous and abnormal" punishments were driven to emotional insanity by the thought of "the ruined woman, worse tortured than he [the lynch victim]." Haygood quoted an article in the *Christian Advocate* in which the Reverend Dr. E. E. Hoss, also a Southern Methodist Episcopalian clergyman, said that he believed, with good reason, that "three hundred white women had been raped by negroes within the preceding three months." Commenting on this judgment, the bishop wrote, "I believe Dr. Hoss's statement to be under rather than above the facts in the case."[53] This persistent mentality justified Wells's continued efforts after her European tour to publicize lynching as a crime and to discredit the rape myth.

FOUR

Introduction
to Chicago

Before she was invited to England in 1893, Ida B. Wells had already made plans to publish and distribute a pamphlet at the World's Columbian Exposition in Chicago. Her intention was to make known the true state of blacks in the United States and to explain to foreign visitors why black Americans were not represented in this show of world progress. She had expected to be able to raise $5,000 to print the booklet in French, German, Spanish, and English and to distribute it without charge. Frederick Douglass and Frederick J. Loudin, one of the famous Fisk University Jubilee Singers, had promised assistance.[1]

Since 1890, American blacks had been protesting their exclusion from the organization of the exposition. The fair was to be financed partly with funds appropriated by Congress. A national committee had been set up by the president of the United States. Although there were representatives from each state and the territories, as well as ten commissioners-at-large, there were no blacks appointed to the board of directors. In 1891, after being entreated by a group of blacks to be given some representation, President Benjamin Harrison named a black man, Hale G. Parker, as an alternate on the board of directors. A board of lady managers was the channel through which all women's organizations were to make application for space in the exhibits. It consisted of nine Chicagoans headed by Mrs. Potter Palmer, originally from Kentucky. There were also representatives from each state and territory, but no black woman's name appeared on the roster of board members and representatives. Realizing, however, the uselessness of appealing to the male board, blacks placed their hope in the influence that their women might exert on the board of lady managers.[2]

Black Americans were divided on whether they should exhibit in appropriate areas of the fair, or whether they should have a separate annex. At a mass meeting in 1890, the Chicago attorney and editor of the *Conservator*, F. L. Barnett, presented a resolution encouraging them to participate in exhibitions throughout the fair. J. C. Price, president of the Afro-American League, was in favor of a separate department. The board of lady managers used the differences of opinion among black women as an excuse for providing that they be represented by a white woman. A patronizing statement from the board urged "the leaders of the various factions to sacrifice all ambition for personal advancement and work together for the good of the whole."[3] In December 1891, Barnett, aware of the "envious structures and vindictive opposition of a few women in Chicago," made an appeal to Mrs. Potter Palmer on behalf of Fannie Barrier Williams. Williams, a highly qualified black woman, was gaining some recognition from the president of the board of lady managers. She had at a recent conference ably presented plans that were subsequently approved by the board of control. In his letter to Palmer, Barnett noted, "The best element of every race is the prey of its moral banditti and we are no exception."[4]

In reviewing for foreign visitors the efforts of blacks to obtain a part in the planning and managing of the fair, Barnett explained that two organizations of black women had similar plans of operation but different officers. Each endorsed its own leader with the hope of implementing its plan through her as a representative to the board. The writer acknowledged the "earnestness, fidelity and sometimes acerbity of temper" with which the women supported their candidates, but he pointed to the minutes of meetings of the lady managers, "enlivened frequently with hysterics and bathed at times in tears." He argued, "The failure of a few colored people of Chicago to agree, could not by any kind of logic, justify the Board in ignoring the seven and one-half millions outside the city."[5]

Ann Massa gives greater significance to the disunity among the black women regarding plans. She states that women following Lettie A. Trent in the Women's Columbian Association accepted the idea of working through a white representative and of putting on a separate exhibit. The rival group, the Women's Columbian Auxiliary Association, led by Mrs. R. D. Boone and supported by integrationists like attorney Barnett and Dr. Daniel Hale Williams, preferred to have their exhibits included with those of white Americans in similar fields. Massa saw the differences of opinion among black women as identical with those among the men.

> Precisely the same problems were involved in the impressive series of collective and individual attempts which both obscure and well-known black women made to secure an effective display of black women's achievement at the Fair. Moreover, the unceasing, embattled flow of ideas and activities from these

women made as effective a display of race pride and talent as any static exhibit in the Fair's pavilions might have provided.[6]

The interests of the black women were put into the hands of Mary Cecil Cantrill. This appointment of a white Kentuckian, whose views on black Americans were suspected of being paternalistic, was unsatisfactory to blacks and to some whites. The result was a resolution to relegate black American concerns to the state and territorial boards of lady managers. From the beginning, the ineffectiveness of this move was clear. States, particularly Southern states in which most blacks lived, would be loath to allocate limited funds for black participation in the fair.

When collective protest failed, individual efforts were made. The most significant application for a representative position was made by Hallie Quinn Brown, a teacher and elocutionist.[7] She was born free in Pittsburgh in the mid-nineteenth century. Educated at Wilberforce University in Ohio, she went South to teach in the Reconstruction public schools. She was dean of Allen University in Columbia, South Carolina, for two years before returning to the public schools of Dayton, Ohio.[8] Her application for membership on the board of lady managers led to an interview with Palmer, who was impressed with her intelligence and rhetoric, but also alarmed at the fact that Brown had been making her own investigation into how much the state boards were doing to contact blacks and to arouse their interest in the fair.

Hallie Brown asked for ordinary board membership with special powers and special funds in order to avoid the discrimination inherent in creating a special position for her as a black woman. Actually, Palmer did not have the power to change the board's composition, but she did not present this fact in dismissing Brown's request. She referred instead to the black woman's failure to name a salary, and used this to make a false assumption. Noting the applicant's present earnings, her secretarial assistant, and her semi-public career, the chief lady manager wrote: "I asked you to name a salary that you would consider the equivalent of your services and as you have not done so, presume you did not find the position one you cared to fill. Lamenting that this is the case, I certainly cannot blame you and hoping we may yet find the proper person to take the place."[9]

One state, New York, saw fit to have a black woman, Joan Imogene Howard, appointed to its board of lady managers. Only one black man, J. E. Johnson, was given a clerical job, although hundreds of white clerks were hired. In January 1893, a black woman, Mrs. A. M. Curtis, was given charge of the black exhibits as they arrived. Curtis was not affiliated with any of the protest groups, and her position was a token gesture to forestall further complaints as the installations were made. Having no real power, she resigned after a few months. Two months before the fair opened, Fannie Barrier Williams was made responsible for the arrangements of all the exhibits in the Women's Building.[10]

Williams had campaigned for representative posts for a black man and a black woman, but had given up and taken a secretarial job in the Department of Publicity and Promotion. It was through the recommendation of this department's head that she was offered a supervisory position. To her surprise she was not paid, but she accepted the offer as some recognition of intelligent black women, who would be interested and inspired by the exhibits.[11]

Fannie Williams was the wife of the attorney S. Laing Williams, but she was recognized in her own right as a writer and lecturer. Born of a free and prominent black family in Brockport, New York, she was well educated and held elitist views.[12] In March 1893, she was invited to give an address at the World's Congress of Representative Women. Her participation opened the doors for several other black women to speak before integrated groups.[13]

In early 1893, a group of blacks on the East Coast suggested that a day be set aside as Colored American Day. Similar days had been scheduled for national groups, such as the Irish and the Germans. Despite the fact that the idea was inspired by blacks who proposed a day of prayer, speeches, and musical celebrations, it raised a furor among newspapermen like F. L. Barnett, who considered it "the refinement of irony."[14] Ida B. Wells wrote a letter to the *Indianapolis Freeman* congratulating it on its stand against "Jubilee Day."[15] "The self-respect of the race is sold for a mess of pottage and the spectacle of the class of our people who will come on that excursion roaming around the grounds munching watermelon will do more to lower the race in the estimation of the world than anything else."[16] In this instance, Wells opposed the aging Frederick Douglass, her ally in producing the protest pamphlet that had become as controversial among black editors as the separate day for black participation. The *Indianapolis Freeman* ran an article with the offensive title "No 'Nigger Day' No 'Nigger Pamphlet.' " George Knox, the editor, printed the letter signed by Douglass and Wells soliciting funds for the publication, but he did not endorse it. Knox disagreed with the assumption of the booklet that blacks would not participate in the fair. He wrote that they would appear in the thousands. "The beauty of mankind, skill, ingenuity, refinement, culture, and erudition of the Negro will be amply represented," he said. Knox objected to presenting the facts of slavery and American race problems to the world. In denouncing the pamphlet project, he refused to contribute to it or to solicit funds from others for it.[17]

Douglass responded immediately to Knox, expressed his annoyance at the editor's use of the despised "nigger," and suggested that denunciation had been mistaken for rhetoric in the article. The elder statesman of the race admonished, "No Brother Freeman, we must not be silent. We have but one weapon unimpaired and that weapon is speech, and not to use this and use it freely, is treason to the oppressed."[18]

The *Freeman* continued to disparage the idea of the pamphlet, insinuating that Douglass's self-esteem would not allow him to admit that he could be wrong. It continued to give space to his opinion, however. In April, it suggested that the ideas for Jubilee Day and the pamphlet were dead, but the July 22 issue admitted that while blacks still disapproved the special day, they looked favorably on the pamphlet.[19]

Financing the booklet was a discouraging task. Douglass had continued to work for funds, with little success, while Wells was in Europe. He was inclined to give up. On her return, Wells was more convinced than ever of what she had written earlier in the first circular letter, which stated, "The necessity for placing ourselves before the world in a true and dignified light is imperative and this seems the best way."[20] She became increasingly aware, nonetheless, that there were obstacles to completing the project.

In July, Wells wrote to Judge Albion Tourgee about her discouragement. Money was not forthcoming, and writers had delayed or neglected the work. She urged him to write a chapter on recently passed Southern laws, the Ku Klux Klan, and methods used to nullify the black vote. "The English people do not understand how state governments can thus nullify the National Constitution regarding the right to vote. It is very necessary that this be made clear and I know no one with the data and the ability and the zeal for the pamphlet, all rolled in one who could help me." She promised to pay him at a later date, indicating that she thought it possible to raise $500 through personal appeals. In a postscript, Wells explained that she respected his desire not to be involved, and so she had made no public reference to him in regard to the pamphlet.[21]

Making use of her popularity after the successful European lecture tour, she gathered about her some Chicago women who could assist in organizing meetings to raise the needed money. On Sunday afternoons, Quinn Chapel,

Bethel, and St. Stephen's Church were alternately filled with audiences who came to hear Frederick Douglass or Ida B. Wells. She had determined that the ideal of a booklet in four languages was beyond reach and had lowered her aim. For $500, a printing of 20,000 copies in English with prefaces in French and German could be provided. In a note to the public, preceding the preface, she gave credit to black Americans for making the pamphlet possible and indicated that 20,000 copies were ready for free distribution.[22]

The eighty-one-page booklet was titled *The Reason Why the Colored American Is Not in the World's Fair* and included contributions by Frederick Douglass, I. Garland Penn, F. L. Barnett, and Ida B. Wells, who also edited the publication. [Pages 189-223 of this book republish the sections by Ida B. Wells and F. L. Barnett.] Well's preface stated that the purpose of the writers was to answer seriously the justifiable questions of visitors regarding the absence of black Americans from the fair. In Douglass's introductory chapter, he explained, "We have deemed it only a duty to ourselves, to make plain what might otherwise be misunderstood and misconstrued concerning us. To do this we must begin with slavery. The duty undertaken is far from a welcome one."[23]

The small book systematically reviewed the history of slavery and the spirit of slavery still existing in the United States in 1893. Douglass's discussion covered both aspects, moving from actual bondage to discriminatory laws and the atrocities of the convict lease system. Wells gave a statistical and descriptive account of lynchings; she also analyzed lynch law. While the chief emphasis of the pamphlet was on racial problems, I. Garland Penn reported on the impressive progress of the race since Emancipation. He pointed out in detail the population increase, the improved literacy rate, the establishment of schools and churches, and the advances made by blacks in the professions, labor, and the arts. The story of the black American's disappointment and protest at being left out of the planning and management of the fair was told by attorney-editor, F. L. Barnett. He concluded the work by saying: "Our failure to be represented is not of our own working and we can only hope that the spirit of freedom and fair play of which some Americans so loudly boast, will so inspire the Nation that in another great National endeavor the Colored American shall not plead for a place in vain."[24] In assessing the value of this project, Ann Massa notes the "proud, ironic subtitle: 'The Afro-American's Contribution to Columbian Literature.' " She believes that despite the reluctance of some blacks to examine the situations leading to the government's disregard of eight million black Americans, the pamphlet was timely, coming when the news that Fannie Williams would speak at the Women's Congress might have taken the edge off the black people's complaint. She considers the publication in itself rare and climactic, of "pioneering significance."[25]

The Reason Why was distributed by Wells from the Haitian Pavilion, where Douglass was in charge. On August 25, Colored American Day was celebrated. A number of representative blacks appeared on the program. The poet Paul Laurence Dunbar and the concert singer Harry T. Burleigh were among the notables. Douglass gave the major address, using the occasion to censure the policies of the fair directors and to proclaim the progress of black Americans in spite of the obstacles of injustice and discrimination. Wells stayed away, but she read the accounts of the speech given by the aging race leader. Realizing that he had seized the opportunity to render a service to the cause of the race, she was filled with remorse and immediately went to him to apologize for her stubborn refusal to participate. In recalling the incident, she wrote, "He persevered with his plans without any aid whatever from us hotheads and produced a program which was reported from one end of the country to the other.[26]

While Ida B. Wells was in Chicago to protest against the slights suffered by blacks during the Columbian Exposition, she turned to good use the example of women's organizations for social improvement in England, by becoming the prime mover in founding the first Afro-American women's club in the city. The Tourgee Club, named in honor of Judge Albion W. Tourgee, had begun as a black men's club. The clubhouse was set up chiefly for entertaining visitors to the city and to the World's Fair. One day each week was left open as "ladies' day." Because the women had not made use of the facility, Wells was invited to act as hostess and to speak on ladies' day. She welcomed the opportunity to point out to her audience the advantage they had in such a meeting place. She encouraged them to use it regularly. She also told them of the English women's groups before which she had lectured and of the club movement in the East, where the women had organized in order to assist her anti-lynching mission.[27]

The first meeting drew a large crowd and initiated weekly gatherings for lectures, discussions, and musical programs. Wells was elected to chair the meetings. She invited other distinguished persons to speak to the group; among them the English editor W. T. Stead, who was writing *If Christ Came to Chicago*. When the women decided to form a separate organization, they elected Ida Wells as president. The following year the club was granted a charter and named in her honor.[28]

Besides this involvement with the clubwomen in Chicago, Wells joined the staff of the *Chicago Conservator*. Ideologically, she was akin to the editor, F. L. Barnett, who had been one of her collaborators in producing the World's Fair protest pamphlet. Like her, he was an agitator. A successful attorney with political ambitions, he prided himself on being of refined family and company. He was nevertheless an outspoken advocate of race unity in achieving full rights for all black Americans.[29] Barnett was a member of the Chicago elite. Born of slave parents in Nashville, Tennessee, his father purchased the family's freedom in 1856 and three years later took them all to Canada. Ten years later the Barnetts migrated to Chicago, where Ferdinand completed high school and college. In 1878, he was granted a law degree from Northwestern University.[30] In that same year, he founded the *Conservator*, one of the first black newspapers in Chicago.[31]

As soon as he had attained professional status, Barnett became active in the protest movement for equal rights. Strongly advocating united, organized effort, he showed impatience with blacks who were comfortable in their individual achievements and oblivious of the needs of others not so fortunate. In a speech on racial solidarity delivered at the National Conference of Colored Men of the United States in 1879, he stressed the value of corporate action rather than individual brilliance. He condemned the "spirit of pomp and display," urging instead frugality and economy. Concerned with respectability, a characteristic of the professional class at that time, he said that education and morality should be the general rule among black Americans. He questioned the jealousies that deterred blacks from aiding their own potential leaders. In the same category as ignorance among the masses, Barnett placed disinterest and lack of cooperation among the educated. The remedies he proposed for blacks in time of government unconcern and inaction were reflective of the self-help tradition. He exhorted his audience to instruct the ignorant, to dissipate jealousies, to aid the downtrodden, to patronize black tradesmen, and to work out problems together.[32]

This emphasis on racial unity did not prevent F. L. Barnett from being basically an integrationist, who also expressed the conviction that black Americans should prepare themselves for full participation in the nation's civic affairs. He counseled economic stability in order that blacks be prepared and prompt to seize opportunities. He urged ambition for leadership and support for those who succeeded in getting into the political arena.[33]

As editor and owner of the *Chicago Conservator*, Barnett provided his readers with items of world interest, but he allowed more space for politics and personalities. The newspaper office was a center for political discussion. It attracted the interest and visits of local and national black leaders. Prominent Chicagoans who were militant integrationists gave Barnett and his news organ enthusiastic support. Among the *Conservator*'s friends was the "old settler"[34] John G. Jones, a lawyer and politician. Because he so fiercely protested any form of segregation and so frequently called indignation meetings, he was referred to as "Indignation Jones." A faithful advocate of equal rights, he was an enemy of separatism. Another ally and sponsor was the eminent dentist Dr. Charles E. Bentley, closely associated with the skilled surgeon and founder of Provident Hospital, Dr. Daniel Hale Williams.[35]

Thus, after the work of the Columbian Exposition, Ida B. Wells found a congenial atmosphere in her associations with the editor, staff, and supporters of the *Chicago Conservator*. She decided to remain in Chicago. Her plans were delayed, however, when she was asked by the Society for the Brotherhood of Man to return to England and Scotland to resume anti-lynching lectures. Before she left on this second trip to Britain, Wells established another tie with the city. She made arrangements with the editor of the *Chicago Inter-Ocean*, a white newspaper, to write a column from abroad. She was the first black American to be hired as a correspondent by that paper.[36]

FIVE

The Second
British Tour

The second invitation extended to Ida B. Wells to lecture in Europe evoked greater reaction in the United States than the first. The Southern press lifted its boycott against her. It was condemnatory of her and disparaging toward the English. The *Memphis Commercial Appeal* commented, "It was only when she had put an ocean between herself and the facts that she could get a patient audience. As to the force of the English public opinion—bah!" The *Mobile Register* insisted, "There are two things about the South that the English people cannot understand: the relationship between the whites and blacks in the counties where the blacks are in the majority; the second is the dilatory character of our legal processes." There was an ever-present reminder that while lynch law was regrettable it was the only means available to the Southerners to "induce the negroes not to commit crime, to cease ravishing, and live peaceful and honest lives."[1]

While Southern white newspapers attacked the position of Ida B. Wells, some black newsmen complained about her tactics. C. H. J. Taylor, editor of the *Cincinnati American Citizen*, was among those who claimed to take exception only to her manner "as champion to remedy race afflictions." He appealed to the *Indianapolis Freeman*, however, to correct the notion that he had attacked Well's character.[2] J. L. Fleming, her former business manager, denied the worth of the lectures. He wrote in his *Chicago Free Speech*, "Fire eating speeches nowhere on the globe will help the situation." Fleming was in turn excoriated for his expression of disapproval by a black woman who challenged him to devise something better than the Wells crusade. She referred to Wells as the Joan of Arc of the race, saying that the young woman journalist had put up with what few men would be willing to endure, and that she had succeeded in winning favorable resolutions from the British.[3]

In England, Wells found that the task before her was more difficult than the tour of 1893. At the end of the first European sojourn, she had become aware of a serious breach in the relationship between Catherine Impey and Isabelle Fyvie Mayo. Impey had been guilty of a personal indiscretion involving one of the East Indians in residence at the home of Mayo. As a result, Mayo took a punitive attitude toward the Englishwoman with whom she had worked so closely in social reform. Ida Wells had refused to reject Impey, who in May 1893 had already been relegated to the background of the Society for the Recognition of the Brotherhood of Man.

The terms accepted by the executive council in November were her expenses plus two pounds per week. Arrangements had been made for her leave of absence from the *Conservator*. In December, Wells received a letter from Isabelle Mayo suggesting that information about Catherine Impey should be publicly revealed. Desiring no part in this personal quarrel, Wells refused. She wrote the same to Celestine Edwards, a black man replacing Impey. Edwards replied that he had no desire that the problem involving Impey be discussed. Mayo, on the other hand, notified Wells that the trip should perhaps be canceled as she, Scottish head of the Society, would now have nothing to do with Wells, who again contacted Edwards to find out whether Mayo's letter represented the sentiments of the Society as a whole. He assured her that it did not, and that she should start for England right away. Despite Edwards's goodwill, the situation that greeted Wells's arrival in Liverpool was not a happy one. Mayo had resigned and withdrawn her share in the expense of the trip. Edwards was ill. The organization was very weak as a consequence of the withdrawal of the friends of Impey. The guest lecturer was left to her own resources in paying her passage and arranging for speaking engagements.[4]

Under these disagreeable circumstances, Wells found herself dependent on other sources for introductions to various audiences. In March she wrote to Frederick Douglass requesting both a letter of thanks in her behalf to the Reverend C. F. Aked, who had welcomed her into his home as a guest and into his church as a lecturer, and a letter of introduction to groups that might require one. Douglass complied with the first part of the request. He addressed a letter to Reverend Aked thanking him for the hospitality he had shown Wells, adding in somewhat restrained tones a denial of the accusations made by Southern papers against her and his own belief in her cause. He refused, however, to be moved by Wells's importunity in requesting a letter of introduction immediately. To her distress, he required another letter from her assuring him that he could "intelligently and truthfully" recommend her to English groups.[5] Although she had failed to explain in detail the reason a letter of introduction was necessary, she received his request for a second letter as a personal insult and responded on April 6 with injured and angry feelings.

> With all the discouragements I have received and the time and money I have sacrificed to the work, I have never felt so like giving up as since I received your very cool and cautious letter this morning with its tone of distrust and its inference that I have not dealt truthfully with you.

She explained that she would not have asked him for a letter, had not the Reverend Aked suggested the possible need for it. She expressed frustration and anxiety, reminding Douglass that she had never asked any favor of him or anyone except "to further the cause." Indicating the uselessness of the letter of introduction after the passage of so much time, she said:

> It will be 20 days at least before that letter can reach me, and then it will be too late, for I shall as soon as I finish the dates made for me this month, throw up and come home. My business in Chicago needs me too badly to be giving my time for a work which nobody else will do, and which I cannot afford to do at such cost to myself and suspicion to my friends.

With this message she enclosed a copy of the invitation she had received from Mayo the preceding September. She also indicated that she had been urged to undertake the second lecture tour by Mayo and Edwards.

In this lengthy explanation of her problems, Wells apologized to Douglass for her inability to repay him $25 she had borrowed and for which she had expected a reimbursement from the British Society. Again she expressed her injured feelings: "While my heart bleeds that you should class me with that large class who have imposed upon your confidence, I still love you as the greatest man our race has yet produced and because of what you have suffered and endured for the race."[6]

Exactly one month later, having seen the letter written by Douglass to Aked, Ida Wells wrote again of her disappointment at his restraint in endorsing her activities. She referred to the miserable failure of the Society for the Recognition of the Brotherhood of Man, the vagueness of the English people about the black population of America, their tendency to believe the impressions left by American visitors, magazines, and newspapers, and their inclination to question the honesty of her interpretations. For the third time Wells made her plea to Douglass for a strong recommendation, enclosing a letter from a Unitarian minister who asked for such an endorsement. Four days later she reinforced this plea with another urgent request. She said that she had been promised a hearing by Members of Parliament at the residence of the Lord Mayor of London at which he would preside. This gathering was contingent upon "letters vouching for my testimony and character, to show that I am speaking for my race and not myself, from persons of influence in America." The outcome of such a meeting, she promised, would be a far more forceful denunciation of lynching than had come forth in the United States. For this occasion Wells said that she had requested a letter from Senator Chandler also, since he had recently spoken out against lynching.[7]

In her autobiographical account of the second European tour, however, Wells-Barnett did not refer to any assistance given by influential Americans. She praised the *Chicago Inter-Ocean* for its consistent publication of the column "Ida B. Wells Abroad" and noted the contribution of Albion W. Tourgee in his "Bystander" column for its fairness to American blacks. The reports of her activities throughout England during 1894 indicate that she needed little introduction. From Liverpool, Manchester, Newcastle, and London she wrote enthusiastic accounts of numerous lectures before very large groups, several of which drew up resolutions condemning the practice of lynching. Among the most memorable events for her was the formation of the Anti-Lynching Committee in London. The long membership list, including many distinguished English personages, was headed by that of the Duke of Argyll, son-in-law of Queen Victoria. The names of some prestigious Americans were added later.[8]

Wells received a good deal of press coverage in England. In the United States, however, the Southern press, never denying the fact of lynchings, continued to defend the practice with the story of the "peculiar and shocking crimes that provoke it."[9] The black crusader became an object of scorn and insult. The *Memphis Daily Commercial* circulated in England articles of its May 26 issue defaming her character "in language more vulgar and obscene than anything the *Police Gazette* ever contained." Wells reported that the effect of the tone and style was to discredit the paper. Since copies of the *Commercial* had reached Britain, she had been honored at a breakfast with members of Parliament at the Westminster Palace Hotel, and an anti-lynching committee had been formed. The only printed comment of which she was aware was a statement of the *Liverpool Daily Post*, which said, "Both the articles are very coarse in tone and could not possibly be reproduced in an English journal." The writer of the *Post* item added that the *Commercial* admitted the lynchings and that was the problem that Wells had brought before the English public.[10]

The American white press eagerly published negative reactions of American blacks to Wells's anti-lynching crusade. A majority of the Colored School Teachers Association of Georgia was reported to have voted down a resolution commending Wells.[11] The *Memphis Appeal-Avalanche* had good copy for its purposes in an interview with former Congressman John M. Langston. He professed disagreement with Wells, intimating that she was less patriotic than eager for "notoriety and revenue." To this demeaning suggestion, Langston added his conviction that the evils that had existed in the South in the past were rapidly being remedied. The interview caused reactions in the black community redounding to the benefit of Wells and her cause.[12] The A.M.E. Bishop Henry McNeal Turner of Atlanta wrote a lengthy defense of her character and her crusade and turned his wrath upon black Americans who had not the courage of their convictions to uphold Wells. Bishop Turner, a strong advocate of emigration to Africa, wrote:

> I know of editors of our colored papers who are in profound sympathy with Miss Wells, but will not say a word through their papers. The bulk of our school teachers are scullions. They sympathize with Miss Wells, commend her labors, spirit and motives, yet when they meet in convention they will adopt no commendatory resolutions; nor will they make a speech favorable to her, and why? Because they are afraid they will lose their positions. They sacrifice their man and womanhood to the will of those who traduce and degrade them and thereby become scullions. Whenever a people are so abnormalized by their environment that they are afraid to lift up their voices in protest against their murderers and exterminators, it is time to leave there or ask for enslavement.[13]

Wells wrote a scathing denunciation of J. Thomas Turner, the black man whom the *Commercial* used to testify to the truth of its libelous articles distributed in England. The *Commercial* had described Turner as a representative of the respectable element of black Memphis. She labeled him a sycophant.[14]

From the security of a sympathetic land, Ida B. Wells was in a position to express the truth as she perceived it about practices in the South. Blacks who remained in that part of the United States continued to be the victims of intimidation and mob violence. There had been a decrease from 155 lynchings in 1892 to 114 in 1893, but there had been a rise again to 128 in 1894.[15]

In focusing attention on what she called the national crime of the United States, Wells was not reluctant to risk offending highly regarded Americans. She bluntly told audiences there that the religious and moral leaders of the North met the lynching of American blacks with silence. Since the Reverend Dwight L. Moody and Frances Willard were reformers well known in Britain, questions were asked about their positions in particular. Wells included them both among those who raised no protest, but she went further in regard to Willard, the leader of the Women's Christian Temperance Union (WCTU).[16]

Frances Willard had given an interview, published in 1890, that expressed sympathy for Southerners, indirectly defending lynchers and denigrating the characters of blacks. Her attitudes were the same as those at which Ida Wells aimed her fiercest arguments. This offensive interview, which drew the criticism of Frederick Douglass as well as Wells, had taken place after the WCTU had been warmly welcomed by Southerners at the October 1890 national convention held in Atlanta. Willard's sentiments of good faith with her Southern hosts had been backed up with a promise of her loyalty to them on her return to the North. Expressing her belief that Southerners had been unintentionally wronged when the North had neglected to put any restrictions on the black man's vote, she had said:

> We ought to have put an educational test upon the ballot from the first. The Anglo-Saxon race will never submit to be dominated by the Negro so long as his attitude reaches no higher than the personal liberty of the saloon, and the power of appreciating the amount of liquor a dollar will buy.

To this comment, she had added:

> I pity the southerners, and I believe the great mass of them are as conscientious and kindly-intentioned toward the colored man as an equal number of white church-members of the North. . . . The problem on their hands is immeasurable. The colored race multiplies like the locusts of Egypt. The grog-shop is its center of power. The safety of women, of childhood, of the home is menaced in a thousand localities at this moment, so that the men dare not go beyond the sight of their own roof-tree.[17]

In a lengthy address before an audience at the Washington A.M.E. Metropolitan Church in 1894, Douglass had countered statements such as those made by Willard. He had systematically analyzed the arguments used to justify disfranchisement, lynching, and other injustices, showing the falsity of the charges used against the black man. Citing the accusations of Willard and others, he announced his readiness to confront these persons, but in a conciliatory tone he asked the Northern friends of the race to show for the victims of lynch law some of the justice and charity they so willingly expressed for the Southern mob. In so doing, he pointed to the mistake people of the North made in overlooking "the natural effect and influence of the life, education and habits of the lynchers." He recalled the evils of slavery, as he had done in other speeches, and the disregard for life to which the South was inured by centuries of this peculiar institution.[18]

Wells had with her in England the issue of the *New York Voice* in which Willard's interview had been published. Wells had the temerity to quote it in an article she wrote for *Fraternity*, the official organ of the Society for the Recognition of the Brotherhood of Man. Because Frances Willard was the guest of the influential socialite Lady Henry Somerset, Wells's article caused embarrassment. Florence Balgarnie, the English lecturer and journalist, who was also an active anti-lynching advocate, apprised Lady Somerset that the Wells article was to be printed in the May edition of *Fraternity*. She hoped to prevent the circulation of the issue. Lady Somerset chose to defend her guest by publishing, in advance, in the *Westminster Gazette*, an interview in which she allowed Willard to explain her position and show that she had been misrepresented in a speech by Wells. Undismayed, Wells, the feisty crusader, answered the accusations of the interview in a letter to the editor of the *Gazette*.

> The fact is, Miss Willard is no better or worse than the great bulk of white Americans on the Negro questions. They are all afraid to speak out, and it is only British public opinion which will move them, as I am thankful to see it has already begun to move Miss Willard.[19]

When she wrote to Douglass in June, Wells told him that Lady Somerset, in her anger, was attempting to misconstrue his words as a commendation of her mission but not of her, personally.

> I published, by request the whole of that interview of Miss Willard's which you mention in your pamphlet in *Fraternity*. Miss Willard has been her guest and feted and flattered until she has been made a fool of. When people asked as to her attitude on the lynching question, I told the truth and quoted her words. For so doing I incurred Lady Henry Somerset's displeasure and then it was she cabled you.

She went on with her account of Lady Somerset's intention to discredit her, but added, "God has raised up powerful friends for the cause, not me, and I have not suffered."[20]

At the national convention of the WCTU held in Cleveland in November 1894, Frances Willard took the opportunity to defend her record regarding race:

> The zeal for her race of Miss Ida B. Wells, a bright young colored woman, has, it seems to me, clouded her perception as to who were her friends and well-wishers in all high-minded and legitimate efforts to banish the abomination of lynching and torture.

She imputed to Wells a slur on the reputations of half the white race. She claimed that Wells had accused white women of taking the initiative in "nameless acts between the races." Wells claimed that her statement had been, "Colored men have been lynched for assault upon women, when the facts were plain that the relationship between the victim lynched and the alleged victim of his assault was voluntary, clandestine, and illicit."[21]

The WCTU president admitted that the sentiments expressed in the *Voice* interview were her true feelings, and that she regretted only that she had not censured immoral white men who had created racial tensions and family discord by their illicit relations with black women. She denied that there was any distinction of color in the national or world temperance unions, and stated that while there were separate temperance societies in the South, blacks were represented in the WCTU at the national level. Willard declared, "It is inconceivable that the WCTU will ever condone lynching, no matter what the provocation."[22].

Wells felt herself vindicated. The "Bystander" of the *Chicago Inter-Ocean* commented at length on the fact that Willard had taken Wells to task for censuring the silence of the WCTU on the problem of lynching. On the criticism of the Union, he commented, "This was literally true—Not until lashed by her words and the condemnation of the English critics did that organization venture even to condemn; it has not yet uttered any vigorous protest." Tourgee, the "Bystander," criticized Christianity, the pulpit, and the press for their complacency and their excuses for keeping silent. Quoting a Northern journalist who expressed his powerlessness to address the crime of lynching, Tourgee pointed out that the pattern of the church and the press in regard to slavery was being repeated. "At first they denied; then they ridiculed; then they excused. When finally forced to condemn, they asked the question of this writer: 'What can we do about it?' "

Urging pulpit and press to declare open war against lynching and to support national anti-lynching legislation, Tourgee showed his sympathy with Wells's crusade. He concluded, "It is because she speaks the truth that American Christianity withers under her gentle rebuke. It does no good to scold or blame her. She is black, but the only way to refute her is not to ask what can be done but to go and do."[23]

Wells thanked Tourgee for the "unequivocal expression in behalf of justice which you alone seem moved to make." She told him that she was distressed at having no opportunity to show that she had not misrepresented the WCTU in England, and that at Cleveland the Southern Caucus had prevented the passage of an anti-lynching resolution by the national WCTU.[24] She had attended the meeting in Cleveland as the delegate of a society of the A.M.E. Church there, had been introduced, and had made a plea for a statement against lynching. She later confronted Willard on the interpretation the WCTU leader had given to her words regarding the complicity of white women in interracial liaisons in which the black was later accused of rape, but Willard made no retraction nor explanation at the convention. The organization's *Union Signal* printed an editorial note in December, however, indicating that Willard had not meant literally that Wells had "put an unjust imputation upon half the white race." She had, she said, only intended to suggest the way the public would construe Well's utterances.[25] Blacks, however, continued to level what Frances Willard's biographer termed "trenchant criticism" at the WCTU.

The renowned reformer's discomfort under fire evidently gained for her the sympathy of one group of civil rights advocates. On February 6, 1895, a letter was addressed to the English press defending Willard against criticisms that the writers said would not be tolerated by persons familiar with her character and work in her own country. Willard's defenders explained the racial policies of the national WCTU, which allowed blacks to be members and representatives at national conventions, although there were racially separate units in the South. The letter also extolled Willard's personal liberalism which, it said, was manifest in her reported threat to withdraw from a Chicago women's club if it did not accept blacks as members. Although the letter was composed and distributed by members of the WCTU, it was signed by ten distinguished Northern civil rights advocates led by Frederick Douglass.[26]

At the World WCTU convention held in London in June 1895, Lady Henry Somerset, reelected president of the British Union, announced a proposed resolution against the lynchings in the southern part of the United States. In her introductory remarks, however, she denounced Wells for her charge that Willard was unsympathetic to American blacks. Florence Balgarnie, secretary of the Anti-Lynching Society of London, gave her hearty approval to the anti-lynching resolution, and defended Wells's contention that the American WCTU had "acted the part of an apologist for, rather than a denouncer of outrages perpetrated upon Negroes." The hostility of the audience to her remarks forced Balgarnie to a tearful retreat. Willard recovered the moment by enthusiastically endorsing the resolution, but she expressed regret that Wells, "by her attitude toward the whites, had stirred up the black blood to strife." Hallie Quinn Brown, who was touring Europe as an elocutionist-lecturer and fund-raiser for Wilberforce University, was another speaker at the convention, and she unequivocally supported Miss Willard.[27]

The *Cleveland Gazette* quoted the *London Daily News*: "The convention of the World's WCTU virtually condoned lynching by expressing the contented attitude of their American sisters, who think it enough to rebuke howling, murdering rioters with the perfunctory remark that human life must not be taken without due process of law." The article continued, "The American visitors should know that no British woman regards such a remark as anything less than a solemn mockery when applied to hideous murderers." A black American in England, writing to the editor of the *Gazette* to express his disappointment in the convention, stated that in his view Willard was a "temporizer," attempting to convince both blacks and Southern whites of her sympathy. The Cleveland paper commented, "Our people of this city are astonished at the stand Miss Hallie Q. Brown has taken."[28]

However, Wells's challenge to Willard's statements and to the unconcern of the temperance union regarding lynching was apparently an effective influence on the WCTU president's interest in her reformer image and her organization's anti-lynching stand. Frederick Douglass had died the preceding February, and Frances Willard wrote to Mrs. Douglass from Lady Somerset's home in Reigate, Surrey, offering sympathy on the death of "our beloved apostle." She reported that an anti-lynching resolution, a copy of which she enclosed, had been unanimously adopted by the British WCTU at their convention, and that another had been passed by the World Union. She promised to try to get the same response at the national WCTU convention at Baltimore in October. She wrote: "I wish to thank you for your kindness and I can but hope that hereafter there can be no doubt as to my attitude."[29]

In recounting her conflict with Frances Willard, Ida B. Wells explained her outspokenness, which took precedence over tact whenever she faced issues that she felt were not being met honestly by persons in positions of power or influence. Of the Willard incident, she wrote:

> I desire no quarrel with the W.C.T.U., but my love for the truth is greater than my regard for an alleged friend who, through ignorance or design misrepresents in the most harmful way the cause of a long suffering race, and then unable to maintain the truth of her attack excuses herself as it were by the wave of the hand, declaring that "she did not intend a literal interpretation to be given to the language used."[30]

In arousing public sentiment in England and Scotland against lynching, Wells affected the reputations of others besides Willard. She had focused her attack mainly on Southern officials of the United States, accusing them not merely of allowing lynchings but also of fostering them. The responses of several governors indicated their irritation with this unpleasant exposure, and their immediate tendency, too, was to discredit Ida B. Wells and her message.

In June 1894, Governor W. J. Stone of Missouri addressed a letter to the *London News* attacking an editorial it printed after one of her lectures. The *Richmond Dispatch* questioned the wisdom of the governor in giving the anti-lynching propagandist his attention, thus dignifying her position. The *Dispatch* reminded its readers that Wells had been "expelled [from Memphis] for heinous conduct." Governor Stone had intimated that the chief object of the anti-lynching agitator, in his estimation, was to turn immigrants away from the South.[31] This notion was also expressed by Governor W. J. Northen of Georgia. His contention was that Ida B. Wells was working with a group of English and American investors who were eager to divert immigrants from the South to the West.[32] A *New York Age* article reprinted in the *Topeka Weekly Call* told of a letter from the Georgia governor, denouncing Wells's statements as outrageous. A leading Georgia congressman countered her attack on lynching by asserting that blacks who assaulted women deserved no less. Again he repeated the notion that Wells was a destitute hireling of a syndicate working in the interest of a Western boom. He accused her of putting obstacles in the way of Southern lawmakers, publicists, and preachers attempting to curtail lynchings by the accusations she made against them.[33] Referring to Southern utterances in reaction to Wells's crusade, an English observer wrote:

> Miss Wells was evidently right in thinking that, on this question, as on Negro emancipation half a century ago English opinion counts in America. We know our national faults, and have no desire to be censorious, but we think that the views of a people like ourselves standing outside the bitter racial, social and political prejudices which vex the United States should have their weight with right-minded Americans, and we are glad to find that, as a matter of fact this is the case.[34]

Lloyd Crawford, who studied American reactions to the crusades of Ida B. Wells, found little evidence of black opposition to her. When it existed, however, it was publicized by the white press. *The New York Times* reported a speech given by the politically ambitious H. C. C. Astwood, who had been a United States consul and was then secretary of the National Negro Democratic Party. At the executive committee meeting of the New York State Cleveland League, he said, concerning Wells:

> I speak for the honest and intelligent masses of my race when I call her a fraud. She has been going about the country gathering notoriety. She knows nothing about the colored people in the South. We all regret that lynchings occur there, but we approve them to the extent that the white people of the South do.
> A reputable or respectable negro has never been lynched, and never will be. Only outlaws have suffered such a fate. It was right and just that they should be outlawed for their crimes.
> All this talk about the pitiable condition of the negro in the South is nonsense and untrue.

Going on in this vein, Astwood made the unlikely statement that "Old habits of old associations are returning. The negro is going to be happy again with associations of the people who once held him in bondage.[35]

This kind of attack on Wells with its defense of Southern policies and practices was ignored by the black press. The Afro-American Press Association stood firmly behind Wells. She was a member of the organization and at one time its secretary. As a crusader against lynching she had its hearty endorsement. Less than one month after Astwood's speech was reported, there was an exchange of letters between officers of the Afro-American Press Association and Virginia's anti-lynching Governor Charles O'Ferrall. It reveals the stance of the black journalists. The national organization had invited the governor to speak at a meeting. He refused on the grounds that the group supported Ida B. Wells "in her slander of the people and civil authorities of the South." As O'Ferrall stated his position against lynching he accused Wells and the press association of excusing "the brutes who commit this crime [rape] too horrible to mention," and implied that if she and the other journalists condemned black criminals, lynchings would cease.

The association officers responded by expressing regret at the governor's refusal to attend their meeting and at the obvious difference of opinion existing between them. In answering his indictment that the journalists and Wells condoned the crimes of blacks, the group resolved to denounce all crime and to demand punishments sanctioned by state and federal laws. In the context of this resolution, there was no place for lynchings. The writers insisted that Wells spoke the truth and they concurred in her statements that blacks were lynched when they were not so much as accused of rape. As for the governor's concern about the South's reputation for lawlessness, since most of the members of the association were Southerners, they stood to suffer with that section, but for them life and liberty were more important than the success and money to be gained through good publicity. Although the press association did not relate the "growing popular sentiment against lynchers" to the activity of the "brave little woman who had dared to champion our cause," they praised Governor O'Ferrall and the governors of North Carolina, Georgia, and Tennessee for their recent determination to put an end to lynchings in their states.[36]

The enthusiastic receptions accorded Wells in New York in late July and in Chicago in August 1894 indicated that these Northern black communities were generally as supportive of her work as the society of the journalists. Several days after her arrival in New York, T. Thomas Fortune introduced her to an overflow crowd at Bethel A.M.E. Church. She explained that having been denied a hearing before the general public in the large cities of the United States and before the president, she had accepted the invitation of prominent British thinkers and had lectured at 102 gatherings. She recounted the sympathetic response of the British people and the antagonistic reactions of the American press. Urging American blacks to form an anti-lynching society, she spoke of the purpose of the anti-lynching movement.

We want the colored race to be placed in the proper light before the people of this country, for there is in literature no true type of the negro as he is today. The lawless lynchings in the south for alleged crimes against the whites are in ninety-nine cases out of a hundred simply outrages against our race. The press is in control of the whites and the attacks upon us are colored to suit themselves.

The colored people of the country should organize themselves. . . . They should at least contribute the sinews of war with which to fight the battle. The south knows that we are very much disorganized.[37]

She insisted on the need to investigate lynchings and the crimes that they purported to avenge, and she denied the accusation that she or any person conscious of civil rights would uphold black criminals.

We do not desire to shield the criminal because he is a black man, but we want at least to have his guilt established by a court competent to try him before he is executed, and we want the black man's home to be as sacred from invasions as that of any other man in the land.[38]

In stating these goals, Ida B. Wells anticipated the National Association for the Advancement of Colored People. To her emphasis on investigation that organization would add legal defense, a process that she attempted with the limitations of her individual resources.[39]

In Chicago, the returning crusader was greeted by another large audience at Quinn Chapel. She was called the "leading African woman in America," and praised for her speech and manner. On this occasion she announced:

At last we have made the American people realize that the world is condemning the awful atrocities of the South. We had to go 3,000 miles to get a hearing and platform from which to speak. That was my mission to England.[40]

The editor of the *Chicago Observer*, however, wrote that the only effect of the Wells tours had been the founding of a league in opposition to the Anti-Lynching League. The *Indianapolis Freeman* considered this a premature judgment and an unfair evaluation.

Before the advent of Miss Wells and the consequent Anti-Lynching movement, the Negro's case in equity had lingered comparatively unnoticed for years, been set back on the calendar, dismissed from public attention, avoided by all as an unpleasant condition of things hard to face with the means of settlement not well in hand.

The South was indifferent and the North accepted its bluff of defiance of public opinion. The South had grown steadily bolder in the game of "nigger killing." No assistance from churches, nor politicians except in the face of defeat or in the perfunctory statement of a newly elected president.

The hour had come, where was the man?

Unfortunately, the man was not forthcoming—Miss Wells was![41]

Ida B. Wells combined assertiveness, the need of the times, and her own experience to assume the task that may have seemed a man's to her supporters and her critics. She did not consider for which sex the work at hand was appropriate. She carried out the mission of agitator and propagandist for which she felt her experiences qualified her. This she did with the self-reliance and independence that black women had been reputed to have since the days of bondage. The discussion, embarrassment, and criticism following her anti-lynching tours motivated Southern officials in the United States to seek remedies against lynching. The anti-lynching legislation enacted by states between 1893 and 1905 provided several preventive measures. These took the form of strengthening law enforcement and increasing community responsibility. The new enactments provided that law officers be given greater power to enforce the law, and that greater responsibility be demanded of them. Penalties for failing to prevent mob violence were prescribed, and citizens were warned of severe reprisals for obstructing legal procedures. Means for discovering, apprehending, and punishing lynchers were established. Finally, communities were made responsible for damages against lynch victims, whose personal representatives were guaranteed the right of recovery.[42]

At the federal level, the most significant effect of Wells's tours was the Blair Resolution. On August 3, 1894, within a month of her return to the United States, Congressman Henry William Blair of New Hampshire introduced a measure calling for an investigation into all the acts of violence committed as punitive measures against alleged criminals during the previous ten years. A commissioner of labor was to be held responsible for the investigation into cases in which charges of assault resulted in mob action against the accused. These official inquiries were to be financed by a maximum appropriation of $25,000. Although the resolution eventually died in committee, Blair was able to present petitions to the committee urging passage from citizens of twelve states, including South Carolina, Alabama, Tennessee, Maryland, and Louisiana. There was greater success at the state level. Between 1893 and 1897, North Carolina, Georgia, South Carolina, Ohio, Kentucky, and Texas passed anti-lynching laws.[43]

When Wells resumed her crusade in the Northern cities of the United States, she was confident that her efforts had been "blessed with the most salutary results." She summarized:

> Since the crusade against lynching was started, however, governors of states, newspapers, senators and representatives and bishops of churches have all been compelled to take cognizance of the prevalence of this crime and to speak in one way or another in the defense of the charge against this barbarism in the United States. This has not been because there was any latent spirit of justice voluntarily asserting itself, especially in those who do the lynching, but because the entire American people now feel, both North and South, that they are objects in the gaze of the civilized world and that for every lynching humanity asks that America render its account to civilization and itself.[44]

The anti-lynching agitation of Ida B. Wells during the early 1890s did affect American public opinion and did influence anti-lynching legislation in the states. The practice of lynching, however, was not eradicated. It was several decades before a decrease in lynching incidents appreciably reflected the anti-lynching protest or the anti-lynching laws. Black Americans required a power base that would enable them to persist in systematic investigations and litigations that would be taken seriously by the nation as a whole.[45]

SIX

White Racism
and Black
Organizational Response

From the 1890s into the 1920s, segregationist thought was crystallized and publicized systematically and authoritatively in the entire nation. Racist ideas were accepted by intellectuals and academicians. I. A. Newby writes, "Anti-Negro racism was the fashion of the day, as white America busied itself defining and implementing the new status of Negro Americans." Segregationists had the biological and social sciences to lean on in developing the rationale for their policies and practices. Newby observes that before the 1920s these disciplines accepted or failed to refute the view that blacks were inferior to Caucasians. Science, history, and religion were used to defend disfranchisement and segregation. Two of the fundamental racist postulates were that black Africa had never developed a genuine civilization and that black Americans had never shown themselves capable of responsible citizenship. Segregationists were not alone in this misreading of history. Historians of the late nineteenth and early twentieth centuries, with the weight of academic training in the best of the nation's graduate schools, believed blacks to be inferior and substantially supported segregationist opinion. Descriptions of racially related episodes of history leading to the conclusion of inherent deficiencies in black people were combined with the historians' assumption that America was the white man's land.[1]

In the South anti-black sentiment became extreme. Blacks were looked upon not merely as inferior, but as immoral and criminal, incapable of reaching the white man's civilization, and prone to revert to barbarism in freedom. C. Vann Woodward explains that elements of the intense racism of the South had been present all along but held in check. Now, opposition to it had been relaxed. Northern liberalism and Southern conservatism with its prestige and influence were weakened and discredited. The radicalism of the South was no longer in constraint.[2]

Aware that lecture tours in Britain were only a beginning in counteracting anti-black sentiment in America, Ida Wells planned a year of lecturing in Northern cities of the United States. Although she did not receive a salary in England, funds were raised by friends of her cause to defray her travel and personal expenses there. In announcing her intention to tour the North in 1894, Wells asked the same kind of financial support in her own country. Finding that her appeals were not being answered, she began to accept invitations from blacks in various places and to charge a fee. She traveled through Northern cities from the Atlantic Ocean to the Pacific, speaking before black audiences, organizing anti-lynching societies, and contacting religious leaders and making appeals through newspapers. These activities made Wells aware that some blacks thought her message too radical. At the end of the year, however, she felt that she had accomplished as much as one person could in affecting public sentiment regarding racism and lynching. She had the satisfaction, also, of having had her work financed entirely by black Americans.[3]

In 1895 Wells published *A Red Record: Tabulated Statistics and Alleged Causes of Lynching in the United States, 1892—1893—1894*. The one-hundred-page pamphlet contained a brief history of the emergence of the Southerner's murderous violence when he no longer had a vested interest in the black man's life. A letter written by Ida Wells to Frederick Douglass indicates that she based this discussion on ideas that Douglass had provided in a pamphlet of his own. Wells contended that during slavery the white owners kept their black slaves in subservience by scourgings, but since the slaves were of economic value to them, they refrained from killing them. It was more satisfactory to sell the incorrigibles "Down South." With Emancipation, the whites no longer had the right to use whips on blacks, and so the new form of intimidation was lynching.[4]

To these ideas, Wells added the materials she had collected on actual lynching incidents. She told her story graphically, using statistics and descriptions culled from publications of white men whose veracity had not been questioned. Along with statistics, she presented names and places, alleged crimes, and descriptions of the inhumane executions of the lynch law's victims. The booklet was punctuated with rhetorical comments to show the pitiable position in which the Southern black found himself when he attempted to make use of his constitutional rights. Regarding the vote, she wrote:

> But it was a bootless strife for colored people. The government which had made the Negro a citizen found itself unable to protect him. It gave him the right to vote, but denied him the protection which should have maintained that right. Scourged from his home; hunted through the swamps; hung by midnight raiders, and openly murdered in the light of day, the Negro clung to his right of franchise with a heroism which would have wrung admiration from the hearts of savages. He believed that in that small white ballot there was a subtle something which stood for manhood as well as citizenship, and thousands of brave black men went to their graves, exemplifying the one by dying for the other.[5]

She gave lengthy recitals of mob brutality, which she attributed to a thirst for blood that could not be put off for justice. The remedy she proposed was respect for law. She did not contend that all the blacks who had been lynched were innocent of crime. "We have associated too long with the white man not to have copied his vices as well as his virtues." But, she did insist that blacks were not given the same opportunity as whites to defend themselves against their accusers. On the contrary, rather than proving the accused guilty, the white accusers demanded that the black prove himself innocent, even though no evidence that he could provide would be accepted by them as satisfactory. She termed the mob's usual report that the lynch victim had made a complete confession of his crime a "monstrous falsehood." In demanding fair trials for accused blacks, Wells assured her readers that, "No maudlin sympathy for criminals is solicited." She urged them to join forces with her, pressing for laws that would secure equal justice for all by disseminating facts about lynching and supporting the Blair Resolution.[6]

As Wells continued her anti-lynching crusade in America, repercussions of a white editor's attempt to undermine her credibility in England were being felt. John W. Jacks, president of the Missouri Press Association, addressed a message to Florence Balgarnie.[7] The letter was a libelous attack on Well's character and an indictment of black American women generally as blatantly immoral. Balgarnie deflected Jacks's damning statement from its intended course. She sent it to Boston to the Women's Era Club of which Josephine St. Pierre Ruffin was president. In the hands of this astute clubwoman, the letter set in motion the organization of a national association of black women.[8]

Ruffin was a native Bostonian, of mixed ancestry, born free, and educated. In 1890, she founded the Women's Era Club and became editor of the club's official organ, *Women's Era.* Her organization was invited to membership by the State Federation of Women's Clubs, and from 1893 to 1896, she was on the board of managers.[9] A group of black women in Washington had banded together in 1892 to form the Colored Women's League. According to Mary Church Terrell, president of the Washington club, this association considered itself a national organization. In 1895, when the Federation of Afro-American Women resulted from Ruffin's invitation to all black club women to convene in Boston, a second national organization came into being.[10]

An association that included women from all parts of the country had been discussed for several years. The call issued in 1895 indicated that one of the pressing needs felt by American black women was the opportunity to gain respect for themselves in the eyes of the public. The insult given by the Southern journalist fused the women's purposes and precipitated action toward a united organization. A copy of the Jacks letter was sent to every black women's club in the country. The women were asked to read it and use it with discrimination. It was never published, and its contents were described only as "too indecent for publication."

The first conference, national in scope, met during the last three days of July in Boston. The resolutions passed began with a denunciation of John W. Jacks as a "traducer of female character." They ended with an endorsement of "the noble and truthful advocacy of Mrs. Ida B. Wells-Barnett."[11] In June 1895, Ida Wells had married F. L. Barnett in Chicago. She did not attend the convention and explained her absence as the result of being "utterly worn out" from the constant pressure of travel and lecture engagements.[12]

Before the meeting, Florence Balgarnie had addressed a letter to Mrs. F. R. Ridley, secretary of the Women's Era Club. She commended the action of the clubwomen, saying, "You have done what I expected brave, true-hearted women would do, that is put on a bold front to the traducers of your race and sex." She asked that her sentiments of sympathy be expressed to the convention and that it be made clear that "in sending you the letter I was convinced of its utter and dastardly falsehood from the first."[13] Ruffin's address to the group pointed out the necessity for black women to meet for a "good talk" about the peculiar burdens under which they labored and the serious concerns of particular interest to them. She noted that courage and inspiration could be derived from their congenial gathering together. As to the most important reason for the conference, she said:

> All over America there is to be found a large and growing class of earnest, intelligent, progressive colored women, women who, if not leading full, useful lives, are only waiting for the opportunity to do so, many of them warped and cramped for lack of opportunity, not only to do more but to be more; and yet if an estimate of the colored women of America is called for, the inevitable reply, glibly given is, "For the most part ignorant and immoral, some exceptions, of course, but these don't count."

Remarking on the many who had achieved in varying measure, she urged, "It is 'mete, right and our bounden duty' to stand forth and declare ourselves and principles, to teach an ignorant and suspicious world that our aim and interests are identical with those of all good aspiring women."[14] At this meeting the name given the new organization was the National Federation of Afro-American Women. Mrs. Booker T. Washington was elected the first president.

On July 19 of the following year, the Federation convened in Washington, shortly after the National League of Colored Women had adjourned their meeting there. The next day a letter was read stating that a committee of seven women from the League would meet with seven members of the Federation in order to effect a union of the two bodies. The League committee had been given full power to negotiate and presented a set of articles of agreement. One of these stipulated that the name of the new organization would be the National Association of Colored Women; another indicated that officers would be elected in proportion to the number of clubs represented in each group. This gave the Washington-based League an advantage. A motion made by Wells-Barnett to give the Federation committee full power in the negotiations carried. Much disagreement ensued over the use of "colored" as opposed to "Afro-American" in the title. By the close of the meeting, however, the joint committee on union had decided on the title National Association of Colored Women (NACW) and Mary Church Terrell had been chosen president.[15]

Wells-Barnett was listed by the credentials committee as a fraternal delegate representing the Anti-Lynching Society of England. She had been sent by the Ida B. Wells Club in Chicago, and since she brought her four-month-old son, her husband had hired a nurse to accompany her. She was an active participant on the Committee of Resolutions and gave a speech on reform. Among the many resolutions adopted was one again commending her work in "arousing the civilized world to the horrors of lynch law." Another resolution indicating that Balgarnie was paying the price for her loyalty to Douglass, whose name she attempted to vindicate in the Willard affair, appealed to the Baptist Women Temperance Association, which had deposed Balgarnie from office, to set up, as she had requested, an arbitration committee to reconcile the differences between herself and the officers of that organization.[16]

Despite the fact that the NACW had been spurred into existence by the need to defend the character of Ida B. Wells and that of American black womanhood that she represented, she was at no time a leader among the women making up that body. In 1899, when the association met in Chicago, she was excluded from any official participation by Mary Church Terrell, the president. For the next ten years she did not attend the biennial meetings. Wells-Barnett was sensitive to the rejection of other clubwomen. Her appraisal of the situation was that in the organization there was the ever present "personal element," deterring race progress.[17] Because she was no respecter of persons in power, she did not see that she was out of step with a new leadership and a new movement.

Others with whom she began her militant career were more adaptable. One of these was T. Thomas Fortune, who with much hesitation had acquiesced to the entreaties of Bishop Alexander Walters to reorganize the National Afro-American League, which Fortune had declared defunct in 1893. He indicated agreement with Walters and other leaders on the need for such an organization, but his strident militancy was gone. He doubted the ability of the masses of blacks to support an organization any better than they had a decade before. He made it known to Walters that a conference would be open to a few race leaders only. His confidence in an all-black league was also weakened. He said, "I am almost persuaded that we cannot accomplish our object any more than we could the abolition of slavery unless the white men and the black men, the white women and the black women, join the movement."

In September 1898, Wells-Barnett attended the unveiling of the Douglass Monument in Rochester, New York, and participated in the formation of the Afro-American Council. At this conference, Fortune was elected president, but because he repeated his doubts about the feasibility of a national organization, Wells-Barnett suggested that someone with more enthusiasm

Ida B. Wells-Barnett and Charles Aked Barnett
(ca. Oct. 1896)

should be president. Fortune agreed with her and resigned. The other officers chosen were John C. Dancy, vice-president; Ida Wells-Barnett, secretary; and John W. Thompson, treasurer. Fortune accepted the chairmanship of the executive committee.[18]

An unscheduled conference was called by the Council in November 1898. This was considered a necessity in the light of President William McKinley's failure to make any comment in his message to Congress about the Wilmington, North Carolina, riot the preceding summer.[19] Despite the urgency of the meeting, a tone of moderation was set by Bishop Walters, who presided. He took a middle ground between the doctrine of accommodation and the stance of militant protest. He combined insistence on equal rights with an attitude of patient waiting for their realization. He urged protest against injustice, but he also recommended hard work, education, and moral growth among blacks. He indicated his respect for academic and professional training, but showed his disdain for the post-Civil War negligence of manual skills and labor in preference for the professions. His message, therefore, was acceptable to both militants and moderates. Dissension between these opposing factions was precipitated by the speech of Wells-Barnett.[20]

In April of the same year, she had led a delegation from Chicago to Washington to protest to President McKinley the lynching of a black postmaster in Lake City, South Carolina. In the name of the blacks of the country and of Chicago in particular, she urged the president to act to redress the crime committed against a federal employee at his post. Pointing to this lynching as a "federal matter," she asked that efforts be made to apprehend the offenders, that indemnity be paid the surviving wife and children, and that a national anti-lynching law be enacted. Although the president gave the delegation assurances of his agreement and promised that the appropriate departments would look into the matter, nothing came of the promises.[21]

With this experience in the recent past, Wells-Barnett at the Council meeting called the accommodationist ideas of Booker T. Washington erroneous. She contradicted the notion that American blacks would be accorded their constitutional rights when they had become a significant part of the nation's economic life. She went farther and condemned McKinley's negligence and inaction regarding blacks' problems. The result of her remarks was the forceful expression of views on both sides of the issues that Washington's 1895 Atlanta Exposition speech had made pivotal. Articulate

Northerners strongly objected to accommodationism. Supporters of Washington and government appointees staunchly defended moderation.[22]

Toward the end of the century, segregation, disfranchisement, and other injustices increased. With this discouraging trend, many blacks saw protest as futile. Louis Harlan, in commenting on Washington's Atlanta speech, perceives it as a reflection of a facet of black American thought that had existed since the Reconstruction years. It represented the tendency of Southern blacks to adjust to their local conditions and to place emphasis on economic development and the industrial education, trades, and small businesses that it required. Public reaction to Washington's speech was slow in coming. A number of black newspapers hesitated to print it, but increasingly many black leaders accepted the viewpoint it expressed. The formerly radical Fortune went so far as to congratulate Washington, comparing him to Douglass in his potential to lead the race.[23]

The spirit of protest was not entirely dead, however. In the spring of 1899, the National Afro-American Council published a call to blacks to set aside Friday, June 2 and Sunday, June 4 as days of fasting and prayer. The proclamation included a recitation of grievances that were described as "unhistoric, unprecedented and dreadfully abnormal," which impelled the Council "to appeal to the Afro-Americans of the United States to put forth some endeavors by ceasing to be longer silent, and to appeal to some judiciary for help and relief." In the absence of an earthly tribunal of justice, the appeal was to be made "to the bar of Infinite Power and Justice."[24]

In 1899, the Afro-American Council held its annual convention in Chicago. It was preceded during the same week by a convention of the NACW. Ida Wells-Barnett was a member of each association. The Ida B. Wells Club now headed a roster of six Illinois black women's organizations. When the NACW decided that their 1899 biennial convention would be held in Chicago, the black clubwomen of the state organized themselves into the "Women's Conference" to make preparations for the event. They chose Fannie Barrier Williams as president of this temporary federation.[25]

Ida Wells-Barnett, who had relinquished the presidency of her club, was not invited to participate in the preparations or on the program of the women's assembly. She considered this a personal slight from Mary Church Terrell, president of the national association. The two women had been acquaintances in their earlier years in Memphis. Although Terrell was the wealthy daughter of a prosperous businessman, Wells had felt an affinity with her in ambitions and hopes. They had begun their careers as lecturers for civil rights at the same time. Wells-Barnett asked Terrell why she had been excluded and was told by Terrell that she had received letters from Chicago club women indicating that if Wells-Barnett was invited to be on the program or was involved with the preparations, they would not participate. This was an even greater blow to the woman who took credit for initiating the club movement among Chicago's black women and on whose account, partially at least, the national organization came into being. As a result of Terrell's explanation, Wells-Barnett would not attend the women's conference, except to convey an invitation from Jane Addams, extended through her, to the Association's officers to have lunch at Hull House. She felt that Mary Terrell had used the antagonism of the Chicago women to prevent her being a contender for the presidency.[26]

The convention, held at Quinn Chapel, was given extensive coverage by the Chicago papers, a fact that Terrell used to good advantage in compiling press notices for sale.[27] The president of the NACW considered the Chicago convention the most successful of the three over which she had presided. She was reelected to the highest office by a large majority and recorded in her autobiography, "Some of the women wept and rushed upon the platform to embrace me. Such a spontaneous outburst of confidence in me more than repaid me for all the strenuous efforts I had exerted to make the Association as a whole and the convention in particular a success."[28] The *Chicago Tribune* reported both confusion about the meaning of the Association's constitution in allowing her a third term and dissatisfaction among the New England delegates who opposed her.[29] A more revealing account of opposition to Mary Terrell and her own sense of vindication in her election was given in a personal letter she wrote. She protested that although she had not desired reelection, "it was one of the greatest triumphs a woman could possibly have." She explained that "our 'Virtuous Friend' had done all in her evil power to prejudice the minds of the Illinois delegates against me and when I reached Chicago, I found them hating me with a zeal worthy of a better cause."

The rivalry that Wells-Barnett thought Mary Terrell feared from her was probably more truly placed in Fannie Barrier Williams and Josephine St. Pierre Ruffin. In the same letter, Terrell wrote, "Fannie and Mrs. Ruffin, who came clear from Boston for the express purpose of getting the presidency by fair means if possible and foul, if necessary, seized the Associated Press reporter, when he came to the meeting and told him that I had been reelected only after a long struggle and with great opposition."

Although she felt it necessary to correct this impression by giving her own version of events to *The Washington Post* and *The Star*, she admitted, "The women who oppsed [sic] me lead [sic] me a dog's life after the meeting on several occasions, but I feel that I came off unscathed."[30]

In a later letter to Mrs. Booker T. Washington, who edited *Notes*, the official news organ of the Association, Terrell called herself "a woman of peace." She wrote, "I have succeeded in placating everybody except two ladies in Chicago and one in Boston who wanted the presidency." Assuring Washington that an article by Ruffin had done her no harm, Terrell congratulated herself on her handling of the Chicago women. She noted that the events following "the mean malicious things" circulated about Washington and herself showed "how careful I am and tactful, where the interests of the Association are concerned."[31]

W. E. B. Du Bois, who had become involved with racial issues, wrote a report of the NACW convention. He stated that the women gathered in Chicago "were rather above the average of their race and represented the aristocracy among Negroes. Their evident intelligence and air of good breeding served also to impress the onlookers."[32] The infighting for position was overlooked in the emphasis placed on the notable personalities participating. The program was filled with humanitarian topics that touched the many needs and problems of the blacks in America. The convention was honored by a welcome from Carter H. Harrison, mayor of Chicago, and the list of guest speakers included Booker T. Washington, Bishop H. M. Turner, and prominent black and white Chicagoans.[33]

Du Bois was a participant at the 1899 meeting of the Afro-American Council and reported on that convention as well as the NACW assembly. In a comparative note, he stated, "Its culture and taste were in painful contrast to the women's session, but its earnestness and faithful striving made it a far more reliable reflex of the mental attitude of the millions it represented." The scholarly writer described the membership as mostly male, "of average ability, rather talkative and excitable." Among the notables whom he chose to point out were the genial Bishop Walters and Wells-Barnett, whom he identified as the initiator of the anti-lynching crusade.[34] The convention sessions were filled with rhetoric and resolutions. Walters expressed his opposition to expansionism and appealed to President McKinley for fair trials and military promotions for black men. At an open meeting, Du Bois gave a talk entitled "The Business Enterprises of the Race and How to Foster Them." Isaiah Montgomery reported on Mound Bayou, Mississippi, the all-black town of which he was the mayor. Bishop Henry McNeal Turner, the advocate of emigration, explained his scheme for moving seven million American blacks to Liberia. Before the conference was adjourned, the pastor of Bethel A.M.E. Church, Reverend R. C. Ransom, denounced Booker T. Washington, who was in the city but had not participated in the convention. He also asked that the name of Mrs. Washington be stricken from the list of delegates. She had been scheduled to speak to the group, but had sent regrets instead. Walters defended Washington's position in not becoming involved with a radical group. Despite the feelings of Ransom, the conference formally upheld the Tuskegeean.[35] Behind the scenes, Fortune, who was ill and not in attendance, had warned Washington not to associate himself with the convention, lest he be held responsible for its results.[36] At this meeting, Wells-Barnett, who was re-elected secretary, asked to be relieved of that office. She was instead made chairperson of the anti-lynching bureau that she had urged the Council to create.[37]

At a banquet held at the Sherman House at the end of the convention, officers of the NACW joined the Council members. On this occasion, Mrs. Washington, who was asked to speak, voiced her indignation at the attack on her husband during the Council sessions. Wells-Barnett recalled that it had been reported during the assembly that Bishop Walters had gone to the Palmer House to confer with Mr. Washington, and that the need for such a secret conference had been questioned by a delegate who inferred that Washington was in the city to hold in check the Council's utterances against the President of the United States. Reverend Ransom's explanation of his own disenchantment with the Council details a similar meeting between Walters and Washington in Chicago en route to a convention in Indianapolis in 1900. The clergyman charged Washington with attempting to weaken the Council's program. He was also aware of the political influence that was entering into the organization in the form of expenses of delegates paid by Mark Hannah, a Republican politician, through A.M.E. Bishop Arnett. In regard to his withdrawal from the Council, Ransom said, "I saw it was useless as a weapon, toward or in favor of political and social justice."[38]

Washington did seek to influence and indeed dominate the Council. He was, at the end of the century, in earnest about creating the nationwide power structure that would be known as the Tuskegee Machine.[39] It has been conjectured that the Council received both publicity and support because it was identified with Washington. On the other hand, its initial purpose was undermined. Dissension between the supporters and the opponents of the man who had emerged as chief race leader prevented the kind of discussion and action for which the organization had been founded. Fortune, the agitator, had in the 1880s formed a personal friendship with Washington. Temperamentally worlds apart, the two men argued about methods, but Fortune judged that their objectives were the same and moved toward Washington's viewpoint. The compatibility of Fortune with Washington, which became increasingly apparent, brought the Council founder under attack by the radicals. Bishop Walters wavered in his support of Washington, but, motivated by the desire for racial unity under one leader, cooperated with him for the most part. By 1902, the Washington takeover was complete. At the convention held in St. Paul, Fortune was elected president with a roster of fellow officers also friendly toward the accommodationist. Washington's secretary reported to him that to the discomfort of W. E. B. Du Bois and Ida Wells-Barnett, the Council was now in the control of Tuskegee.[40]

Not only had Washington usurped control of this national organization, he had begun also to exert power over individual blacks through his influence at the White House. In 1901, with Washington's advice, Theodore Roosevelt appointed Robert H. Terrell to a judgeship on the Municipal Court of Washington, D.C. Commenting on the selection of Terrell, Louis Harlan observes that Judge Terrell's wife, Mary Church Terrell, "was more sharp-witted and ambitious than her easy-going husband, but 1901 was no year for a woman, least of all a black woman, to aspire to high station except through her husband."[41]

In 1903, Du Bois published *The Souls of Black Folk*. One of the essays was a direct criticism of Booker T. Washington's racial policies. Wells-Barnett had had some correspondence from the author in April and wrote to him in May to comment on his publication. Her husband and she had attended a conference held at the home of Celia Parker Wooley, whom she described as a "very good friend of the race." The group was racially mixed, including whites whom Wells-Barnett considered among the most literary, as well as Dr. and Mrs. Charles Bentley, Mr. and Mrs. S. Laing Williams, and several other blacks. The group's discussions had concentrated on Du Bois's criticism of Washington and had concluded that that essay weakened the whole work. Of Barnett and herself, she added, "Of course you know our sentiments." Assuring Du Bois that interest in the book had been aroused, she told him of her plan to have another discussion in two weeks at "a meeting of our best brained."[42] Wells-Barnett did not indicate who the "best brained" were.

In the group who met at the Wooley residence, she had included the most notable leaders of Chicago. It is possible that she anticipated a different outcome in a discussion without the presence of whites.

The year after W. E. B. Du Bois published *The Souls of Black Folk* with its criticism of Booker T. Washington, Wells-Barnett joined in the published attack on the Tuskegeean. As part of a symposium entitled "The Negro Problem from the Negro Point of View," she wrote an article entitled "Booker T. Washington and His Critics" for *World Today*. [Reproduced here pages 255-260.] She denounced Washington in vituperative language, directing her wrath at what she considered his denigration of the character of black Americans in order to please Southern whites. She expressed resentment at Washington's emphasis on industrial education and his implication that, until the coming of Tuskegee, blacks were illiterate and immoral. She referred to the men and women who had with industry accumulated land, livestock, and money, and whose children had benefited from the honest toil of their parents and the generosity of Northern educators. She considered Washington's rejection of college education a "bitter pill," stating that the Tuskegeean had made popular the belief that the black was inherently inferior. As for industrial education, she argued, "This gospel of work is no new one for the Negro. It is the South's old slavery practice in a new dress. It is the only education the South gave the Negro for two and a half centuries." She pointed to specific results of the concentration on Tuskegee as the model of appropriate education for the black African. These generally tended to limit the types of education and the number of schools open to aspiring young blacks. She accused Washington of assuming the same pose as those who blamed mob violence on the lasciviousness of the black, and further, of forfeiting the "fundamental rights of American citizenship to the end that one school for industrial training shall flourish."[43]

Although Wells-Barnett remained opposed to the philosophy of the Tuskegee principal, she was not totally allied with his opponents. After 1895, Washington was presumed by whites and many blacks to be the spokesman for black Americans, but by 1905 Du Bois had emerged as the second most influential American black. The intellectual from Massachusetts had intended to keep a middle course between radical elements and the Tuskegee followers. The power of the Tuskegee Machine, which eventually touched his position and work at Atlanta University, proved more than Du Bois could tolerate. Urged by friends to organize a national radical strategy, he invited fifty-nine black men from seventeen states to a meeting at a small hotel at Fort Erie, Ontario. On January 31, 1906, the Niagara Movement was begun. The purpose of the meeting was to set down the demands that the conferees felt they could legitimately make of white Americans, whom they charged with full responsibility for the problems of black Americans. James Weldon Johnson was of the opinion that the Du Bois organization split American blacks into two parties. His observation was based on the contention that any protest movement was anti-Washington, and that the accommodationist was relentlessly anti-Niagara Movement.[44] It disregarded, however, blacks whose radicalism went beyond that of Du Bois.

The Niagara Movement was designed to provide discussion among the educated black elite on racial topics, to spread propaganda that would reach the masses, and to agitate for the rights that the race was being denied. It survived with difficulty until 1910. By the time of its demise, the National Negro Conference had been called by a group of white liberals in New York. William English Walling, Mary White Ovington, Charles Edward Russell, and Henry Moskowitz were the chief organizers. Oswald Garrison Villard, who had associations with Booker T. Washington as well as with radical civil rights advocates, joined them later and composed the call for the National Negro Conference, which initiated the National Association for the Advancement of Colored People (NAACP).

Villard presented the injustices inflicted on black Americans in that year of the centenary of Lincoln's birth and concluded with the summons, "Hence we call upon all the believers in democracy to join in a national conference for the discussion of present evils, the voicing of protests, and the renewal of the struggle for civil and political liberty." The call was signed by more than fifty persons of both races, among them W. E. B. Du Bois and Ida Wells-Barnett. One thousand invitations were issued, including one to Washington. Villard contacted the powerful school principal personally, however, to make the proposed organization's aggressive stance clear and to present the opportunity for Washington to decline without misunderstanding.[45]

The conference was held in New York on May 31 and June 1, 1909. The theme of the meetings was a refutation of the theories of black people's inferiority. Some twenty-five speeches were given on the condition of American blacks. Wells-Barnett's talk on "Lynching, Our National Crime" included a discussion of the Springfield riot that had been the touchstone to the indignation of Walling and the New Yorkers, who had initiated the idea of an integrated organization. Villard presented the need for a permanent organization and laid before the group the organizing committee's views of what its functions and procedures would be.[46]

The gatherings went smoothly until the final session to which had been relegated the discussion of resolutions and the announcement of the Committee of Forty on Permanent Organization. The black radicals in attendance argued long and vociferously about points deemed irrelevant by the more conservative members. Villard, in distress, commented, "I suppose we ought really not to blame these poor people who have been tricked so often by white men, for being suspicious, but the exhibition was none the less trying." Du Bois noted that at one point, "A woman leapt to her feet and cried in passionate, almost tearful earnestness—an earnestness born of bitter experience—'They are betraying us again—these white friends of ours.' "[47]

Although the new organization proposed to address racial injustices with protest and radical action, the organizers were careful to maintain a moderate tone. Du Bois had experienced the futility of an organization directly opposed to Washington. He was, therefore, reluctant to have members of the militant Niagara Movement participate. With its interracial character, the NAACP could expect a large audience, prestigious membership, and strong financial support. The power of Washington to influence philanthropists to contribute and to affect membership was not ignored in the leaders' concern with balancing the radical element in their midst with middle-of-the-roaders, such as Mary Church Terrell and Dean Kelly Miller of Howard University, as active participants.[48]

In choosing the Committee of Forty, the nominating team took a middle course. It avoided followers of Washington and extremists like Ida Wells-Barnett and William Monroe Trotter. The list read on the night of June 1, however, pleased no one. Barnett and Trotter were disappointed and angry at their omission from the Committee, which included well-known moderates. Negotiations were carried on for several days after the close of the conference in order to rectify the situation. Wells-Barnett's name was the first to be added by Russell, who had been chairman of the meetings. Walling wrote to Du Bois that he thought "strong and energetic personalities" should be included. Referring to the fact that of the forty on the Committee there were only twelve blacks, he said, "It is impossible that twelve colored members could thoroughly represent all the ideas, sentiments, standpoints, and organizations which ought to receive a constant hearing inside our committee."[49]

In her account of the radicals at the birth of the NAACP, Mary White Ovington observed:

> In their experience, the boasted bond of brotherly love had always a loose strand, and a good pull broke the white from the black. They asked questions freely and they made many speeches. I especially remember Monroe Trotter of Boston, and Ida Wells Barnett. . . . They were powerful personalities who had gone their own ways, fitted for courageous work, but perhaps not fitted to accept the restraint of organization.

Regarding Barnett's and Trotter's omission from the Committee of Forty, Ovington wrote, "Their anger as they went out was perhaps justified. Mrs. Barnett took her complaints to Russell who quite illegally, but wisely, put her on the Committee."[50]

In May 1910, W. E. B. Du Bois was the only black elected to an office; he was named director of publicity and research. Du Bois was recognized as a radical, but he was an elitist whose arrogance turned away many blacks. Although Wells-Barnett had praised his anti-Washington essay published in 1903, at the 1909 meeting he became the object of her fury. In her account, he had deliberately deleted her name from the original list of the Committee of Forty. Later she recalled his explanation, "Mrs. Barnett, I knew that you and Mr. Barnett were with Mrs. Wooley in the Douglass Center and that you would be represented through her. I took the liberty of substituting the name of Dr. Charles Bentley for yours." Since Bentley was not present, Du Bois proposed to reverse his action. In her anger Wells-Barnett spurned his offer.[51]

Being named to the Committee by Russell did not assuage the hostility that Wells-Barnett continued to feel toward Du Bois. He, in turn, ignored her activity entirely in the pages of the *Crisis*, the official organ of the NAACP. Writing to Joel Spingarn, who came to be interested in the NAACP through the case of Steve Green, with which she was involved before the NAACP, Wells-Barnett referred to an NAACP branch meeting to which she had not been invited in time to attend.

> Both Mr. Villard and Prof. Du Bois gave me the impression that they rather feared some interferance [sic] from me in the Chicago arrangements. They also gave me very clearly to understand at the executive meeting there in New York that I was not expected to do anything save to be a member. Candidly,

I don't expect a great deal to result from their activity, for the very good reason that Miss Addams whom they desire to mother the movement simply has not the time nor strength even if she had the inclination to lead this new crusade. Unfortunately, a few of our own "exclusives" have the same idea that Mr. Villard has, that the organization should be kept in the hands of the exclusive academic few. This same academic few are perfectly willing to be identified with a movement that has Miss Jane Addams as its head in order that they may bask in the light of her reflected glory and at the same time get credit for representing the race that they ignore and withdraw themselves from on every occasion of real need. Of course I am not very popular with the exclusive few, and I cannot say that I look with equanimity upon their patronizing assumptions.

As I see the matter now, I shall not bother much with the Chicago branch, but confine my efforts more and more to the work of the Negro Fellowship League.[52]

This she did. In the late twenties, her convictions had not changed. With characteristic self-assurance, she wrote:

I cannot resist the conclusion that, had I not been so hurt over the treatment I had received at the hands of the men of my own race and thus blinded to the realization that I should have taken the place which the white men of the committee felt I should have, the NAACP would now be a live, active force in the lives of our people all over this country.[53]

When Wells-Barnett moved from her role as lone crusader to that of organization woman, she experienced disillusionment and rejection. The mood of black America was less one of protest than of adjustment. Fortune turned to Washington, and Du Bois dared not turn too completely away from him. Wells-Barnett was less attuned to the rules of diplomacy and less adroit at accepting society's role for her than her contemporaries Mary Terrell and Fannie Williams. She did not fit easily into their patterns of achievement and recognition. What Fortune had written of her as a young journalist could be applied to her later in other spheres.

As a writer Miss Wells lacks in the beauties and graces affected by academicians. Her style is one of great strength and directness. She is so much in earnest that there is almost an entire absence of the witty and humorous in what she writes. . . .

Few women have a higher conception of the responsibilities and the possibilities of her sex than Miss Wells.[54]

But twenty years later the time was out of joint.

SEVEN

Social and Civic Activity in Chicago

The black population of the Chicago to which Ida B. Wells returned in 1895 numbered 15,000. The majority lived in a section south of the downtown district and west of State Street, the directional dividing line. Others were scattered about the city in small enclaves of a few blocks. According to Allan Spear, segregation was not complete. Blacks lived among whites and there were few entirely black neighborhoods. As professionals and businesspeople, the black Chicagoans maintained friendly working relationships with their white counterparts. Although black churches and clubs increased, most civic institutions remained open to both races. Unlike other ethnic groups, the blacks were not yet involved in the industrial expansion of the city. Neither were they a part of the organized labor movement. They earned their livelihoods in service trades and in domestic employments. In these capacities they were inconspicuous, causing neither care nor hostility on the part of the white population. A small upper class of professionals and service tradesmen constituted the leadership in the black community. These men and women were generally Northern born descendants of families free before 1865. Many were of racially mixed heritage. They had formed strong associations with whites who were their professional colleagues or business clients. As the culturally and socially elite, they influenced the ideals and behavior of the lower classes of blacks. Respectability and refinement were characteristics of this group and the standards of acceptance that they urged others to emulate. Educated in integrated schools and associated with whites in their occupations, they were proud of their achievements and militant in their pursuit of equal rights and assimilation into the general society.[1]

The reason given by Ida Wells for her decision to make Chicago her permanent residence was F. L. Barnett's proposal of marriage.[2] During her year of lecturing in the United States, he had had her itinerary and sent letters to greet her on her arrival in each new city. Although Barnett was a widower, thirteen years older than Wells, their common interest and work on the Columbian Exposition pamphlet and the *Chicago Conservator* had created a bond of mutual respect and affection between them.[3] On June 27, 1895, they were married in Chicago at Bethel Church. The *Chicago Tribune* noted the event with the heading "Two Notable People Are Married." Ferdinand Barnett was described as "prominent among the colored people of the city." Of the bride, the *Tribune* said, "Miss Wells has a wide reputation both here and abroad as an earnest and conscientious woman who has devoted her life to her people."[4]

Four days after the wedding, Ida Wells-Barnett took over the editorship of the *Conservator*, and her husband entered fully into his law practice and politics. She became engaged in local affairs as president of the Ida B. Wells Club and as a lecturer before audiences of white clubwomen. Within a year, Barnett had been appointed assistant state's attorney by the newly elected Charles S. Deneen.[5]

The Barnetts were a prominent couple in the black community, which the researchers St. Clair Drake and Horace Cayton separate roughly into three categories. At the top of the social scale, they place the people of refinement, established by education and breeding as the social elite. In the middle is the "respectable" element, less decorous in their behavior, but a churchgoing group of poor or moderate means. At the bottom are the "riffraff," who were generally neither religious nor disciplined. This class was looked down upon by their racial fellows. Seeing themselves as the image of progress to be imitated, the "refined' prodded and preached education to the "respectables" as well as to the "riffraff."

A continuous migration of Southern blacks to Chicago between 1890 and 1910 swelled the black population from 15,000 to 40,000. With this influx came successful clergymen, Reconstruction politicians, and the more or less educated who had become restless under the new encroachments of Southern laws upon their rights.[6] By 1895, most Southern blacks had been disfranchised. In 1896, the Supreme Court had decreed that segregation was legal. Educational appropriations for black children had been reduced. Booker T. Washington's accommodationist doctrine was being advanced to the satisfaction of the white South.[7]

Black Chicagoans had begun to develop institutions of their own, despite the ideal of complete assimilation held by the guiding elite.[8] Contact with the white community continued, as several of the city's prominent businessmen took philanthropic interest in the black institutions. Blacks maintained a hold on domestic jobs and work in skilled and unskilled trades. As the number of European immigrants increased, however, they began to see their job security threatened. The tendency of blacks was to take the condescending attitudes of American whites toward the immigrants. The European newcomers similarly learned and expressed the attitudes prevalent among whites about blacks, but no serious friction arose between the two groups. They found living in the same blocks and buildings conducive to neighborliness until a later period. Around 1905, there was a move among blacks to push out of their traditional employments and to challenge the restrictions unions placed on them as craftsmen. There was growing emphasis on self-reliance, which was identified with acquiring political power and developing a strong business and professional base.[9]

F. L. Barnett and his wife were among Chicago's black leaders. For the 1890s, however, Allan Spear considers their ideas and activities representative of a new type of leadership. They "foreshadowed Negro leaders who were to emerge in World War I." Pointing out their forceful insistence on racial solidarity, he contrasts them with others of the old elite, such as Daniel H. Williams and Charles E. Bentley, who took a less militant approach to civil rights activity. Spear judges that Williams, a physician, and Bentley, a dentist, were "torn between professional and civic duties." He notes that the Barnetts were "publicists by trade," a fact that determined their dependency on the black community for economic support of their news organ, which necessarily spoke out on racial matters. The new leaders of the World War years emphasized black business and professional services, and they contributed to the institutional life of black Chicago. Unlike the Barnetts, however, they were neither educationally well prepared for their professional careers nor culturally endowed for maintaining standards of respectability and gentility. The new leaders were tied to the black belt by practical business acumen. The Barnetts exhibited a solidarity with the masses of blacks, which grew out of a racial ideology. Like the new leaders described by Spear, the Barnetts opposed segregation but urged unity among blacks in resisting economic and political exploitation.[10] In a more recent interpretation of Chicago's black leadership, Albert Kreiling characterizes Ferdinand Barnett as "a prototype of the Afro-American Agitators," and he identifies Ida Wells-Barnett as "Chicago's most famous Afro-American Agitator." In describing the Afro-American agitators, Kreiling states:

True, the agitators demanded equal treatment and often opposed separate racial institutions. Moreover, like later middle class blacks, they felt divided loyalties between an attachment to white ideals and sentiments of racial identity. However, the thrust of the agitator's activity was the introduction of a heightened sense of collective racial identity, which became a substitute for increasingly moot moral absolutes grounded in otherworldly and libertarian-individualist outlooks.[11]

This description represents tendencies that the Barnetts manifested both as publicists and as civil rights advocates in other areas.

Early in her life as a Chicago resident, Wells-Barnett showed the inclination of the Afro-American agitator to rely on the resourcefulness of blacks when the benefits of integration were too slow in coming and the waiting too costly. Although she caused some consternation among assimilationist blacks, she directed, as one of the first projects of the Ida B. Wells Club, the establishment of a kindergarten for black children at Bethel A.M.E. Church. The public school system had not begun to provide this type of training.[12] There existed a small number of private kindergartens, but the only one accessible to the black children of the South Side was at the Armour Institute. While it was open to both races, the waiting list convinced Wells-Barnett that it could not accommodate all the children who needed it.

There was considerable objection to the project. The feeling was that establishing classes for black children would be setting up the color line that would bar the children from admittance to the integrated Armour Institute. Wells-Barnett was persuaded that the immediate need was training for black children, that the existing institutions were not providing for this need, and that the only alternative was for the black community to provide for its own. Her reaction to the arguments against the club's proposal was expressed many years later:

> To say that I was surprised does not begin to express my feeling. Here were people so afraid of the color line that they did not want to do anything to help supply the needs of their own people. The reasoning was that it would be better to let our children be neglected and do without the kindergarten service than to supply the needs of our own. We had a battle royal, but the club was very loyal to the president and proceeded to give an entertainment with which to raise funds to equip a kindergarten.

Reverend Reverdy C. Ransom, pastor at Bethel Church from 1896 until 1900, supported the project. Two young women, trained for kindergarten work and looking for employment in a situation like that proposed, added to the feasibility of the venture. A lecture room was made ready, and the neighborhood mothers were invited to send their children for the half-day sessions.[13] Ransom was a race militant who brought to his ministry the reform spirit of the social gospel. He was a supporter of Wells-Barnett, who was a member of his congregation, and he was an advocate of her agitation for civil rights and her work among the clubwomen for social improvement.[14]

At the time that the Ida B. Wells Club was becoming active in Chicago, there was a general movement among clubwomen to engage in programs of racial self-help. Fannie Barrier Williams was considered, like Wells-Barnett, one of Chicago's leading spokeswomen of the club movement.[15] In an appraisal of the club activity of black women, she wrote:

> The club movement among colored women reaches into the sub-social condition of the entire race. Among white women clubs mean the forward movement of the best women in the interest of the best womanhood. Among colored women the club is the effort of the few competent in behalf of the many incompetent; that is to say that the club is only one of many means for the social uplift of the race.[16]

Black women's clubs had sprung into being between 1890 and 1895 in the principal cities of the land. They anticipated the work of the Urban League, according to August Meier, and led the field of welfare activity for two decades. Their projects included day-care centers, kindergartens, places for mothers to meet, sewing and cooking classes, penny savings banks, employment bureaus, and programs to aid orphans, homeless girls, the elderly, and, in one instance, youth in a reformatory. In many cases contributions to these various efforts were limited by the humble resources of the clubwomen. The significant factor was, nonetheless, the emphasis on self-help and racial unity motivating the women.[17]

The emergence of the black women's clubs followed the development of the white General Federation of Women's Clubs. Fannie Barrier Williams indicated that the white organization had been a guide and an inspiration, but she pointed out that black women had not simply imitated their sisters. Their club movement was, "nothing less than organized anxiety of women who have become intelligent enough to recognize their own low social conditions and strong enough to initiate the forces of reform."[18]

Early histories of the black clubwomen's movement were self-conscious records of club historians. Gerda Lerner conjectures that as the national white women's movement resulted from the needs of the urban poor at a time when a "sizeable group of educated women with leisure" was available for club activities, the black women's clubs originated under similar circumstances. Black women organized for philanthropic purposes and welfare. Membership was related to social class among both black and white, and while blacks bridged social gaps more readily, in both groups there were class prejudices.[19]

The Ida B. Wells Club was the first black women's club in Chicago. Its motto was "Helping Hand" and its stated objective was "Elevation of Woman, Home, and Community."[20] The historian of the Illinois Federation of Colored Women credits the club with three outstanding achievements: the founding of the first kindergarten for black children in the city, assistance in forming the first black orchestra in Chicago, and charter membership in the League of Cook County Clubs. This last achievement was significant because it opened the way for participation of other black clubs in the formerly all-white organization. Mrs. George W. Plummer, one of the women responsible for the Cook County League, befriended the Ida B. Wells Club by donating to it a course in parliamentary law. Elizabeth Lindsay Davis, founder of the Phillis Wheatley Club, recognized the benefit derived by later organizations from the associations and activities of the first club.

> From these helpful programs of club work, race unity and parliamentary drill in the mother club, have sprung all the other clubs of Chicago and the state and from the ranks of its members have come many of our club presidents, our leading business women and our leading church and social service workers.[21]

One important factor in the invitation extended to the Ida B. Wells Club by the League of Cook County Clubs was the fact that the white women's clubs were generally not disposed to integration. There had been great agitation in the Chicago Women's Club when Fannie Barrier Williams was admitted. Black women had been barred from the State Federation of Illinois.[22] At the 1900 convention of the General Federation of Women's Clubs in Milwaukee, a greeting from Mary Church Terrell, president of the National Association of Colored Women, was not accepted. At the same meeting, the presence of Josephine St. Pierre Ruffin was the occasion of much unpleasantness related to the color line. Ruffin, who held membership in the Massachusetts State Federation and in the New England Press Association, would have been accepted as a representative of either of these clubs, but when she chose to represent the New Era Club, which was a black women's club, there was great dissatisfaction and an attempt to take from her physically the badge issued to her as a convention delegate. Citing the Georgia Women's Press Club threat to withdraw from the Federation, the *Chicago Tribune* in 1895 predicted the kind of dissension that showed itself in the Ruffin affair.[23]

Although Chicago's black clubwomen were making some progress toward integration in women's organizations, white hostility against the black population generally grew as the number of blacks in the city increased. By 1915, there were 50,000, the majority of them migrants from outside Illinois. One profound outcome of this concentration in Chicago was the shaping of the black ghetto. Allan Spear attributes this development primarily to white hostility rather than black poverty or choice, although these were resulting factors. White Chicagoans became anxious about job competition and the expanding housing needs of blacks. They viewed blacks as pawns in the city's corrupt political system. Their growing fears and prejudices were strengthened by the rash of racist literature being circulated throughout the United States.

Housing became a crucial issue. Resistance from residents and real estate agents effectively prevented blacks from moving into white neighborhoods and pushed some who had lived in racially mixed areas back into the well-defined black sections. Newcomers had no alternative except to settle in the burgeoning black area of the South Side that gradually extended its borders.[24]

Unlike the temporary enclaves in which other Chicago ethnics made their beginnings, the black ghetto expanded and became fixed. Drake and Cayton note that in 1910 there had been no neighborhood in Chicago with more than 61 percent blacks, that more than two-thirds lived in sections that were less than 50 percent black, and that one-third resided in neighborhoods less than 10 percent black. Ten years later, 87 percent were residents in areas more than half black. By 1930, this figure had risen to 90 percent, and almost two-thirds lived in black concentrations of from 90 to 99 percent.[25]

Friction between the races mounted. There had been a decline in the number of lynchings in the entire country in the late 1890s, but there was a rise again in the early 1900s. The figure rose from eighty-nine in 1900 to

101 in 1901; for the next ten years the average was seventy lynchings. Race riots, too, were on the increase in Northern and Southern cities.[26]

Like Southern blacks, the leaders of the black community of Chicago met their hostile environment by gaining skills and establishing their own economic and civic organizations. They did not abandon the civil rights struggle, but they focused their energies increasingly on building a black community that could supply its inhabitants with the benefits that white Chicagoans enjoyed. Churches were the oldest and most stable institutions of the black ghetto. Quinn Chapel had been established in 1847. Blacks had from that time responded to hostility from white congregations by founding their own. By 1900, there were twelve or more. Between 1900 and 1915, the number doubled. Provident Hospital, which had been set up as an interracial institution, was staffed in 1916 almost entirely by blacks. Blacks assumed a greater share of its financial burden and considered it their hospital. The black YMCA, which had been fiercely resisted in 1889 as a deterrent to integration, was strongly endorsed in 1910 by some of its former opponents. New black businesses, particularly those offering services, came into being. Jesse Binga represented the new successful businessman. Buying property in the changing areas adjacent to the black slums, he built up a profitable real estate agency. In 1908, he opened Binga Bank, the first such black enterprise in Chicago.[27]

This industry on the part of black leaders to provide for the needs of their community was not completely successful. For the majority of black Chicagoans, the job market was severely limited. In 1900, most were still employed in domestic and personal service occupations, a pattern that was to persist for another ten years. In comparing the position of blacks with that of other Chicago ethnics, Ray Ginger says that they were at the bottom of the social scale. Employed chiefly as domestics and for menial tasks, they feared that even these jobs might be taken by the immigrants. Occasionally they were given a chance to perform skilled labor when there was a strike. At these times they were recruited from all over the South as strikebreakers.[28] During the 1904 stockyard strike and the following year when the Teamsters struck, this situation caused a great deal of resentment and hostility against them.

Several reasons have been given for industry's refusal to hire blacks under normal circumstances: employers feared the objections of white employees; blacks trained in the South were insufficiently skilled by Northern standards; and most unions, if they did admit blacks, had discriminatory practices.[29]

When Reverend Reverdy Ransom was appointed pastor of Bethel A.M.E. Church in 1896, a large portion of the black population was living in flimsy frame houses on Dearborn Street, Armour Avenue, and adjoining streets back to the Chicago River. Bethel was near this neighborhood, at the corner of Dearborn and 30th Street. Quinn Chapel, at which Ransom was assigned to preach each Sunday, was at Wabash Avenue and 24th Street, in an area where few blacks lived. Because both churches had large seating capacities, the new minister was duly surprised at having overflow crowds. He was to learn that his flock was swelled by migrants from the South, whose needs went beyond ordinary Sunday services. Ransom was one of the first blacks to attempt to provide social services through his church. He organized the Men's Sunday Club, which attended to the intellectual, social, and business needs of its members; eventually its membership was five hundred. After four years, Ransom resigned this pastorate in order to take up work at the Institutional Church and Social Settlement at Dearborn near 39th Street.[30]

In his new pastorate, which Ransom referred to as the first social settlement for blacks, rather than an ordinary church, he was able to organize a day-care center, a print shop, and a gymnasium. In this church-settlement, classes in home arts and music, and various activities such as concerts, meetings, and civic affairs were held. A forum provided lectures by black and white speakers. Ransom compared the Institutional Church and Social Settlement with Hull House and the Chicago Columns.[31] He numbered among his associates Jane Addams, Mary MacDowell, Ida Wells-Barnett, and Fannie Barrier Williams, whom he described as "some of the finest personalities I have known." Each of these women was or would be involved in settlement work.[32]

Poverty was a problem for all of Chicago's newly arrived ethnic groups, but none was so complex as that faced by blacks.[33] Influenced by the self-help theory and aware of the charity organizations and settlement movement, black leaders were inclined to attempt similar activities. Although the charity organizations were involved with aid to the destitute and the unemployed, the settlement houses seemed to have more appeal to socially conscious blacks. The settlement workers, unlike the charity agents, were concerned with more than the immediate alleviation of poverty and the problems in individual cases. These social workers were reformers and they were concerned about the socio-economic conditions causing poverty.

Allan Davis comments that settlement workers were not always free of bigotry and hatred, or of sentimentality and condescension toward those in need. On the other hand, some efforts to aid blacks were made at a time when progressivism was primarily directed at whites. Of the woman who led the settlement movement in Chicago, Davis notes that Jane Addams did not avoid all racial prejudice, but she came as close to doing so as most of the reformers of the time.[34]

The most prominent white settlement worker involved with blacks was Celia Parker Wooley. In 1904, she founded the Frederick Douglass Center at Wabash Avenue and 30th Street. The location was on the boundary of the black section. The purpose was to attract a racially mixed group. Wooley's chief concern was not the poor downtrodden blacks, but middle-class, educated blacks. They were, she felt, discriminated against entirely because of skin color. The by-laws of the Center indicated that the purpose was the promotion of good relations between the races, the removal of the disabilities confronting blacks in civic, political, and industrial matters, and the pursuit of equal opportunities for both races. It was clear that the Center would not be a forum for protest. It would foster instead a sense of mutual responsibility.[35]

In her autobiography, Ida Wells-Barnett recorded that Wooley had consulted with the Williamses, the Bentleys, and the Barnetts, the three black couples whom she knew. Apparently they responded positively to her proposed integrated settlement. She proceeded to look for a building that would be accessible to blacks and whites on Wabash Avenue, the racial dividing line. Her efforts to rent such a place were futile, because she intended to have black aides, not servants. With the help of some white contributors, she made the first payment for the purchase of a building at 3032 Wabash Avenue. Wells-Barnett urged a group of black women to make a collection among themselves and contribute to each of the succeeding payments. Once the Center was established, a women's club was organized. Wooley suggested that the president should be a white woman, Mrs. George W. Plummer. Wells-Barnett resented this. She had expected to be nominated, but she observed that the other black women seemed content. Under the circumstances she accepted the vice-presidency. Wells-Barnett, however, was not a follower. Neither was she willing to accept quietly what she suspected was a patronizing attitude or a subtle sense of superiority in her white co-workers. About an incident in which she felt that she had been publicly humiliated by Wooley, she wrote:

Ida B. Wells-Barnett, with Charles A. Barnett, 14, Herman K. Barnett, 12, Ida B. Barnett, Jr., 8, and Alfreda M. Barnett (1909)

From that time on Mrs. Wooley never failed to give me the impression that she did not propose to give me much leeway in the affairs of the center. I felt at first that she had been influenced by other colored women who, strange to say, seemed so unwilling that one of their own race should occupy a position of influence, and although I was loath to accept it, I came to the conclusion before our relations ended that our white women friends were not willing to treat us on a plane of equality with themselves.[36]

Unlike Fannie Barrier Williams, who would become the leading black woman in the operation of the Douglass Center, Wells-Barnett was not content with being a member of an integrated social group. Williams agreed with Wooley's view that the settlement was to be a meeting place at which whites would get to know the level of respectability to which many blacks had risen. It was not set up to do "slum work." As a result of its emphasis on social exchange, forums and teas were a significant part of the Center's program. There were a women's club, a boys' club, and athletic organization. Religious services and domestic science classes were held, and there was a library.[37] The fact that Wooley's chief aim was to establish amity between middle-class whites and blacks led to dissatisfaction in those concerned with the needs of the poor.

The Center came under criticism by the outspoken editor of the *Broad Ax*, Julius Taylor, on another score. He was critical of the condescending attitudes of the white director and of the acquiescence of the black members under her leadership. In a lengthy article entitled "Afro-American Women 'Jim Crowed,' " he reported that Wooley had indicated in a speech that black women, even though highly educated, lacked executive ability and were incapable of leading reform activities. He noted that her policy of having only white presidents for the various departments of the Center was evidence of her belief. Of Wells-Barnett's vice-presidency of the women's club, he wrote, "We believe she is a lady of too much prominence to accept such a minor or unimportant position in any women's club." Taylor criticized the aloofness of the other prominent black women associated with the Center, saying that none except Wells-Barnett would step inside the doors of the clubs of their less fortunate sisters. He summed up what he considered the insidious bigotry of the Center by suggesting that Wooley had learned an effective technique in controlling blacks, that of belittling leading men and women while occasionally appearing in public with blacks. As far as poor blacks were concerned, Taylor thought the Center irrelevant.[38]

Steven Diner states that the only successful settlement in any black neighborhood was the Wendell Phillips Settlement. It was founded in 1907 by a group of blacks for blacks. It had an interracial board, however, which included well-known social reformers; among them Sophonisba Breckenridge and Louise Bowen. This settlement provided a meeting place for the West Side community and it offered a variety of activities for betterment of the neighborhood adults and children.[39]

The Negro Fellowship League, founded by Ida Wells-Barnett, came into existence as an indirect result of the 1908 race riot in Springfield. It was one of four settlements near black neighborhoods.[40] Wells-Barnett had transferred her church membership from Bethel A.M.E. to Grace Presbyterian and was teaching a Bible class for young men when violence erupted in the state capital. She was distressed at the happenings there and at the apathy of blacks who seemed undisturbed about the outbreak and the three lynchings "under the shadow of Lincoln's tomb." She spoke of these things with her class, and with her encouragement several members met at her home to discuss what they could do. Sunday afternoon discussions at the Barnett home became regular events to which the men brought others, including their women friends.

One of the causes given for the violence in Springfield was the idleness of young men out of work. There were idle young men in Chicago, also. State Street had become what Wells-Barnett called the "Great White Way" for migrant blacks who spent their time in the saloons, pool halls, and gambling houses. She had visited inmates at the Joliet prison and had heard the stories of those who had gotten into trouble in Chicago. Convinced that the crime rate among blacks was disproportionately high because there were no public facilities available to young blacks, she urged her followers to consider setting up a "lighthouse" on State Street to aid other young people.

Wells-Barnett had continued to write and lecture against lynching. After one of her speeches at the Palmer House, she met Mrs. Victor Lawson, wife of the *Daily News* editor. This woman questioned Wells-Barnett's statement that black men were not allowed in the city's YMCAs. Her interest led to a private interview in which Wells-Barnett told her of the need for an uplifting influence in the State Street area. As a result of this meeting, Mrs. Lawson provided money for the Negro Fellowship League to set up a reading room and social center for men and boys at 2830 State Street. She also made it possible for the League to hire a secretary who would visit the disreputable places along the way to invite men to the League facilities and to take charge of activities. It was not easy to find a young man with the necessary qualities willing to work in the area. Despite this obstacle, the center opened its doors on Sunday, May 1, 1910.[41]

Before the League had facilities of its own, and later in order to accommodate large audiences, the members sponsored activities, such as the Emancipation Day celebrations, at the Institutional Church and Quinn Chapel. The group was composed of young people interested in their own intellectual and moral progress as well as that of the less fortunate. The events that they organized often featured lectures by notable blacks and musical programs provided by the League orchestra. Wells-Barnett usually presided at these functions. Other black church and civic organizations cooperated in making the activities successful by their attendance.[42]

The kind of serious discussions with which the League had begun continued. The influence of the agitator-founder on the group showed itself in its attempts at reform activity. The evil of lynching was addressed in a protest letter to the Christian Endeavor Union. The Negro Fellowship League criticized a number of Christian groups that had met after the Springfield riot and had found no one to indict for what was termed an "outrage against human principles and Christianity."[43] Local politics and the unionization of Pullman porters were other topics of lectures and discussions. On one occasion the League met with the Chicago Federation of Colored Women's Clubs to celebrate Frederick Douglass Day, and Wells-Barnett gave the principal address. The fiery William Monroe Trotter, editor of the *Boston Guardian*, spoke to the group when the National Equal Rights League was established in Chicago.[44]

On May 7, 1911, the League launched the *Fellowship Herald*, its four-page news organ, edited by Ida Wells-Barnett. The newspaper was published weekly with an excellent layout, pictures, and ads. The June 22, 1911, issue is the only one known to be extant, but it gives some indication of the scope of the *Herald*. It touched on a number of race-related items, including an Illinois Supreme Court decision denying black children the right to attend a neighborhood school in Quincy, Mary Church Terrell's impending resignation from the school board of the District of Columbia, and Jim Crowism in baseball in Detroit. Special notice was given to lectures and other activities sponsored by the League during the preceding week and those planned for the coming week. News on local personalities and organizations was also featured.

One lengthy editorial was devoted to the problem of young black men on the street corners. The writer pointed out, "There is no service which our race leaders in Chicago could perform which is so badly needed as this one of showing our young men the harm they do the race by these gatherings of idle men on street corners and in front of saloons, etc." The article noted that loafing was a trait among young blacks in places other than Chicago and quoted a Mississippi speaker who blamed "organized labor of the other race" for the idleness of black men.

There had been some internal dissension in the League over the fact that the president was a woman. Wells-Barnett had responded that a woman headed the movement because of the indifference of the men. She had indicated that when the organization produced a male leader who would work for the concerns of the race she would relinquish the position. This response was recorded in the eight-page June 22 issue, which promised a woman's edition of twelve pages on July 13. The proposed special was to include articles about and by prominent race women.[45]

During its first three years, the League was able to add to its program an employment office and some lodging provisions for men. Although forty or fifty persons visited the center daily, the membership had not grown as Wells-Barnett had hoped. Neither was the organization self-sustaining. An additional burden was placed on it when a license was required for the employment office. Secretaries continued to be unwilling to go into the shady places along State Street to distribute League information, so the president found it necessary to go daily to the center herself. The death of Mrs. Lawson, and Mr. Lawson's withdrawal of financial assistance, necessitated a move to smaller quarters at 3005 State Street. Although the lodging house had to be given up, the League functioned in the new location for another seven years.[46]

Wells-Barnett kept the League in operation from 1913 through 1916 with the salary she earned as an adult probation officer. Judge Harry Olson of the Chicago Municipal Court had appointed her to the position with the understanding that she would have her probationers report to her at the League office. During the three years that she held the appointment, the center continued the work of finding employment and providing cards to the needy for food and lodging at nearby facilities.[47]

Ida Wells-Barnett attributed the demise of the Negro Fellowship League to the founding activities of the Chicago Urban League from 1915 to 1917. "It seemed that the Urban League was brought to Chicago to supplant the activities of the Negro Fellowship League." She was convinced that her social center was reaching the population that could not afford the Wabash Avenue YMCA facilities. She therefore resented the fact that organizations which had contributed to its support had turned their assistance toward the establishment of the Chicago Urban League, which she considered a rival for funds. T. Arnold Hill, the organizer of the Urban League in the city, had obtained the enthusiastic aid of Dr. George Cleveland Hall, a member of the new business and professional elite in the black community. Hall was chairman of the YMCA board of directors and later president of the Douglass Center, which Wooley had invited the Urban League to make its headquarters in 1918.[48]

During the beginning years of the Urban League, its representatives made a concerted effort to win acceptance from a select leadership group of blacks and whites. They secured the cooperation of prominent white social workers and civic notables, as well as the services of the sociologist Robert E. Park. Many black leaders were reluctant to give support. Dr. Hall was the first to do so, followed by Robert S. Abbott, editor of the *Chicago Defender*. One of the first group endorsements came from the Chicago Federation of Colored Women.[49] Wells-Barnett expressed her feelings about the growing interest in the new endeavor: "In the strange way we take hold of the new to the detriment of the old, almost every organization among the women's clubs promised support to Mr. Hill."[50]

She was not alone in her resistance. Many church-affiliated agencies, settlements, and social clubs questioned their fate with the coming of the umbrella organization. The broader scope and the plan to coordinate their activities were threatening. The Urban League was set up to address industrial, economic, and social problems. One of its objects was to act as an intermediary between the existing agencies and their sources of funding. It promised to study and interpret problems in order to direct those in need to the most helpful sources of assistance. Despite the opposition of those who saw their efforts at social welfare being replaced by this large operation, the Chicago branch of the Urban League succeeded in winning support. According to Arvarh Strickland, historian of the early years of the Chicago Urban League, the complex adjustment needs of the blacks moving into the industrial North required the more elaborate system of aid that it proposed.[51]

During the years that Wells-Barnett directed the Negro Fellowship League, she continued to be active in other social and civic affairs that brought attention to the cause of black advancement. In February 1913, the fiftieth anniversary of the Emancipation Proclamation was celebrated at Orchestra Hall. She was one of the organizers of the celebration, which was reportedly attended by several thousand blacks and whites. Among the outstanding guest speakers were W. E. B. Du Bois, Jane Addams, and Rabbi Emil G. Hirsch. A one-hundred-voice choir directed by James A. Mundy provided the musical program. This was the first time that black musicians had performed at Orchestra Hall.[52]

At the beginning of the same year, Wells-Barnett founded, with the aid of several other suffragists, the Alpha Suffrage Club. Illinois women were making strides toward obtaining the vote in their state. Feeling that black women were apathetic about this cause and fearing that they would be excluded from the political rights gained by others, she attempted to create interest and enthusiasm among them. She had been a member of the Illinois Equal Suffrage Association from the early days of her Chicago residency[53] and was also a member of the Chicago Political Equality League.

The purpose of the Chicago Political Equality League was "to promote the study of political science and government, and foster and extend the political rights and privileges of women." Ida Wells-Barnett was listed as a member in each of the annuals from 1900 through 1909. She was apparently an active participant at meetings. On January 3, 1903, she spoke to the group on "The American Negro Woman, Her Past, Present and Future." She was scheduled to handle the question box on December 1, 1906, after a talk on "The Initiative and Referendum, the Hope of Woman's Suffrage."[54]

Although the March 18, 1914, issue of the *Alpha Suffrage Record* gave January 13, 1913, as the date that the Alpha Suffrage Club was organized, it also claimed that the organization had been in existence for three years. Among the accomplishments listed was a membership of 200, fifteen of whom had acted as judges and clerks in city elections for the past year. The Club had succeeded in getting black women of the city to register to vote and through its members had initiated other political clubs in Hyde Park, the South and West sides of Chicago. Wells-Barnett was the president of the Alpha Suffrage Club, which had the distinction of being the first such organization among black women in Chicago. Members met weekly at the Reading Room of the Negro Fellowship League.[55]

The cause of women's suffrage had been alive among leaders of the National Association of Colored Women's Clubs for some time. In September of 1912, an issue of *Crisis* carried "A Woman Suffrage Symposium," which included articles by a number of women. In the section

"Men of the Month," the work of Mary Church Terrell and Margaret Murray Washington was cited with that of other clubwomen. An editorial by Du Bois urged black men to support women's suffrage, reminding them that any agitation for the ballot was related to black suffrage.[56]

The Alpha Suffrage Club was the result of the effort of Wells-Barnett to interest the ordinary black women of Chicago in the issue. Before the club was formed, she had spent several years overcoming their disinterest and fear of ridicule from their male counterparts. She succeeded by showing the women that their votes would aid black men seeking elective offices. She used her position as adult probation officer in Chicago to hold a meeting on suffrage with the women inmates of Bridewell prison, encouraging them to prove themselves worthy of the opportunity.

The first major project of the new organization was to send its founder and president to Washington to participate in the suffragists' parade on March 3, 1913, the day before President Woodrow Wilson's inauguration.[57] An account of that event was sent to Julius Taylor by an eyewitness and reported in the *Broad Ax* five days later. Taylor's correspondent went to some length to emphasize that no color line was evident in the spectacle viewed by thousands from all parts of the United States. There was, however, a separate black contingent in which Terrell was included. The article pointed out that Ida Wells-Barnett had "proudly marched with the head officials and with the head ladies of the Illinois delegation showing that no color line existed in any part of the first parade of the noble women who are in favor of equal suffrage."[58]

The *Broad Ax* failed to detail the events leading up to Wells-Barnett's joining the Illinois group after the parade was underway. Because the National American Women's Suffrage Association was doing its utmost to maintain unity with the women of the South, the leaders had requested publicly that Wells-Barnett not march with the Chicago women. Some Southerners had threatened to withdraw if integrated sections were allowed. Wells-Barnett was apparently disappointed in expecting the immediate support of the women of her state. Aileen Kraditor states, "Eventually she was banished to the Negro women's contingent." Her response to this was an ultimatum that either she would walk with Illinois or not at all. Some compromise seems to have been made in the Illinois ranks. At the beginning of the procession she was not seen. Along the route, however, she stepped out from among the spectators, was flanked by two white women, and continued to the end.[59]

Ida B. Wells-Barnett,
with Ida B. Barnett, Jr., and Alfreda M. Barnett. (ca. 1914)

The *Broad Ax* reported shortly after this incident that the Alpha Suffrage Club would honor Wells-Barnett, Belle Squire, and Virginia Brooks as three heroines of the Washington demonstration. The two white women were recognized as the loyal supporters of Wells-Barnett in her bid for equal black representation. They were billed as the chief speakers on the program to which members of the Chicago Federation of Women's Clubs were invited. The Alpha Club continued to hold its regular weekly meetings, sometimes featuring other noted white clubwomen, and it participated in the local suffrage parades. The main effort, however, was to reach as many black women in the community as possible to familiarize them with civic and political issues and the mechanics of voting.[60]

In 1910, Wells-Barnett had expressed her evaluation of the ballot in an article entitled "How Enfranchisement Stops Lynching." [Reproduced in this volume pages 267-276.] The black American's vote was "the only protection of his citizenship." Considering the deteriorating condition of the blacks in the South, she pointed out that despite their acquisition of property and education, laws continued to be passed against them. Without the ballot protest was useless because blacks could neither choose lawmakers nor retire those who legislated against them. They would continue to pay taxes but have no voice in the use of those taxes. Not even life was secure. "Having successfully swept aside the constitutional safeguards to the ballot, it is the smallest of small matters for the South to sweep aside its own safeguards to human life."[61]

In 1913, the Illinois legislature gave women the right to vote for presidential electors, for certain non-constitutional officers, and on issues submitted to voters in municipalities and other political divisions in the state.[62] In urging the black women of Chicago to use their newly acquired right, Wells-Barnett was concerned not only with protecting life, but also with improving the quality of life in the black ghetto. Their efforts could help to put a black man on the city council to represent the needs of the South Side.

The most highly regarded elective office was a seat on the city council, and no black Chicagoan had attained one. Composed of seventy aldermen, two from each ward, the council was responsible for the people's health, personal and property protection, sanitation, and recreation. It was empowered to pass the budget, create departments, grant franchises, recommend or reject appointments, and oversee the administration of individual wards.[63] In the first issue of the *Alpha Suffrage Record* (the only issue known to be extant), the club announced its enthusiastic endorsement of Oscar DePriest as a candidate for alderman of the Second Ward and of William Hale Thompson for mayor. The announcement in the form of a resolution added, "We pledge ourselves to leave no stone unturned to secure their election on April 6; we realize that in no other way can we safeguard our own rights than by holding up the hands of those who fight our battles."

Admonishing blacks to carry out their voting responsibility, the paper reprinted an editorial from *The New York News*, which praised Chicago for pointing "the way to the political salvation of the race." The article proclaimed Chicago the only place in the United States where blacks had been given "adequate political recognition," and emphasized that this was true because only in Chicago had they demanded it.[64]

In 1914, an independent black candidate, William Randolph Cowan, had gotten 45 percent of the Republican vote in the Second Ward, which by 1920 was 70 percent black.[65] The day after the primary, which Cowan had lost by only 167 votes, Oscar DePriest appeared at a meeting of the Alpha Suffrage Club to ask the women to support the party's candidate. He promised that the Republican organization would nominate a black man for the next opening. By Wells-Barnett's account, "The women began to fire broadcast at him." They insisted on knowing when there would be a vacancy and how they could be sure that the party would keep its promise.[66]

In November of that year, George F. Harding, a Second Ward alderman, was elected to the state senate. DePriest was nominated by the Republicans to run for Harding's vacant city council seat. The following February the three black aldermanic candidates—Charles B. Griffin, Louis B. Anderson, and Oscar DePriest—presented their platforms to the Alpha Suffrage Club and answered questions. The *Broad Ax* reported that at this meeting a motion was unanimously passed that any member of the club who supported a white candidate would be expelled.[67]

William Hale Thompson was at this time a candidate for the office of mayor. He, too, sought the black vote of the South Side. Mr. and Mrs. Barnett attended the meeting at the Sherman Hotel where Thompson's friends introduced his pledge-card campaign. She was called on to speak, but instead asked for the politician's program in reference to black Chicagoans. Satisfied with his responses, she and her clubwomen actively supported his campaign for six months. They had obtained several thousand pledges before Judge Harry Olson's candidacy for the Republican organization was announced. She abruptly terminated her efforts for Thompson's election, disappointed but convinced that she could not oppose Olson. Both Thompson and DePriest were victorious in 1915, but the Barnetts were on Olson's losing side when the votes were counted.[68]

EIGHT

Politics and Legal Action in Illinois

One feature that distinguished Ida Wells-Barnett from other black women in Chicago was her political interest and activity. As early as 1885 she published her philosophy on political choice. Analyzing the one-party mentality as narrow and lacking in knowledge of history, she proclaimed herself neither Democrat nor Republican. "This is my position. I can see plainly how one can sanction some particular phase of each party without being able to endorse either as a whole and thus be independent—and because this is my position I naturally wonder that others do not 'see as I do.' " She noted that blacks who supported the Democratic Party were ostracized and accused of being bought. She pointed out, however, that in view of the Republican Party's contemptuous behavior toward black Americans in recent years, the only feature attracting the black vote was the promise of appoitive offices. She added that the willingness of the officeholders to retain their jobs under the Democratic administration without reference to party was an indication that interest in the Republicans was not a matter of principle but of personal gain. Criticizing those who avoided political discussion altogether, she said that they did not indicate their independence, but acknowledged submission to conditions as they existed. She stressed the right and the need for rational political discussion among blacks.

> It is not in favor, nor against the interest of either party that I write this. Let a man be Democrat, Republican or Independent as his judgement dictates, if he is obeying honest and intelligent convictions. It is the spirit of intolerance and narrowmindedness among colored men of intelligence that is censured and detested. This is a free country and among other things it boasts the privilege of free speech and personal opinion.[1]

In 1888, Wells-Barnett attended the Indianapolis Conference of Colored Democrats. At this meeting, T. Thomas Fortune was chairman of the

Committee on Resolutions, which strongly endorsed Grover Cleveland.[2] Later, she was associated with William Monroe Trotter, who supported the Democrat Woodrow Wilson in the 1912 campaign.[3] Wells-Barnett was tolerant of political choices with which she did not agree, but aware as she was of the weaknesses of the Republicans in their increasing indifference to the blacks in America, she actively supported the party of Lincoln in Chicago.

She valued the right to participate in politics and had desired a legal career, which was out of reach.[4] In marrying the politically ambitious attorney F. L. Barnett, she became involved in politics and law. To some extent practicality played a part in the Barnett marriage. By her own admission, marriage was more a necessity than an ambition. She seemed to believe with other women of the time that a career and marriage could not be combined. On the other hand, she knew that in order for the professional woman of the nineteenth century to survive, she had to have a personal income or patronage of some sort.[5] She had neither. When Susan B. Anthony reflected her disappointment that the young black agitator had forsaken a promising career for family life, Wells-Barnett recorded, "I could not tell Miss Anthony that it was because I had been unable like herself, to get the support which was necessary to carry on my work that I had become discouraged in the effort to carry on alone."[6]

There was a practical aspect in Barnett's consideration of a second marriage, as well. His secretary recalled that in answer to her curiosity about his social life some time after his first wife's death, he had confided to her, "I am not thinking of marriage as I have not forgotten my first wife enough, yet; and when I do think of marriage it will be to a *woman*—one who can help me in my career."[7]

In Ida B. Wells he had apparently found the partner who shared his political interests and views. Early issues of the *Conservator* and individual articles from later issues indicate that F. L. Barnett, while remaining loyal to the Republican Party, honestly admitted its failures and complained about its neglect of the American black. He, too, was of the mind that mere sentimental allegiance to the Republicans was out of place. Concerned with encouraging political consciousness among blacks, he instructed the *Conservator* readers on their voting strength as a power bloc to be used in the interest of the race and urged political aggressiveness.[8]

Well known and highly regarded as an attorney and political thinker among Chicago's black professionals,[9] Barnett was a reasonable choice for a political appointment. In 1896, a year after his second marriage, his opportunity presented itself. He was named assistant state's attorney by Charles S. Deneen. It was, however, the political maneuvering of the astute Edward H. Wright that secured for Barnett the office that he held for almost fifteen years.

Wright was a native New Yorker, who began his successful ascent as a Chicago politician in the 1880s. When Charles Deneen was elected state's attorney, Ed Wright showed both his political influence and determination. When Deneen sought the Republican nomination for state's attorney, he made an agreement with County Commissioner Wright to appoint a black assistant in exchange for the commissioner's support at the county convention. After he was nominated and elected, however, Deneen failed to keep his part of the bargain. Wright reminded him of the promise to appoint Barnett. The reminder did not motivate the state's attorney to act. At the time for the appropriation of funds by the county board for the various offices, Wright withheld the money for Deneen's office. Despite his evident intention to ignore the agreement regarding Barnett, Deneen was forced to bow to Wright's power over funds and appointed Barnett one of his assistants.[10]

Wells-Barnett, too, entered into political activity a short time after her marriage. Members of the Women's Republican State Central Committee and their husbands had attended the Barnett wedding as a group. Despite the fact that by the fall of 1896 Wells-Barnett had an infant son, she was asked by the same women's political organization to travel around the state to lecture in anticipation of the coming election. She toured Illinois, where in each town a nurse was provided for the care of the child while his mother lectured. In her autobiography she noted, "I honestly believe that I am the only woman in the United States who ever traveled throughout the country with a nursing baby to make political speeches." She was enthusiastic about the project because it gave her the opportunity to instruct white and black women on organizing themselves to take advantage of any privilege of political participation as it came. When the series of lectures was over, she expressed regret that in most places no black women were in the audiences. She commented, "If the white women were backward in political matters, our own women were even more so."[11]

Until the birth of a second son in 1897, Wells-Barnett edited the *Conservator*, which she had taken over in July 1895. No issues from this period exist, but judging from reprints of articles in other newspapers, Albert

Kreiling concludes that, "Under her the paper took stands on political and other affairs across the country." The *Conservator* was later sold, but the Barnetts retained the mortgage and continued to influence its positions and to write for it.[12]

Wells-Barnett decided in 1897 to retire from her active career to the duties of her home. This was a matter of conviction and necessity for her. She believed that children should grow up under the care and guidance of their mother at home. With two small children demanding her attention, she decided that marriage and motherhood were a full-time job and that, "It was hopeless to try to carry on public work." Two sons of Ferdinand Barnett's first marriage were approaching adolescence by the time the last of the Barnett children was born in 1904. The responsibility for six children curtailed for several years Wells-Barnett's usual intense activity. She did not take any position that would keep her away from home regularly until the youngest child was eight years old. During the growing-up years of all the children she was careful that they were sufficiently supervised and provided for in her absence.[13]

During this more or less quiescent period of her life, her husband was proposed by the Deneen faction of the Republican Party as a candidate for a judgeship on the Municipal Court. By this time, 1906, he had already served ten years as assistant state's attorney. According to Harold Gosnell, white Republican newspapers opposed his candidacy; nonetheless, early returns of the election seemed to indicate that he was a winner. The final tally showed, however, that he had lost by 304 votes. That he was "counted out" as some observers charged was not proved,[14] but it was twenty years before any black was elected a judge in Chicago.[15]

A letter to the editor of the *Chicago Chronicle* may be indicative of the prevailing sentiment on the subject at the time of Barnett's nomination. The writer, who signed himself "White Man," noted that the black attorney was the only Republican defeated in the election. He blamed the Republican leaders for lack of good judgment in putting a black man's name in nomination. His explanation was, "The Negro is a man, a brother and a citizen but he belongs to an inferior race, and while white people are perfectly willing to see him in public offices in which the point of inferiority is not raised they violently resent any effort to place him in a position in which he will exercise authority over them." Barnett was described by this white as "a fair and an upright and amiable man," "naturally courteous," and of a "compliant rather than a firm and obstinate disposition." These qualities,

The Barnett family in 1917

Standing: Hulette D. Barnett (wife of Albert G. Barnett),
Herman Kohlsaat Barnett, Ferdinand L. Barnett, Jr., Ida B. Barnett, Jr.,
Charles Aked Barnett, Alfreda M. Barnett, and Albert G. Barnett;
seated: Ferdinand L. Barnett, Sr., Beatrice Barnett, Audrey Barnett,
Ida B. Wells-Barnett; *foreground*: Hulette E. Barnett, Florence B. Barnett.
The four little girls are the children of Albert and Hulette Barnett.

he said, were detrimental because "while his race would make obstinacy dangerous to him his yielding disposition would make him dangerous to the public."[16]

In retrospect, Wells-Barnett blamed the opposition of the clergyman-politician A. J. Carey for her husband's defeat. According to her account, Carey opposed Ferdinand Barnett because she had, with his concurrence, given enthusiastic endorsement to the Pekin Theater, which had been converted from a saloon. Although Robert T. Motts, the owner, was a reputed gambling lord, Wells-Barnett approved his theater venture as a means of encouraging interest in a higher type of entertainment and culture among blacks. The minister, on the other hand, expressed the opinion that the theater was an extension of a "low gambling dive." The Barnetts showed their good faith by attending the opening of the Pekin at the invitation of Motts. For this they incurred Carey's censure from the pulpit, which Wells-Barnett accused him of using for political and pecuniary purposes.[17]

The times were such that whether or not Carey's influence was a factor in Barnett's defeat, it was undoubtedly true that white Chicago was not ready for a black man with "absolute authority."[18] In that year, hostility between the races began to show itself in the nation in the form of riots. The black-hating political speeches and the sensational reporting of the local press in Georgia led to the scandalous "Atlanta massacre" in September of 1906.

J. Max Barber, editor of *The Voice of the Negro*, an Atlanta-based magazine, had been forced to leave the city because he had repudiated an article by John Temple Graves of the *Georgian*, justifying the events in the Georgia capital.[19] He took refuge in Chicago, where he was a guest speaker at a meeting of the Douglass Center Women's Club. In his talk, he described the horrors of organized violence against blacks in Atlanta. The response of the club's president, Mrs. George W. Plummer, was an exhortation addressed to Barber "to drive the criminals out from among you." To Wells-Barnett, this was a disappointment and an affront. She answered for Barber, saying that to give that advice to a man in Barber's position was to offer a stone to one who asked for bread. Wells-Barnett learned from the experience that Mrs. Plummer had not been convinced of her account of the happenings that drove her from Memphis. Her motion that the club offer resolutions condemning the atrocities and asking that the legal authorities take action was ignored. Ferdinand Barnett calmed the temper of his wife after the incident: "My husband told me that I had to learn to take my friends as I found them, making allowances for their shortcomings, and still hold on to their friendships."[20]

Less than two years after the Atlanta violence there was rioting in the capital of Illinois for three days. On September 5, 1908, the *Springfield Forum* reported "two weeks of excitement caused by rioting and attacks upon the colored people," but the city had a price to pay. The *Forum* listed claims against Springfield for loss of life and property damage, grand jury investigations, and the maintenance of the national guard. The black newspaper credited the governor with quick and efficient action. After inquiring into the disturbance at four in the afternoon of August 14, Charles S. Deneen had remained in his office all night. Two local companies of militia were ordered in at eight in the evening. Jailed black prisoners were transferred to Bloomington. More troops were required by nine. Companies from six Illinois towns, the Fifth Infantry, and cavalry troops were called. When the mob disregarded shots fired over their heads, permission was given for the troops to fire small bullets at their legs. This action scattered the crowd, described as "drunken and reeling men and boys who, fired by lust for blood and excited by the burning buildings, were anxious to drive all colored people from the city." Troops were stationed in five sections of the town to protect the homes of blacks.[21]

The seriousness with which Charles Deneen gave his attention to the racial crisis in Springfield was a matter of law established just three years before. In 1905, through the efforts of the black legislator Edward Green, a bill to suppress mob violence was passed by the state lawmakers.[22] That act defined a mob as a group of five or more persons intent upon violating any person or property for whatever reason. It determined fines for conspiring to form a mob, and designated mob action a felony. It guaranteed restitution for the loss of life and property by the state to the victims or survivors of such violence. Finally, the law provided that the sheriff or deputy who allowed the lynching of a person in his custody be dismissed from his office with the provision that he could petition the governor for reinstatement within ten days of the lynching.[23]

The Springfield riot took the lives of two blacks and four whites. The spree of racial violence had been touched off by the old story of a black man's assault on a white woman. Although the accusation was retracted by the woman who made it, two innocent, unimplicated black men were lynched. One was a barber, hanged in the backyard of his shop, which was destroyed along with other black businesses. The other, the eighty-four-year-old owner of half the block in which he lived with his white wife of more than thirty years, was hanged and mutilated in his own yard. In the frenzy of the riot, three white men were shot, one accidentally. Another man was found at the bottom of a stairway leading to a barroom. According to the Chicago Commission on Race Relations, one fundamental cause of the riot was the laxity of the law enforcement agencies and the "vicious conditions" tolerated in the community, especially in the black sections.[24]

Determined to avoid activity that would take her away from her family obligations, Wells-Barnett contained her inner agitation after the Springfield affair and confined her activity to preventive measures against potential conflict in Chicago. One year later, however, she was compelled to take a challenge in Cairo, Illinois. On November 11, 1909, William "Frog" James, accused of raping and murdering a white woman, was taken from the custody of Alexander County sheriff Frank Davis and lynched by a mob. When rumors of a lynching were heard on November 10, the black prisoner was taken from the Cairo city jail, where he had been incarcerated for one day, and was placed in the custody of Sheriff Frank Davis. The sheriff with one deputy took James by train to a town some distance north. Hearing that the mob was gathering to pursue them, the three left the train with no particular destination. Davis was identified in a town in which he bought some provisions. His location was reported to the Cairo mob, which overtook the men and returned them to the city. Although the sheriff and the deputy were armed, they put up no resistance except to make a plea that James not be harmed. The sheriff returned to his office while the prisoner was hanged, shot, and burned.

In its hysteria, the throng followed Davis to the county jail and took a white prisoner accused of murder. In this instance, Davis was reported to have asked some bystanders to assist him against the mob. His request ignored, he went so far as to point out the cell of the second lynch victim. Eventually the sheriff called the governor for aid. When the troops arrived, order was restored.[25]

The law required the dismissal of the Alexander County sheriff, but he had the right to petition for reinstatement. This he did promptly, with the support of the white community and blacks who considered Davis a friend because he had appointed black deputies. A group of black Chicagoans met and sent a communication to Deneen expressing their feelings of indignation at the lynchings, which the sheriff had made no real effort to prevent. As a result, the governor notified them of the time at which he would hear Davis's plea.

Attorney Barnett had attempted to interest some Chicago men in going to Springfield to protest the sheriff's reinstatement. His efforts failed. He reported this at dinner to his wife and four children on the Saturday afternoon preceding the sheriff's scheduled appearance before Deneen. Wells-Barnett recorded that at the end of his statement, her husband added, "And so it would seem that you will have to go to Cairo and get the facts with which to confront the sheriff next Wednesday morning. And your train leaves at eight o'clock." She responded that she had been accused by black men earlier of taking over situations before they could get involved. In this instance, she had no intention of assuming their responsibility. Before the night was over, however, she was moved by her oldest son's words, "Mother if you don't go nobody else will." The boy later relayed to his father her message that she would take the morning train.[26]

Wells-Barnett's objective in going to Cairo was to gather facts regarding the lynchings. Barnett undoubtedly relied on his wife's refusal to allow an anti-lynching law to be thwarted because black men could not be motivated to act. His urging her to go indicates also his faith in her ability to present her findings effectively before the governor. In Cairo she met individuals and groups, none of whom could testify that the sheriff had actually held William James in the jail, or that he had made any reasonable effort to secure assistance in protecting the prisoner in his charge. She drew up a resolution against the reinstatement of Davis and secured a representative number of signatures, in some instances men who had previously supported the reinstatement petition by letter to the governor. She found "the ubiquitous 'Uncle Tom' " and those who feared involvement, but she was generally satisfied that she had a case to take to Springfield. Her husband wrote a legal brief using information he obtained from Chicago newspapers. He had assured her that she could easily insert any additional data accrued in her interviews. The brief was awaiting her in Springfield on Wednesday morning.[27]

By her account, Davis was flanked by his lawyer, who was also a state senator, his parish priest, a state and a federal official, and a group of Cairo supporters. She was the sole representative in opposition to his reinstatement. To her disappointment, "Not a Negro face was in evidence!" Her situation was alleviated during the day by the presence of a black lawyer, A. M. Williams, who came to invite her to dinner but stayed with her throughout the remainder of the proceedings. Despite the testimony offered in behalf of Davis, the letters read, and the petitions presented, Wells-Barnett felt she had won the day by distinguishing fact from opinion and by her strong plea that, "If this man is reinstated, it will simply mean an increase of lynching in the State of Illinois and an encouragement to mob violence."[28]

The *Springfield Forum* praised Wells-Barnett's performance in presenting the petition for the permanent retirement of the delinquent sheriff. A week later it also printed a letter from F. L. Barnett thanking A. M. Williams for his assistance in supporting the petitions of the citizens of Chicago, represented by his wife. "I think the action of the governor will set such a precedent that lynching will be banished from the State of Illinois, and in so successful a proceeding you deserve the unqualified thanks of all law abiding citizens." Barnett indicated that his wife had commended the "splendid ability" of the lawyer who aided her in the "law phase of the contest."[29]

On December 6, Governor Deneen issued his decision not to grant the petition of reinstatement. He pointed out that, "The measure of the duty of the sheriff is to be determined from a consideration of his powers. He is vested in his county with the whole executive power of the state." He explained this sweeping implication, listing the sheriff's power to call into action any person eighteen years or older in his county to keep the peace, to deputize any number of men and to arm them in special cases, to take the lives of offenders if necessary in order to suppress violence, and finally to call on the governor for the state militia. Deneen reviewed the duties of a sheriff as prescribed in the 1905 mob violence statute. These obligated him to guarantee the life and safety of prisoners by taking every available precautionary measure to forestall injury to persons in his custody. The judgment of the governor after hearing the testimony of both sides in the case was unequivocal. Frank Davis had failed to fulfill his duty as sheriff in allowing the lynchings of William James and Henry Salzner.

Wells-Barnett considered this pronouncement one of the finest to come forth during Charles Deneen's term as governor. She referred particularly to his insistence on the execution of the law. He had written:

> Mob violence has no place in Illinois. It is denounced in every line of the Constitution and in every statute. Instead of breeding respect for law, it breeds contempt. For the suppression of mob violence, our legislature has spoken in no uncertain terms. When such mob violence threatens the life of a prisoner in the custody of the sheriff, the law has charged the sheriff, at the penalty of a forfeiture of his office, to use the utmost human endeavor to protect the life

of his prisoner. The law may be severe. Whether severe or not, it must be enforced.[30]

The *Springfield Forum* honored the anti-lynching crusader's triumph and "the great work she has done in the last twenty years along this line."[31] The *Chicago Defender*, reporting on the meeting at which Wells-Barnett gave details of her investigation to a large audience at the Bethel Literary and Historical Club, suggested that, "If we only had a few men with the backbone of Mrs. Barnett, lynching would soon come to a halt in America."[32] However, the NAACP publication *Crisis*, in an article referring to the firing of the Cairo sheriff, "whom the Governor held responsible for the mob in that city," made no mention of Wells-Barnett's activity.[33]

During the summer of the following year, Wells-Barnett published an article showing that it was the power of the ballot used by blacks in Illinois that made the victory in Springfield possible. She recalled that in 1904 only one black man was elected to the state legislature. That black legislator, however, was chiefly responsible for the passage of the law Deneen was bound to uphold. She noted the precarious position for justice in the case, had there been no mob violence statute, for Davis, she said, represented a pivotal county and the Republican faction that had secured the governor's reelection in 1908. As a consequence of Deneen's decision in which the law was placed above the protection of friends, she contended that three lynchings had been deterred.[34] Indeed, in January, the *Forum* had noted the action of the sheriff in Vienna, Illinois, in preventing a lynching and had commended the governor for his swift dispatch of troops with the order to defy the mob.[35]

Once called into action, Wells-Barnett became involved shortly after the Cairo incident with the case of a black accused of murdering his employer. Steve Green had insisted on leaving a job with which he was dissatisfied. When the man for whom he worked attempted to take his life in retaliation, Green killed him. The slaying took place in Arkansas, but Green made his way to Chicago, where he was jailed. An order of extradition was filed by the Southern state and honored by Illinois. The fact was brought to the attention of a number of prominent Chicago blacks including, the *Defender* noted, "that watchdog of human life and liberty Ida Wells-Barnett." A writ of habeas corpus was asked in order to stay the extradition, but the prisoner had already been taken from the Chicago jail. From the office of the state's attorney, an order was secured to have Green stopped on his way south and returned. The sheriff who would apprehend him was offered a $100 reward.

Green was arrested by the successor of Sheriff Davis in Cairo. Back in Chicago, he appeared before Circuit Court Judge Tuthill, who found the extradition papers faulty and dismissed the man. By the time the extradition order could be corrected and demand again made for Green, Wells-Barnett, with voluntary financial assistance, had put him on his way to Canada.

Charles Flint Kellogg, in his history of the early years of the NAACP, gives credit to Wells-Barnett for managing the entire affair, from securing the writ of habeas corpus to Green's escape into Canada. He notes, however, that the *Crisis* failed to mention her involvement. In a letter to Joel Spingarn, she said that the Negro Fellowship League was responsible for devising the "Steve Green plan," and in her autobiography she acknowledged the assistance of lawyer Edward Wright in the legal proceedings.[36]

A later development left her questioning Wright and taking an unfavorable stand against him. When Joel Spingarn became interested in the case, he offered the National Association $100 to assist with the legal defense of Green. He also contacted Wright to be sure of the facts and to notify him of his financial assistance to the NAACP in order that there be no obstacles or delays in the legal process. Aware that Wright had appealed to Spingarn for more funds, and distrustful of the intentions of the lawyers involved, Wells-Barnett notified Oswald Villard, disbursing treasurer of the NAACP, that the Negro Fellowship League had already started Green on his way to Canada. She added that since the man was illiterate, she had had no word of his arrival, but she would find a means of communicating with him and notify Villard if Green needed funds.

Villard sent this information to Spingarn, commenting, "It is an unfortunate fact that the colored lawyers, as we have learned to our cost . . . usually take advantage of philanthropic interest of this kind to make money for themselves. . . . Either Mr. Wright is ignorant, or he deliberately seeks to mislead you on account of pelf."[37]

During her period of quasi-retirement, Wells-Barnett had continued to carry on her anti-lynching crusade with her pen. In 1900, she published a pamphlet, *Mob Rule in New Orleans*. The booklet reported on an episode of violence in the Crescent City during the summer of that year. She used it to show again that blacks in the South were lynched because they were blacks and to point out that if white men respected the laws of the land, lynchings would not occur, "for every individual, no matter what the charge, would have a fair trial and an opportunity to prove his guilt or innocence before a tribunal of law."[38] She published articles in the popular *Arena* and the *Independent*. In 1913, she identified herself with the Chicago NAACP and the Negro Fellowship League in writing an article for *Survey*. In this denunciation of lynch law, Wells-Barnett referred to the fact that the South's method of dealing with the black had moved to the North. She lamented that the principles of the North gave way, invariably, to the prejudices of the South. Mindful of the fiftieth anniversary of the American black's emancipation that year, she asked, "Does it seem too much to ask white civilization, Christianity and Democracy to be true to themselves on this as all other questions?"[39]

During that year of celebration Ida Wells-Barnett broke with her life of relative inactivity when Judge Harry Olson of the Municipal Court appointed her an adult probation officer. In a letter to Joel Spingarn, she boasted that she was the first black person appointed to that position. Her work with eighty-five probationers, she explained, was a full-time job that required her presence at the Harrison Street Court every morning for three hours, while much of the rest of the day and into the night she worked in the field.[40] During the year following her appointment, she negotiated with Olson to name the young secretary of the Negro Fellowship League a bailiff in the court.[41]

Once back in action, Wells-Barnett assumed an aggressive role. In May 1917, an outbreak of racial violence in East St. Louis, Illinois, demanded her attention. Several days after the conflict a meeting was held in Chicago to study the relationship between the influx of Southern black workers and the riot. The report emanating from the conference indicated that shifting large groups of laborers of either race intensified already bitter feelings and prepared the way for violence. It recommended organization by experienced leaders who would take into account the welfare of the workers.[42] Racial hostility erupted again on July 2. The toll in lives lost and property destroyed was great. Thirty-nine blacks and eight whites were killed; hundreds were injured.[43] Wells-Barnett did not await a request to go to the site. Before the town had resumed a state of normalcy, she went to investigate the situation in order to present to Governor Frank O. Lowden resolutions based on fact in condemning the riot. She spoke with officials and visited the devastated homes from which black residents had been driven. On her return she discovered, however, that her fact-finding mission was not appreciated by leading black politicians. The Barnetts were censured as radicals by a delegation including Ed Wright, Oscar DePriest, Louis

Anderson, and R. R. Jackson, who visited Lowden and assured him of the good faith of the blacks of Chicago.

Wells-Barnett made her report to an audience at the Bethel A.M.E. Church and set out with another delegation for Springfield to see the governor. Assured that a full-scale investigation would be made, she went to St. Louis, where many of the dispossessed had found refuge and where she mistakenly expected to be able to gather more information.[44] A congressional investigation was conducted, however, and to her satisfaction its results were published.

Among the conditions leading to the riot, the congressional committee noted the large increase of black laborers, but it also pointed out that since the warning incident in May no action had been taken by local authorities to strengthen police protection in the town. The major cause of the riot was identified as corrupt politics, which involved "an almost unbelievable combination of shameless corruption, tolerance of vice and crime, maladministration, and debauchery."[45]

By July 17, Wells-Barnett had made a second visit to East St. Louis and had given a report to a citizens' group at Quinn Chapel in Chicago.[46] She was dismayed at the fact that attention had been turned to a number of East St. Louis blacks who, fearing such an outbreak, had appealed to the governor for preventive action. Nothing having been done, they armed themselves. A prominent dentist, Dr. Leroy Bundy, was accused of instigating violent action among blacks. Although he had fled to Cleveland and had fought extradition for three months, he was returned to Illinois, where he awaited trial in Belleville.[47]

The indignation of Illinois blacks was expressed in an article in the *Defender*:

> The whole power of the state under the direction of Attorney-General Brundage is being used to punish the rioters and yet we have the spectacle of outraged justice sending ten men to the penitentiary for the two white officers killed and only four white men found guilty among all the hundreds of brutal murderers who made a two-day orgy of butchering our people, burning their homes, and driving into exile 5,000 peaceable law-abiding citizens.

There was widespread contention that Bundy would be used as an example. If he escaped lynching, he would be legally murdered. A conspiracy against Bundy's life among officials from the governor down the ranks was believed

Ida B. Wells (December 1917) wearing her controversial button:
"In Memorial MARTYERED NEGRO SOLDIERS" after the execution of the
soldiers following the incident in Brownsville, Texas.

to be a "cold-blooded effort to put an end to the man who dares to think and act in defense of the race."[48]

In a letter to the editor of the *Broad Ax* printed on October 27, Wells-Barnett indicated that prayers and protest were not enough in the aftermath of the riot. Money was needed for legal aid. Although empty-handed, she planned to go to Belleville in the name of the National Equal Rights League, of which she was a member, and the Negro Fellowship League, to visit Bundy, who had asked financial assistance of the people of Chicago.[49]

The *Chicago Defender* received requests that someone be sent to interview Bundy and to write a report of the case. On the day that Wells-Barnett's letter appeared in the *Broad Ax*, Robert Abbott, editor of the *Defender*, made an appeal for funds for the legal defense of Dr. Bundy and promised to send a representative to visit him at the Belleville jail. Abbott asked Wells-Barnett to represent his paper. On November 3, her report appeared in the columns of the *Defender*.[50]

She indicated that during the three days of her investigation she had visited Bundy twice. She had also interviewed the two East St. Louis lawyers whom he wanted on his case. Although the Masonic Fraternity and the NAACP had promised assistance in retaining an attorney, neither had hired one. She proposed that adequate funds could be accumulated in one day if people could be sure of the honest use of their contributions. A financial committee was organized among Bundy's friends and Wells-Barnett assured them that *Defender* readers would cooperate.[51]

Wells-Barnett's hopefulness about the fund for Bundy was not realized as quickly as she had supposed. In late December, the *Defender* registered its disappointment with the response. When Bundy was released on bail he began to make speeches on his own behalf. Eventually he was freed and returned to Cleveland.[52]

The nation was rife with racial tension during the summer of 1919. James Weldon Johnson dubbed it "The Red Summer." Twenty-five riots rocked urban centers. Hostility grew against blacks as they continued to migrate to Northern cities. Job competition, high rents in segregated sections, and disillusionment and distrust of whites put blacks on the defensive.[53] Friction frequently resulted when members of the two races encountered one another.

On July 7, 1919, the *Chicago Tribune* published a letter to the editor from Ida B. Wells-Barnett. It was dated June 30 and warned Chicago of what lay ahead if nothing were done about its race problem.

With one Negro dead as a result of a race riot last week, another one very badly injured in the county hospital; with a half dozen attacks upon Negro children, and one on the Thirty-fifth street car Tuesday, in which four white men beat one colored man, it looks very much like Chicago is trying to rival the south in its race hatred against the Negro. Especially does this seem so when we consider the bombing of Negro homes and the indifference of the public to these outrages.

It was just such a situation as this which led up to the East St. Louis riot two years ago. There had been a half dozen outbreaks against the colored people by whites. Two different committees waited upon Governor Lowden and asked him to investigate the outrages against the Negroes before the riot took place. Nobody paid any attention.

Will the legal, moral, and civic forces of this town stand idly by and take no notice here of these preliminary outbreaks? Will no action be taken to prevent these law breakers until further disaster has occurred?

An ounce of prevention beats a pound of cure. And in all earnestness I implore Chicago to set the wheels of justice in motion before it is too late, and Chicago be disgraced by some of the bloody outrages that have disgraced East St. Louis.[54]

The predicted outbreak occurred on Sunday, July 27. Rioting raged uncontrolled for four days and continued sporadically for three more. The casualty list included thirty-eight dead and 537 injured. One thousand were left homeless. The violence which began at the beach off Lake Michigan at 29th Street, swept the south and southwest sections of the city, and reached the West Side and the Loop. Organized gangs of young toughs played a major part in clashes, which resulted in destruction of life and property. The state militia was called into action on Monday and was not withdrawn until August 8.

A committee, requested by citizens and set up almost immediately by Governor Lowden to investigate the Chicago riot, pointed out three factors affecting racial hostility. First, the commission noted the influx of blacks seeking industrial opportunities, but it added that conflict in industry was much less significant than expected. Housing presented a much worse situation. The doubled black population had no recourse other than spreading into the section adjoining the black belt. This, nonetheless, aroused the hostility of whites, who bombed the property of the blacks and the whites who sold or rented houses to them. The third factor was Mayor Thompson's political control in the black section. Black politicians in his faction of the Republican Party influenced the black voters so that other Republican contenders had no chance in that ward.[55]

One year after the Chicago race riot, Wells-Barnett closed the Negro Fellowship League. The State Street "lighthouse" had become too great a financial burden. Within a week of its closing she was hospitalized for five weeks and spent another eight weeks recovering from surgery. Her health was a problem for almost a year. During these months of illness, she attempted to assess the work she had done and decided that it was time for her to think about the future in a personal way.[56] She did not record the results of her ruminations, but in 1924, she renewed her interest in the women's club movement sufficiently to seek the presidency of the NACW. In this endeavor she failed. In 1928, she gave her energies again to politics, organizing the black women's vote for the Hoover-Curtis ticket in the national election.

In September, she circulated a letter from the Republican Committee Headquarters in Chicago. She announced that she had been appointed national organizer of Illinois black women voters, and she reminded black women that although they had had the franchise for almost ten years, less than one-fourth of them used it. She warned them that by neglecting to use it intelligently they could lose it: "The ballot is the right which safeguards all our rights."[57]

A month later she wrote Claude Barnett, director of the Negro Associated Press, about the publication of some of her political propaganda. She sent him a copy of a speech, "Why I Am for Hoover," which she had delivered at a mass meeting of the Illinois Colored Women's Republican League in Chicago and which she had had printed at her own expense. She told Barnett that she had distributed 3,000 copies, and she gave him permission to use it as extensively as he wished.

Privately she expressed to him her disappointment and frustration at the Republican Party's disregard of the blacks' moving toward the Democratic Party. She recited a list of her activities and the expense she had incurred in getting blacks to support Hoover.[58] In another letter, intended for publication, she wrote, "This time the wolf in sheep's clothing is spending money like water to hire our folks in the Democratic camp, but very few of them are going to betray our race for 30 pieces of silver or for the prospect of a drink of liquor."[59] Some time later, Wells-Barnett sent another item for release by the Negro Associated Press. In the cover letter to the director, she revealed the reason for her vigorous campaigning:

As I told you in the other letter, I have been worried over the apathy of those to whom was confided the duty of combatting Democratic Propaganda. Is it indifference, or ignorance of their duties? Something is radically wrong.

All of which will excuse to you, my stewing over the situation. Hoover is going to win but he must not win without us. If he does, our Republican friends (white) will be more indifferent to us than ever.[60]

She was convinced that white politicians must be aware that blacks had a decisive vote and effective political influence.

In 1930, Chicago had the second largest black population in the nation. Blacks there were more politically aggressive than in any other American city. Women, particularly those with a Southern background, were as interested in politics as were men.[61] In that year Wells-Barnett decided to make a bid for political office. She entered a campaign for a state senate seat. Just two years before, she had traveled through ten Illinois counties making speeches and setting up the political organizations of black women for the presidential campaign. She could boast of having helped to raise the number of registered female black voters by almost 50 percent.[62]

She began her campaign in January and carried it on with vigor, seeking endorsements, having petitions signed, and making speeches. By February 12, she was able to send to Springfield petitions for her candidacy signed by 500 persons. She had arranged for a clerk of elections to manage her campaign. Several women were generous in donating funds, enabling her to pay printing expenses. Her attempt to gain the support of the politician Ed Wright, however, failed. "He is still stubborn about helping women," she wrote. During the campaign she contacted Senator Deneen, who was engaged in a fight to retain his seat in the United States Senate against Ruth McCormick, widow of the late Senator Medill McCormick.

Wells-Barnett distributed thousands of cards and letters, posted hundreds of window ads, and was assisted by her husband in setting up her headquarters at 3449 Indiana Street. She was promised the support of the leader of the Second Ward independent group and through him was introduced at the Abraham Lincoln Republican Club, where she was invited several times to speak.[63] On April 8, however, when the votes were tallied, she had received only 585. Adelbert Roberts had won with a count of 6,604.[64]

The Barnetts had been political supporters of the Deneen faction of the Republican Party, but in this campaign, Wells-Barnett ran as an independent. Warren B. Douglas, a former representative in the Illinois legislature, had the backing of the Deneen followers, and Adelbert Roberts, another experienced politician and former state legislator, was supported by the regular organization.[65] When Roberts was elected, Wells-Barnett wrote, "He wd [sic] be with the veteran machine behind him which always wins because the independent vote is weak, unorganized and its workers purchasable." Her observation indicates that she recognized the power of the political machine that she opposed, but it proposes a question as to why she ran against such odds. One might conjecture that she felt the time opportune to show black women of Chicago what their political potential was. She campaigned for a state senate seat at the same time that Mrs. McCormick successfully contended for a United States Senate seat, and she had expected greater interest and response from women than her campaign had received. She also planned a conference after the election with her supporters, the outstanding ones all women, in order to learn from the campaign.[66] It was characteristic of Ida Wells-Barnett to feel that she could perform as well in the state legislature as any of the men who were running for office,[67] and it is likely that she dared to campaign against the entrenched male politicians to show that to do so was her prerogative and that of any other qualified woman.

Within a year of her bid for elective office, Ida B. Wells-Barnett's life was spent. She died after a brief illness on March 25, 1931. W. E. B. Du Bois, who had maintained silence on her activities for twenty years, was moved to write:

> The passing of Ida Wells-Barnett calls for more than the ordinary obituary.
> Ida Wells-Barnett was the pioneer of the anti-lynching crusade in the United States. As a young woman in Memphis, she began her work and carried it over the United States and even to England. She roused the white South to vigorous and bitter defense and she began the awakening of the conscience of the nation.[68]

In this brief appraisal, Du Bois acknowledged Wells's early achievement in "the awakening of the conscience of the nation," but he ignored the almost continuous civil rights activity of Wells-Barnett for the last thirty-five years of her life. She was a pioneer in the anti-lynching crusade, but she was also a pioneer in the struggle for justice in the courts and for the political rights of black men and women.

A Brand-
New Thing

This study began with a question posed by T. Thomas Fortune regarding the impact of Ida B. Wells on her time. Fortune seemed at the beginning of Wells's career to foresee problems that she would face with her contemporaries, despite her early prominence.[1] He was aware of her forceful personality, and he envisioned the political prowess she might have developed had she been a man. When she was twenty-six he wrote, "If Iola was a man she would be a humming independent in politics. She has plenty of nerve; she is as smart as a steel trap, and she has no sympathy with humbug."[2] His insight into the qualities of the young woman whose journalistic career he encouraged was keen. He saw the humorless "strength and directness" with which she approached her work and her "conception of the responsibilities and the possibilities of her sex," which went beyond the dreams of most women. His question remained, "If she fails to impress her personality upon the time in which she lives, whose fault will it be?"[3]

Ida Wells's youthful experience as guardian and provider for five siblings was preparation for the independence and determination that she exhibited throughout her life. In 1889, Fortune described the Afro-American agitator as "a brand new thing under the sun. His mission is to force the concession to him of absolute justice under the State and Federal Constitutions."[4] Five years earlier, however, at the age of twenty-two, Ida Wells had already sued a railroad that had violated her right to be treated with dignity and equality. She proved herself a successful journalist and businesswoman when a black middle class was just beginning to emerge in the South. She brought attention to and influenced the making of anti-lynching laws when the South showed its intolerance of black advancement in the form of mob violence. But by 1895, when she took up residence in Chicago, the black protest scene was changing, and she was no longer a subject of comment or record.

Her work in Chicago began with the publication of the Columbian Exposition protest pamphlet and the organization of black women for the improvement of themselves and others. In 1895, she continued to publish as editor of the *Conservator*, founded by her husband, F. L. Barnett, and to work with the Ida B. Wells Club women. Early in her Chicago years she became a center of conflict. Realizing the plight of young black children who could not be immediately fitted into the only existing integrated kindergarten, she established one for them in their South Side neighborhood. Blacks intent on integration objected, but Wells-Barnett saw the immediate need, and she called on blacks to be aware of their resourcefulness and responsibility to provide for themselves at such times. In this she showed the propensity that she shared with F. L. Barnett to emphasize racial unity even as she pressed for the black's rightful place in an integrated society. Working with the Ida B. Wells Club, she was at least partially responsible for organizing the city's first black orchestra. But while she was president, the club also gained membership in the formerly all-white League of Cook County Clubs.

Women's club work was a middle-class endeavor. Wells-Barnett's conception of racial solidarity and united effort embraced the lower class as well. It extended to encouraging a saloon keeper in his attempt to establish a respectable theater for blacks. It motivated her to call on young black men to organize the Negro Fellowship League "down in the heart of that section of the city which has been the most neglected hitherto by the religious, social and moral influences."[5] The League of young men with their woman president provided shelter and food, a reading room, and an employment agency for downtrodden blacks, usually newcomers to the city. Wells-Barnett indicated the principle of operation of the Negro Fellowship League when she wrote, "We take up all matters affecting the civil and legal affairs of the race, and when we have not been able to start the wheels of justice we have at least affected public sentiment."[6] In compliance with this principle, in 1910, the League maneuvered the escape of Steve Green, a black accused of murder, to sanctuary in Canada when a fair trial in Arkansas seemed unlikely for him. From 1913 to 1916, Wells-Barnett made the League's State Street center the headquarters for her work as a probation officer in charge of eighty-five probationers.

At the same time that she was involved in civil and legal action in behalf of the less fortunate of the city, she was committed to developing political awareness among black women. In 1913, she fought against the embarrassment of the women and the ridicule of the men in forming the

Alpha Suffrage Club, the first organization of its kind for black women. She encouraged the women to study political issues and to learn the mechanics of voting, pointing out their ability to influence the black male vote. She had been an active member of the Illinois Equal Suffrage Association and the Chicago Political Equality League, a lecturer on political issues before women's groups, and a supporter of her husband's political ambitions since her arrival in Chicago. By 1915, she had organized the black women of the South Side for the first election in which they could participate. Having heard the positions of the three black candidates for the office of alderman of the Second Ward and having questioned them to their satisfaction, the women of the Alpha Suffrage Club passed a motion that any member not voting for a black candidate be expelled from the club. Oscar DePriest was elected that year, the first black alderman in Chicago.

Perhaps the most outstanding achievement of Ida Wells-Barnett during her years as a Chicago resident was her challenge to the reinstatement of Frank Davis, sheriff of Cairo, Illinois, who had allowed two lynchings in his jurisdiction. Representing the blacks of Chicago, she interviewed Cairo residents to establish the sheriff's negligence. Armed with a legal brief written by her attorney husband and petitions signed by Cairo residents, she successfully presented a case against the sheriff's reinstatement before the governor of the state. Moreover, she pointed out that the statute that Governor Charles Deneen had upheld in enforcing the retirement of the sheriff, the Anti-Mob Violence Statute of 1905, had been spirited into law largely through the efforts of the one black state legislator elected five years before. She also showed that the governor's action in upholding the statute was a determining factor in eradicating lynching in Illinois.

When Ida Wells married Ferdinand Barnett, she entered into a partnership of ideology. Professionally and socially they belonged to Chicago's black elite, but by 1915 theirs was the mentality of a bygone era. In 1896, Barnett had secured the position of assistant state's attorney through the machinations of the astute politician Edward Wright, but he did not realize his ambition to be elected to a judgeship. In 1913, Ida Wells-Barnett was appointed adult probation officer, but her loyalty to the judge who had appointed her deprived the Barnetts of the political rewards that would have been theirs had they continued to support William Hale Thompson as they had at the beginning of his campaign. Eschewing the pragmatism of the new leadership in the city, the Barnetts refused to compromise the virtues of respectability for power or position.

In 1930, Ida Wells-Barnett made a bid for a state Senate seat. She lost to a black man, but she showed that it was within the power of a black woman to participate as a contender in an election for which she was qualified. Despite the fact that Wells-Barnett initiated and led several organizations and was in the forefront of much protest action, she was not an organization personality. She could not merely participate. Neither could she abide by the rules of compromise. Aware as she was of political machinery, she ran for office as an independent.

The years of Ida B. Wells's journalistic successes in the South and the anti-lynching crusades in Britain and the northern part of the United States were followed by years of unheralded activity. Fortune's question on where the blame should lie if she had no impact on the time can probably best be answered by citing Wells-Barnett's strength and directness and by considering the black middle-class tendency during those years to adjust to white society's roles for men and women and to dependency on white philanthropy and power.

The agitator spirit of the 1880s and the early 1890s had given way to adjustment among middle-class blacks. The accommodationist regime of Booker T. Washington was replaced on the national scene by the NAACP, but it was dominated by white liberals, in spite of its protest stance and radical spokesman, W. E. B. Du Bois. The elite integrationists of the Daniel Hale Williams mold were superseded by the businessman-professionals of the George Cleveland Hall stamp in Chicago. The Urban League became the funnel for philanthropy and the dispenser of the various kinds of assistance to the masses of blacks formerly served by smaller, independent organizations. And the concern with women's suffrage in the black community continued to mean the marshaling of the women's votes in order to elect black men.

Wells-Barnett was stronger and more direct than a race woman was expected to be. She was less impressed than her contemporaries with the usefulness of moneyed white liberals in organizations or with power machines in politics. She resisted the economic pragmatism of the time. Recognition of her place in history, however, has come full circle in an age in which women conceive of their responsibilities and their possibilities much as she did. National Educational Television has just aired an entire program devoted to her accomplishments. She would have been excited and pleased at this acknowledgment of her place in history.

Notes

CHAPTER ONE

1. T. Thomas Fortune, "Ida B. Wells, A.M.," in *Women of Distinction*, ed. Lawson A. Scruggs (Raleigh: L. A. Scruggs, Pub., 1893), pp. 35-39; John Hope Franklin, editor's foreword to *T. Thomas Fortune, Militant Journalist* by Emma Lou Thornbrough (Chicago: University of Chicago Press, 1972), pp. vii-viii.
2. Ida B. Wells-Barnett, Diary 1930, Ida B. Wells Papers, University of Chicago, Chicago, Ill. Carter G. Woodson founded the Association for the Study of Negro Life and History at the Wabash Avenue YMCA in Chicago in 1915. He first published his history of the Negro in 1922.
3. Pauli Murray, "The Liberation of Black Women," in *Voices of the New Feminism*, ed. Mary Lou Thompson (Boston: Beacon Press, 1970), pp. 87, 91.
4. Fortune, "Ida B.Wells, A.M.," p. 39.
5. Monroe A. Majors, M.D., *Noted Negro Women, Their Triumphs and Activities* (Chicago: Donahue and Henneberry, 1893; reprint ed., Freeport, N.Y.: Books for Libraries Press, 1971), p. 188.
6. *Indianapolis Freeman*, February 23, 1889.
7. Roland E. Wolseley, *The Black Press, U.S.A.* (Ames, Iowa: Iowa State University Press, 1971), p. 28.
8. Murray, "The Liberation of Black Women," pp. 88-89, 91; E. Franklin Frazier, *The Negro Family in the United States*, rev. and abr., with a Foreword by Nathan Glazer (Chicago: University of Chicago Press, 1966), p. 102.
9. E. Franklin Frazier, *Black Bourgeoisie* (London: Collier-Macmillan Ltd., Collier Books, 1962), pp. 19, 193; Frazier, *The Negro Family*, pp. 127-128, 140-141, 161-162, 327.
10. Murray, "The Liberation of Black Women," p. 89.
11. St. Clair Drake and Horace R. Cayton, *Black Metropolis: A Study of Negro Life in a Northern City*, 2 vols., 2nd ed., rev. and enl., with an introduction by Richard Wright (New York: Harper & Row, Harper Torchbooks, 1962), pp. 394-395.
12. Fortune, "Ida B. Wells, A.M.," p. 39.
13. Herbert Aptheker, ed., *A Documentary History of the Negro People in the United States*, 2 vols., 4th ed. (New York: Citadel Press, 1951), 2:792.
14. Ida B. Wells, *Crusade for Justice: The Autobiography of Ida B. Wells*, ed. Alfreda M. Duster (Chicago: University of Chicago Press, 1970), p. xxxii.

15. Interview with Alfreda Duster, Chicago, Illinois, February 25, 1976. Papers that Barnett had collected for her memoirs were destroyed in a fire in her home.
16. Wells, *Crusade for Justice*, pp. 8-9; Frazier, *The Negro Family*, p. 130.
17. Frazier, *Black Bourgeoisie*, p. 193.
18. Ida B. Wells-Barnett, "Booker T. Washington and His Critics," *World Today*, April 1904, p. 519.[Page 257 in the present volume.]
19. *Detroit Plaindealer*, October 18, 1889; *New York Age* December 21, 1889.
20. Franklin, editor's foreword to *T. Thomas Fortune*, pp. vii-viii; Louis R. Harlan, *Booker T. Washington: The Making of a Race Leader, 1856-1901* (New York: Oxford University Press, 1972), p. 204.
21. Francis L. Broderick, *W. E. B. Du Bois: Negro Leader in a Time of Crisis* (Stanford: Stanford University Press, 1959), pp. 64, 229-230.
22. W. E. B. Du Bois, *The Correspondence of W. E. B. Du Bois: Selections, 1877-1934*, ed. Herbert Aptheker (Amherst: University of Massachusetts Press, 1973), pp. 55-56; Ida B. Wells-Barnett to Joel E. Spingarn, April 21, 1911, Joel E. Spingarn Papers, Howard University, Washington, D.C.
23. Wells, *Crusade for Justice*, pp. 281, 327-328, 372-373; Arvarh E. Strickland, *The History of the Chicago Urban League* (Urbana: University of Illinois Press, 1966), pp. 27-28.
24. Wells, *Crusade for Justice*, pp. 294, 351-352,

CHAPTER TWO

1. Wells, *Crusade for Justice*, pp. 7-9.
2. Hodding Carter, "A Proud Struggle for Grace," in *A Vanishing America*, ed. Thomas C. Wheeler (New York: Holt, Rinehart and Winston, 1964), pp. 68-70.
3. Wells, *Crusade for Justice*, pp. 8-9.
4. Ibid., pp. 12-13, 15-16; Carter, "A Proud Struggle," p. 72.
5. *Cleveland Gazette*, July 6, 1889; Carter, "A Proud Struggle," p. 71.
6. Wells, *Crusade for Justice*, pp. xviii, 16-18.
7. Ida B. Wells to Albion Tourgee, February 22, 1893, Albion W. Tourgee Papers; Ida B. Wells, Diary 1885-1887, April 3, 1886, Ida B. Wells Papers.
8. *Memphis Appeal*, December 25, 1884; Ida B. Wells to Albion Tourgee, February 22, 1893, Albion W. Tourgee Papers, Chautauqua County Historical Society, Westfield, N.Y.; Wells, *Crusade for Justice*, pp. 18-19.
9. Tennessee, *Reports of Cases Argued and Determined in the Supreme Court of Tennessee*, by George Wesley Pickle (Nashville: Marshall and Bruce Stationers and Printers, 1887), pp. 614-615. The report indicates that the incident occurred on the train going from Woodstock to Memphis.
10. Wells, Diary 1885-1887, April 11, 1887.
11. Wells, *Crusade for Justice*, p. 18; Wells, Diary 1885-1887, June 7, 1886; David M. Tucker, *Black Pastors and Leaders: Memphis 1819-1972* (Memphis: Memphis State University Press, 1975), p. 43.

12. Ibid.; Wells, Diary 1885-1887, June 7, 1886; David M. Tucker, *Black Pastors and Leaders: Memphis, 1819-1972* (Memphis: Memphis State University Press, 1975), p. 43.
13. Wells, Diary 1885-1887, April 11, 1887.
14. Wells, *Crusade for Justice*, p. 21; Wells, Diary 1885-1887, April 18, 1887; Tucker, *Black Pastors and Leaders*, pp. 28-29, 41-42.
15. Wells, *Crusade for Justice*, p. 23; Wells, Diary 1885-1887 passim; *Cleveland Gazette*, April 4, 1885, March 26, 1887, July 6, 1889.
16. Wells, *Crusade for Justice*, pp. 23-24; Tucker, *Black Pastors and Leaders*, p. 39.
17. Wells, Diary 1885-1887, February 2, 1886, December 28, 1886; *New York Freeman*, January 15, 1887.
18. I. Garland Penn, *The Afro-American Press and Its Editors* (Springfield, Mass.: Wiley and Co., 1891; reprint ed., New York: Arno Press and *The New York Times*, 1969), pp. 409-410; Wells, Diary 1885-1887, December 29, 1885, October 12, 1886, April 18, 1887; *New York Freeman*, December 26, 1885; *New York Age*, February 18, 1888.
19. Wells, *Crusade for Justice*, pp. 24-26; Wells, Diary 1885-1887, February 2, 1886, July 20, 1886, July 29, 1886, August 2, 1886, October 2, 1886.
20. *New York Freeman*, January 15, 1887.
21. Wells, Diary 1885-1887, September 4, 1886.
22. *New York Freeman*, August 8, 1885; Wells, Diary 1885-1887, January 13, 1886.
23. Wells, Diary 1887-1889, November 28, 1886; December 21, 1886; December 28, 1886.
24. Wells, *Crusade for Justice*, pp. 17, 43; Wells, Diary 1885-1887, October 2, 1886, December 28, 1886; *New York Freeman*, December 26, 1885, January 1, 1887.
25. *New York Age*, February 18, 1888.
26. Ibid.
27. Wells, Diary 1885-1887, February 1, 1887.
28. Ibid., March 1, 1886.
29. Ibid., April 11, 1886, April 29, 1886, June 15, 1886, June 28, 1886, February 1, 1887.
30. Wells, Diary 1885-1887, August 12, 1887; Wells, *Crusade for Justice*, p. 31; *New York Freeman*, August 20, 1887.
31. *New York Age*, August 11, 1888.
32. Ibid., June 29, 1889; Wells, *Crusade for Justice*, pp. 31, 35-37; Tucker, *Black Pastors and Leaders*, p. 44. The name of the newspaper was officially changed to *Free Speech* when Wells joined the staff. *Indianapolis Freeman*, October 12, 1889.
33. Wells, *Crusade for Justice*, pp. 41-42; *New York Freeman*, August 13, 1887.
34. *New York Freeman*, November 7, 1885; *Cleveland Gazette*, July 6, 1889.
35. *New York Freeman*, May 28, 1887.
36. Emma Lou Thornbrough, "The National Afro-American League, 1887-1908," *Journal of Southern History* 27 (February 1961): 495-496.
37. *Detroit Plaindealer*, October 18, 1889; *Indianapolis Freeman*, June 29, 1889.

38. *New York Age*, December 21, 1889.
39. *Indianapolis Freeman*, April 19, 1890.
40. Ibid., May 10, 1890.
41. Wells, *Crusade for Justice*, p. 35.
42. *Indianapolis Freeman*, November 7, 1891, December 12, 1891, March 18, 1892, April 30, 1892.
43. Ibid., September 26, 1891. *Cleveland Gazette*, May 28, 1892.
44. Thornborough, *T. Thomas Fortune*, p. 111.
45. Tucker, *Black Pastors and Leaders*, pp. 44-46.
46. *New York Age*, February 6, 1892; *Indianapolis Freeman*, January 16, 1892; Penn, *Afro-American Press*, p. 409.

CHAPTER THREE

1. August Meier, *Negro Thought in America, 1880-1915* (Ann Arbor: University of Michigan Press, Ann Arbor Paperbacks, 1968), p. 20; Rayford Logan, *The Negro in the United States* (Princeton: D. Van Nostrand Co., 1957), p. 54.
2. James Elbert Cutler, *Lynch Law: An Investigation into the History of Lynching in the United States*, with a foreword by William Graham Sumner (New York: Longmans, Green, 1905; reprint ed., Montclair, N.J.: Patterson Smith Pub., 1969), pp. 1, 13-39.
3. Ibid., p. v.
4. John Walton Caughey, *Their Majesties the Mob* (Chicago: University of Chicago Press, 1960), p. 5.
5. Cutler, *Lynch Law*, pp. 269-270, 276-277.
6. Ibid., p. 273; Caughey, *Their Majesties the Mob*, pp. 1, 18-19.
7. Cutler, *Lynch Law*, pp. 157-158; Carter G. Woodson and Charles H. Wesley, *The Negro in Our History*, 11th ed., rev. and enl. (Washington: Associated Publishers, 1966), p. 547. In Ida B. Wells-Barnett, *On Lynchings: Southern Horrors [1892], A Red Record [1895], Mob Rule in New Orleans [1900]*, with a preface by August Meier (New York: Arno Press and *The New York Times*, 1969), preface. August Meier indicates that Ida Wells-Barnett chose to use the *Chicago Tribune* statistics in order to avoid the charge of inaccuracy or distortion. The NAACP credited the *Chicago Tribune* and Tuskegee Institute with "more or less accurate records" from 1885 in *Thirty Years of Lynching in the United States* (New York: National Association for the Advancement of Colored People, 1919; reprint ed., New York: Negro Universities Press, 1969), p. 7.
8. Donald Lee Grant, *The Anti-Lynching Movement, 1883-1932* (San Francisco: R and E Associates, 1975), pp. viii-ix, 22-27; I[dus] A. Newby, *Jim Crow's Defense: Anti-Negro Thought in America, 1900-1930* (Baton Rouge: Louisiana State University Press, 1965), p. x; Cutler, *Lynch Law*, pp. 207, 223-224.
9. Quincy Ewing, "The Heart of the Race Problem," *Atlantic Monthly*, January-June 1909, p. 389.

10. Ibid., p. 393.
11. Grant, *The Anti-Lynching Movement*, p. 13,
12. Ida B. Wells-Barnett, *Southern Horrors*, reprinted in *On Lynchings*, p. 18.
13. David M. Tucker, "Miss Ida B. Wells and Memphis Lynching," *Phylon* 32 (Summer 1971): 115-116.
14. Wells, *Crusade for Justice*, p. 52.
15. Ibid., pp. 50-51. Wells notes that details of the lynching of the night of March 9, 1892, were given in the March 10 morning edition of one of the white Memphis newspapers.
16. *Indianapolis Freeman*, May 7, 1892, p. 2. Wells, *Crusade for Justice*, pp. 57-58; Tucker, "Miss Ida B. Wells and Memphis Lynching," p. 117.
17. One such instance involving a minister's wife in Columbus, Ohio, was reported in the *Cleveland Gazette*, January 16, 1892.
18. Wells, *Crusade for Justice*, pp. 64-65.
19. Ida B. Wells, "Lynch Law in All Its Phases," *Our Day*, May 1893, p. 339 [page 178 of the present volume]. This article is the text of an address given by Wells at Tremont Temple in Boston on February 13, 1893. In it she quoted from the *Memphis Daily Commercial* and the *Memphis Evening Scimitar* of May 25, 1892, the Wednesday following her May 21 editorial.
20. *Topeka Weekly Call*, April 22, 1893, p. 1; Wells-Barnett, *Southern Horrors*, p. 5. Wells used the Duke incident to show that she was not the first to question the rape myth, but that she made no apology for so doing.
21. *Nashville Daily American*, May 26, 1892; *Indianapolis Freeman*, June 11, 1892; *Memphis Appeal-Avalanche*, June 30, 1892; Wells, "Lynch Law in All Its Phases," p. 340 [Page 179 of the present volume.]; Wells, *Crusade for Justice*, pp. 61-62, 66-67, 71.
22. Wells-Barnett, *Southern Horrors*, preface.
23. Wells, *Crusade for Justice*, p. 72.
24. Ibid., pp. 78-82.
25. Ida B. Wells to Frederick Douglass, October 17, 1892, Frederick Douglass Papers, Library of Congress Manuscript Division, Washington, D.C.
26. Wells-Barnett, *Southern Horrors*, Hon. Fred. Douglass's Letter, dated October 25, 1892.
27. Ibid., p. 6. That the double standard in sexual conduct so apparent in the miscegenation practices of the South was a source of bitterness to white women is pointed out in "Discontent" by Anne Firor Scott in *The Southern Lady, From Pedestal to Politics 1830-1930* (Chicago: University of Chicago Press, 1970).
28. Wells-Barnett, *Southern Horrors*, pp. 7-11; *Nashville Daily American*, May 20 and 21, 1892; *Chicago Inter-Ocean*, September 24, 1892.
29. Wells-Barnett, *Southern Horrors*, pp. 11, 14-15.
30. Wells, *Crusade for Justice*, p. 62.
31. Wells-Barnett, *Southern Horrors*, p. 23.
32. Albert L. Kreiling, "The Making of Racial Identities in the Black Press: A Cultural Analysis of Race Journalism in Chicago, 1878-1929" (Ph.D. dissertation, University of Illinois, 1973), p. 115.
33. Wells-Barnett, *Southern Horrors*, pp. 22-24.

34. Wells, *Crusade for Justice*, pp. 81-82. The author indicates that in the many Northern cities in which she lectured she used the text of the first paper delivered in New York.
35. Wells, "Lynch Law in All Its Phases," pp. 337-338 [pages 176 in the present volume].
36. Ibid., pp. 341-342 [pp. 180-181]; Cutler, *Lynch Law*, pp. 228-229.
37. Wells, "Lynch Law in All Its Phases," pp. 344-346 [p. 184].
38 Ibid., p. 346 [p. 186].
39. *Memphis Appeal-Avalanche*, June 30, 1892, p. 5.
40. Ida B. Wells to Albion W. Tourgee, February 22, 1893, Albion W. Tourgee Papers.
41. Ibid., February 10, 1893.
42. Ibid., February 22, 1893.
43. F. L. Barnett to Albion W. Tourgee, February 23, 1893, Albion W. Tourgee Papers.
44. *Indianapolis Freeman*, July 16, 1892, p. 4, and August 20, 1892, p. 4; *Topeka Weekly Call*, January 8, 1893, p. 1; *Topeka Call*, April 15, 1893, p. 2.
45. Wells, *Crusade for Justice*, p. 82; Mary B. Hutton, "The Rhetoric of Ida B. Wells: The Genesis of the Anti-Lynch Movement" (Ph.D. dissertation, Indiana University, 1975), pp. 22-23.
46. *Topeka Call*, April 15, 1893, p. 2. The *Call* quotes the letter Catherine Impey sent from Scotland and Ida B. Wells's press release on her proposed trip as printed in *New York Age*.
47. Ibid.; Wells, *Crusade for Justice*, p. 85.
48. Wells, *Crusade for Justice*, p. 89.
49. Mrs. N. F. Mossell, *The Work of the Afro-American Woman* (1894; reprint ed., Freeport, New York: Books for Libraries Press, 1971), pp. 35-36.
50. Wells, *Crusade for Justice*, pp. 100-101.
51. *Indianapolis Freeman*, July 8, 1893, p. 6.
52. "Writers in the October Forum," *Forum*, October 1893, p. 261. The Slater Fund was set up to aid in the education of Southern blacks.
53. Atticus G. Haygood, "The Black Shadow in the South," *Forum*, October 1893, pp. 167-169.

CHAPTER FOUR

1. *Indianapolis Freeman*, March 25, 1893, April 1, 1893; Wells, *Crusade for Justice*, pp. 115, 117.
2. Elliott M. Rudwick and August Meier, "Black Man in the 'White City': Negroes and the Columbian Exposition, 1893," *Phylon* 26 (Winter 1965): 354-355; Ann Massa, "Black Women in the 'White City,' " *Journal of American Studies* 8 (December 1974): 320; F. L. Barnett, "The Reason Why," in *The Reason Why the Colored American Is Not in the World's Columbian Exposition*, ed. Ida B. Wells (Chicago, 1893), pp. 65-66 [page 212 of the present volume].

3. Rudwick and Meier, "Black Man in the 'White City,' " pp. 355, 357-358.
4. F. L. Barnett to Bertha Palmer, December 20, 1891, Bertha Palmer Board of Lady Managers Records, Chicago Historical Society, Chicago, Illinois.
5. Barnett, "The Reason Why," p. 68 [p. 213 of the present volume].
6. Massa, "Black Women in the 'White City,' " pp. 319, 322-323.
7. Ibid., pp. 323-325, 330-331.
8. Sadie Iola Daniels, *Women Builders*, rev. and enl. by Charles H. Wesley and Thelma D. Perry (Washington: Associated Publishers, 1970), pp. 291, 296-297.
9. Massa, "Black Women in the 'White City,' " pp, 331-333.
10. Barnett, "The Reason Why," pp. 69, 74 [pp. 214, 218]; Rudwick and Meier, "Black Man in the 'White City,' " p. 355; Massa, "Black Women in the 'White City,' " p. 333.
11. Barnett, "The Reason Why," pp. 74-75 [p. 218]; Massa, "Black Women in the 'White City,' " p. 334.
12. Allan H. Spear, *Black Chicago: The Making of a Negro Ghetto, 1890-1920* (Chicago: University of Chicago Press, 1967), p. 69.
13. Massa, "Black Women in the 'White City,' " p. 334.
14. Barnett, "The Reason Why," p. 80 [p. 222].
15. A variety of names was used by journalists who were scornful of the special day for black Americans. Among these were Afro-American Jubilee Day and Colored Jubilee Day. Wells-Barnett referred to the day as Negro Day in her autobiography.
16. *Indianapolis Freeman*, March 4, 1893 and March 25, 1893; Rudwick and Meier, "Black Man in the 'White City,' " pp. 359-360.
17. Rudwick and Meier, "Black Man in the 'White City,' " pp. 359-360; Wells *Crusade for Justice*, p. 115; *Indianapolis Freeman*, March 25, 1893.
18. *Indianapolis Freeman*, April 8, 1893.
19. Ibid., April 15, 1893 and July 22, 1893.
20. Wells, *Crusade for Justice*, p, 116; *Indianapolis Freeman*, March 25, 1893.
21. Ida B. Wells to Albion Tourgee, July 1, 1893, Albion Tourgee Papers.
22. Wells, *Crusade for Justice*, p. 117; *Indianapolis Freeman*, July 22, 1893; Wells, *The Reason Why*, "To the Public."
23. Wells, *The Reason Why*; Frederick Douglass, "Introduction," in Wells, *The Reason Why*, p. 2.
24. Barnett, "The Reason Why," p. 81 [p. 223].
25. Massa, "Black Women in the 'White City,' " pp. 336-337.
26. Rudwick and Meier, "Black Man in the 'White City,' " pp. 360-361; Wells, *Crusade for Justice*, pp. 115, 117-119.
27. Wells, *Crusade for Justice*, pp. xix, 120-121.
28. Elizabeth Lindsay Davis, *The Story of the Illinois Federation of Colored Women's Clubs* (n.p., n.d.), pp. 26-27.
29. Kreiling, "The Making of Racial Identities in the Black Press," pp. 124-128.
30. Albert Nelson Marquis, ed., *The Book of Chicagoans* (Chicago: A. N. Marquis, 1917), p. 37.
31. Spear, *Black Chicago*, p. 60.

32. Conference of Colored Men of the United States, *Proceedings*, Nashville, Tennessee, May 6-9, 1879 (Washington, D.C.: Rufus H. Darby, 1879), pp. 83-86.
33. F. L. Barnett, Scrapbook. Personal Files of Mrs. Alfreda Duster, Chicago, Illinois.
34. "Old settler" was the term used to designate an established resident of Chicago before World War I as explained in Drake and Cayton, *Black Metropolis*, p. 66.
35. Stella Reed Garnett to Alfreda M. Duster, April 25, 1951, Ida B. Wells Papers; Spear, *Black Chicago*, pp. 56-57.
36. Davis, *The Story of the Illinois Federation of Colored Women's Clubs*, p. 26; Wells, *Crusade for Justice*, pp. xix, 121-125.

CHAPTER FIVE

1. "How Miss Wells' Crusade Is Regarded in America," *Literary Digest*, July 28, 1894, pp. 366-367.
2. *Indianapolis Freeman*, January 6, 1894; January 20, 1894. In a letter to Frederick Douglass, December 20, 1892, Frederick Douglass Papers, Ida B. Wells indicated that she had earlier appealed to Douglass to defend her against the attacks of Taylor.
3. *Indianapolis Freeman*, April 28, 1894; May 12, 1894.
4. Ida B. Wells to Frederick Douglass, April 6, 1894, Frederick Douglass Papers.
5. Ibid., March 18, 1894; Frederick Douglass to Rev. C. F. Aked, March 27, 1894, Frederick Douglass Papers.
6. Ida B. Wells to Frederick Douglass, April 6, 1894, Frederick Douglass Papers.
7. Ibid., May 6 and 10, 1894, Frederick Douglass Papers. William Eaton Chandler was United States Senator from New Hampshire, 1897-1901.
8. Wells, *Crusade for Justice*, pp. 127, 215-217; *Chicago Inter-Ocean*, April 2, 9, 23, 1894; May 19, 28, 1894; June 4, 25, 1894; July 7, 1894.
9. "English Feelings on America's Lynchings," *Literary Digest*, July 14, 1894, p. 308; "How Miss Wells' Crusade Is Regarded in America," pp, 366-367.
10. *Chicago Inter-Ocean*, July 7, 1894.
11. "How Miss Wells' Crusade Is Regarded in America," p. 366.
12. *Indianapolis Freeman*, June 16, 1894.
13. *Topeka Weekly Call*, August 4, 1894. In the available copies of the *Weekly Call* only the second portion of Turner's article is printed.
14. *Chicago Daily Inter-Ocean*, July 7, 1894.
15. NAACP, *Thirty Years of Lynching*, p. 29.
16. *Chicago Inter-Ocean*, August 13, 1894; Wells, *Crusade for Justice*, pp. 111-112.
17. Ida B. Wells-Barnett, "A Red Record," reprinted in *On Lynchings*, pp. 83-84; Frederick Douglass, *Address of Hon. Frederick Douglass Delivered in Metropolitan A.M.E. Church, Washington, D.C.* (Baltimore: Press of Thomas and Evans, 1894),

p. 7; Wells and Douglass quoted from the October 23, 1890, issue of the *New York Voice*, an organ of the WCTU.

18. Douglass, *Address of Hon. Frederick Douglass*, pp. 7-8, 16-17.
19. Wells, *Crusade for Justice*, pp. 202-209; Wells-Barnett, "A Red Record," pp. 84-86.
20. Ida B. Wells to Frederick Douglass, June 3, 1894, Frederick Douglass Papers.
21. Wells-Barnett, "A Red Record," pp. 80-81.
22. *Chicago Inter-Ocean*, November 27, 1894; Mary Earhart Dillon, *Frances Willard, from Prayers to Politics* (Chicago: University of Chicago Press, 1944), p. 360.
23. *Chicago Inter-Ocean*, November 24, 1894.
24. Ida B. Wells to Albion W. Tourgee, November 27, 1894, Albion W. Tourgee Papers.
25. Wells-Barnett, "A Red Record," p. 89.
26. Dillon, *Frances Willard*, pp. 361-362. This letter was a source of conflict between Lady Somerset and Florence Balgarnie, who sought to vindicate the name of Douglass. Balgarnie stated that Douglass had signed the letter before the nature of the Cleveland resolution was known. (*The Address of Lady Henry Somerset* [Holburn Viaduct, E.C., 1895]), Frederick Douglass Papers.
27. *Cleveland Gazette*, June 29, 1895; Daniels, *Women Builders*, pp. 297-298.
28. *Cleveland Gazette*, June 29, 1895.
29. Frances Willard to Mrs. Frederick Douglass, July 1, 1895, Frederick Douglass Papers.
30. Wells-Barnett, "A Red Record," p. 89.
31. *Topeka Weekly Call*, July 7, 1894.
32. "An Anti-Lynching Crusade in America Begun," *Literary Digest*, August 12, 1894, pp. 421-422.
33. *Topeka Weekly Call*, September 22, 1894.
34. Ibid.
35. *New York Times*, September 4, 1894. In 1892, Wells referred to Douglass's opposition to Astwood's political ambition, indicating that he was not representative of the race. (Ida B. Wells to Frederick Douglass, December 20, 1892, Frederick Douglass Papers.)
36. *Topeka Weekly Call*, September 22, 1894.
37. *Chicago Herald*, July 31, 1894.
38. *New York Times*, July 30, 1894.
39. Charles Flint Kellogg, *NAACP: A History of the National Association for the Advancement of Colored People* (Baltimore: Johns Hopkins Press, 1967), pp. 62-63.
40. *Chicago Inter-Ocean*, August 8, 1894.
41. *Indianapolis Freeman*, September 29, 1894.
42. Cutler, *Lynch Law*, pp. 229, 245-246.
43. Lloyd W. Crawford, "Ida B. Wells: Her Anti-Lynching Crusades in Britain and Repercussions from Them in the United States," paper presented at the meeting of the Association for the Study of Negro Life and History, Xenia, Ohio, October 1962, pp. 17-20.
44. Wells-Barnett, "A Red Record," pp. 71-72.

45. Crawford, "Ida B. Wells: Her Anti-Lynching Crusades in Britain," pp. 22-24.

CHAPTER SIX

1. I. [dus] A. Newby, ed., *The Development of Segregationist Thought* (Homewood, Illinois: Dorsey Press, 1968), pp. 3-8.
2. Meier, *Negro Thought in America*, p. 161; C. Vann Woodward, *The Strange Career of Jim Crow*, 3rd ed., rev. (New York: Oxford University Press, 1975), p. 69.
3. Wells, *Crusade for Justice*, pp. 218-223, 238.
4. Wells-Barnett, *On Lynchings*, Preface; Wells, *Crusade for Justice*, p. xxii; Ida B. Wells to Frederick Douglass, June 3, 1894, Frederick Douglass Papers; Wells-Barnett, "A Red Record," pp. 7-8.
5. Wells-Barnett, "A Red Record," pp. 8-10.
6. Ibid., Chaps. III-VI passim, pp. 96-98.
7. Emma L. Fields, "The Women's Club Movement in the United States, 1877-1900" (M.A. thesis, Howard University, 1948), pp. 63-64.
8. *A History of the Club Movement among the Colored Women of the United States of America* (n.p., 1902), pp. 4-5, 28-29, Ida B. Wells Papers, University of Chicago, Chicago, Ill. This booklet is a compilation of the minutes of the conventions held in Boston in 1895 and in Washington in 1896; Wells, *Crusade for Justice*, pp. xix, 242.
9. Elizabeth Lindsay Davis, *Lifting As They Climb* (Washington, D.C.: National Association of Colored Women, 1933), pp. 236-237.
10. Mary Church Terrell, *A Colored Woman in a White World* (Washington: National Association of Colored Women's Clubs Inc., 1968), pp. 148-149.
11. *A History of the Club Movement*, pp. 3-5, 11-12. After her marriage, Ida B. Wells signed her name Ida B. Wells-Barnett.
12. Wells, *Crusade for Justice*, pp. 239, 242.
13. *A History of the Club Movement*, pp. 28-29.
14. Ibid., pp. 30-32.
15. Ibid., pp. 34-35, 38, 44-45, 60; Terrell, *A Colored Woman in a White World*, pp. 150-151.
16. *A History of the Club Movement*, pp. 37, 39, 43, 46, 50, 51; Wells, *Crusade for Justice*, pp. 242-243.
17. Wells, *Crusade for Justice*, pp. 258, 328.
18. John W. Thompson, *An Authentic History of the Douglass Monument* (Freeport, N.Y.: Books for Libraries Press, 1971), pp. 196, 201, 204; Thornbrough, *T. Thomas Fortune*, pp. 122, 180.
19. Wells, *Crusade for Justice*, p. 257.
20. Meier, *Negro Thought in America*, p. 172.
21. *Cleveland Gazette*, April 9, 1898, quoted in Aptheker, *A Documentary History of the Negro People in the United States*, 2: 796-798
22. Meier, *Negro Thought in America*, pp. 172-173.

23. Ibid., p. 171; Harlan, *Booker T. Washington*, p. 225.
24. *New York Tribune*, May 4, 1899, quoted in Aptheker, *A Documentary History of the Negro People in the United States*, 2: 799-800.
25. Davis, *The Story of the Illinois Federation*, p. 2.
26. Wells, *Crusade for Justice*, pp. 83, 258-260; Wells, Diary 1885-1887, July 13, 1887; Davis, *Lifting As They Climb*, p. 47.
27. Davis, *Lifting As They Climb*, p. 46.
28. Terrell, *A Colored Woman in a White World*, pp. 152, 154-155.
29. *Chicago Tribune*, August 20, 1899; Terrell, *A Colored Woman in a White World*, pp. 154-155.
30. Mary Church Terrell to Frances [Settle], September 5, 189[9], Mary Church Terrell Papers, Library of Congress Manuscript Division, Washington, D.C.
31. Mary Church Terrell to Margaret Murray Washington, May 1900, Margaret Murray Washington Papers, Tuskegee Archives, Tuskegee, Alabama.
32. *Independent*, September 7, 1899, pp. 2425-2427, quoted in Aptheker, *A Documentary History of the Negro People in the United States*, 2: 776-777.
33. Davis, *Lifting As They Climb*, pp. 46-47.
34. *Independent*, September 7, 1899, pp. 2425-2427, quoted in Aptheker, *A Documentary History of the Negro People in the United States*, 2: 775-778.
35. *Chicago Tribune*, August 18-20, 1899.
36. Harlan, *Booker T. Washington*, p. 264.
37. *Chicago Tribune*, August 20, 1899; Wells, *Crusade for Justice*, p. 262; Spear, *Black Chicago*, p. 60.
38. *Chicago Tribune*, August 20, 1899; Wells, *Crusade for Justice*, pp. 261-262 Reverdy C. Ransom, *The Pilgrimage of Harriet Ransom's Son* (Nashville: Sunday School Union, n.d.), pp. 84-85.
39. Harlan, *Booker T. Washington*, p. 254.
40. Thornbrough, "The National Afro-American League," pp. 502-504.
41. Terrell, *A Colored Woman in a White World*, p. 193; Harlan, *Booker T. Washington*, p. 311.
42. Ida Wells-Barnett to W. E. B. Du Bois, May 30, 1903, quoted in W. E. B. Du Bois, *The Correspondence of W. E. B. Du Bois*, 2 vols. (Amherst: University of Massachusetts Press, 1973-1976), 1: 54-56.
43. Wells-Barnett, "Booker T. Washington and His Critics," pp. 519-521 [page 259 in the present volume].
44. W. E. B. Du Bois, *Dusk of Dawn* (New York: Harcourt Brace and Co., 1940), pp. 86, 88-89, 93; Elliott M. Rudwick, "The Niagara Movement," *Journal of Negro History* 42 (October 1957): 177-179, 181-182, 196. James Weldon Johnson was an NAACP official between 1916 and 1930.
45. Charles Flint Kellogg, *NAACP: A History of the National Association of Colored People*, vol. 1: 1910-1920 (Baltimore: Johns Hopkins Press, 1967), pp. 9-12, 19; "How the NAACP Began," *Crisis* 66 (February 1957): 73-75.
46. *Proceedings of the National Negro Conference 1909* (New York: n.p., 1909), pp. 174-179, 197-206.

47. Kellogg, *NAACP: A History*, p. 21; Elliott M. Rudwick, *W. E. B. Du Bois: Propagandist of the Negro Protest* (New York: Atheneum, 1969), p. 125. Du Bois did not identify the woman, but Lerone Bennett in *Before the Mayflower* (Chicago: Johnson Publishing Co., 1961), p. 284, suggests that she was Wells-Barnett.

48. Du Bois, *Dusk of Dawn*, p. 224; Kellogg, *NAACP: A History*, p. 22; Meier, *Negro Thought in America*, pp. 182-183.

49. Kellogg, *NAACP: A History*, pp, 22, 29-30; Rudwick, *W. E. B. Du Bois: Propagandist of Negro Protest*, p. 124.

50. Mary White Ovington, *The Walls Came Tumbling Down* (New York: Harcourt, Brace and Co., 1947), pp. 106-107.

51. Wells, *Crusade for Justice*, p. 325.

52. Ida B. Wells-Barnett to Joel E. Spingarn, April 21, 1911, Joel E. Spingarn Papers, Howard University, Washington, D.C.; Kellogg, *NAACP: A History*, pp. 62-63. Ida Wells-Barnett worked through the Negro Fellowship League, which she founded to aid homeless black men in Chicago and those in need of various kinds of assistance.

53. Wells, *Crusade for Justice*, p. 328.

54. Fortune, "Ida B. Wells, A.M.," p. 39.

CHAPTER SEVEN

1. Spear, *Black Chicago*, pp. 7, 11-12, 54-56.

2. Wells, *Crusade for Justice*, p. 239.

3. Interview with Alfreda Duster, Chicago, Illinois, February 25, 1976.

4. *Chicago Tribune*, June 28, 1895.

5. Ibid., 28 June 1895, p. 5; Wells, *Crusade for Justice*, 242-243; Spear, *Black Chicago*, p. 60; Harold F. Gosnell, *Negro Politicians: The Rise of Negro Politicians in Chicago*, with an Introduction by James Q. Wilson (Chicago: University of Chicago Press, 1935; Phoenix Books, 1967), pp. 154-155.

6. Drake and Cayton, *Black Metropolis*, pp. 48, 53.

7. Meier, *Negro Thought in America*, pp. 100, 162.

8. According to Allan Spear in *Black Chicago*, p. 97, Provident Hospital was established in 1891.

9. Drake and Cayton, *Black Metropolis*, pp. 56-57.

10. Spear, *Black Chicago*, pp. 58-59, 71-72, 79.

11. Kreiling, "The Making of Racial Identities in the Black Press," pp. 116, 125, 144.

12. Davis, *The Story of the Illinois Federation of Colored Women's Clubs*, pp. 26-27.

13. Wells, *Crusade for Justice*, pp. 249-250.

14. Spear, *Black Chicago*, p. 63; Reverdy C. Ransom, "Deborah and Jael," sermon delivered at Bethel A.M.E. Church, Chicago, Illinois, June 6, 1897.

15. Spear, *Black Chicago*, p. 101.

16. Booker T. Washington, N. B. Wood, and Fannie Barrier Williams, *A New Negro for a New Century* (Chicago: American Publishing House, 1900; reprint ed., New York: Arno Press and *The New York Times*, 1969), pp. 382-383.

17. Meier, *Negro Thought in America*, pp. 134-135.

18. Washington, Wood, and Williams, *A New Negro*, p. 384.

19. Gerda Lerner, "Community Work of Black Club Women," *Journal of Negro History* 59 (April 1974): 158-160.

20. Membership Blank, Ida B. Wells Woman's Club, Ida B. Wells Papers.

21. Davis, *The Story of the Illinois Federation*, pp. 27-28; Wells, *Crusade for Justice*, pp. 271-272.

22. Wells, *Crusade for Justice*, pp. 269-270.

23. Rayford W. Logan, *The Betrayal of the Negro*, 4th ed., enl. (London: Collier-Macmillan, Collier Books, 1965), pp. 238-239.

24. Spear, *Black Chicago*, pp. 8, 11, 16, 26-27.

25. Drake and Cayton, *Black Metropolis*, p. 176.

26. NAACP, *Thirty Years of Lynching*, p. 29; Meier, *Negro Thought in America*, p. 162.

27. Spear, *Black Chicago*, pp. 53-54, 91, 96, 100-101, 112-111

28. Ibid., p. 29; Ray Ginger, *Altgeld's America, the Lincoln Ideal versus Changing Realities* (New York: Funk and Wagnalls Company, 1958), p. 98.

29. Spear, *Black Chicago*, pp. 34-36.

30. Ransom, *The Pilgrimage of Harriet Ransom's Son*, pp. 81-83, 103.

31. Spear, *Black Chicago*, pp. 95-96.

32. Ransom, *The Pilgrimage of Harriet Ransom's Son*, pp. 87-88.

33. Steven J. Diner, "Chicago Social Workers and Blacks in the Progressive Era," *Social Service Review* 44 (December 1970): 393.

34. Allan Davis, *Spearheads for Reform: The Social Settlements and the Progressive Movement 1890-1914* (New York: Oxford University Press, 1967), pp. 18-19, 84, 94; Allan Davis, *American Heroine, the Life and Legend of Jane Addams* (New York: Oxford University Press, 1973), p. 129.

35. Diner "Chicago Social Workers," p. 403.

36. Wells, *Crusade for Justice*, p. 283; Spear, *Black Chicago*, p. 104.

37. Diner, "Chicago Social Workers," pp. 403-405.

38. *Chicago Broad Ax*, July 7, 1906, p. 1, and June 30, 1906, p. 1.

39. Diner, "Chicago Social Workers," p. 405.

40. Louise DeKoven Bowen, *The Colored People of Chicago* (n.p., 1913), pp. 12-13.

41. Wells, *Crusade for Justice*, pp. 298-305; *Chicago Broad Ax*, May 7, 1910.

42. *Chicago Broad Ax*, January 8, 1909; December 31, 1910; December 30, 1911.

43. *Crisis*, May 1911, p. 53.

44. *Chicago Broad Ax*, January 9, 1915; February 13, 1915; April 24, 1915.

45. *Chicago Fellowship Herald*, June 22, 1911. This issue is housed at the DuSable Museum in Chicago. In *Black Metropolis*, p. 339n, Drake and Cayton state that the *Fellowship Herald* was begun in 1916. In his article "The Black Press in Illinois," *Journal of Illinois State Historical Society* 68 (September 1975), p. 347,

A. Gilbert Belles states that the *Fellowship Herald* edited by Ida Wells-Barnett was published in 1916 only.

46. Wells, *Crusade for Justice*, pp. 330-332. Allan Spear in *Black Chicago*, p. 106, implies that the League was disbanded when the location was changed. Steven Diner, referring to Spear's work, in "Chicago Social Workers and Blacks in the Progressive Era," p. 406, concludes also that the Negro Fellowship League was in operation for only three years.

47. Wells, *Crusade for Justice*, pp. 332-333; Gosnell, *Negro Politicians*, p. 204.

48. Wells, *Crusade for Justice*, pp. 372-373; Spear, *Black Chicago*, p. 72; Arvah E. Strickland, *History of the Chicago Urban League* (Urbana: University of Illinois Press, 1966), pp. 38-39.

49. Strickland, *History of the Chicago Urban League*, pp. 26-28, 36.

50. Wells, *Crusade for Justice*, p. 273.

51. Strickland, *History of the Chicago Urban League*, pp. 34-35, 40-42.

52. *Chicago Broad Ax*, February 15, 1913; interview with James A. Mundy, Olivet Baptist Church, Chicago, Illinois, July 14, 1975.

53. Wells, *Crusade for Justice*, p. 345; Bessie L. Pierce, "The Women of Illinois," *Chicago Tribune Supplement*, February 4, 1968, p. 62; *Alpha Suffrage Record*, March 18, 1914, Ida B. Wells Papers.

54. "Chicago Political Equality League Annual," 1895-1911.

55. *Alpha Suffrage Record*, March 18, 1914. The date of this issue seems to be incorrect. It announces the endorsement of DePriest and Thompson, whose campaigns were run in 1915.

56. *Crisis*, September 1912, pp. 223, 240-247; "Votes for Women," *Crisis*, September 1912, p. 234.

57. Katherine E. Williams, "The Alpha Suffrage Club," *Half Century*, September 1916, p. 12; Wells, *Crusade for Justice*, pp. 345-346.

58. *Chicago Broad Ax*, March 8, 1913.

59. Aileen S. Kraditor, *The Ideas of the Woman Suffrage Movement 1890-1920* (Garden City, N.Y.: Doubleday, Anchor Books, 1971), pp. 167-168.

60. *Chicago Broad Ax*, March 29, 1913; November 15, 1913; May 30, 1914; Eunice Rivers Walker, "Ida B. Wells-Barnett, Her Contribution to the Field of Social Welfare" (M.S.W. thesis, Loyola University, 1941), p. 71.

61. Ida B. Wells-Barnett, "How Enfranchisement Stops Lynching," *Original Rights Magazine*, June 1910, pp. 44-45 [page 269 in the present volume].

62. Pierce, "The Women of Illinois," p. 62.

63. Gosnell, *Negro Politicians*, pp. 73-74.

64. *Alpha Suffrage Record*, March 18, 1924.

65. Gosnell, *Negro Politicians*, p. 74.

66. Wells, *Crusade for Justice*, pp. 346-347,

67. Gosnell, *Negro Politicians*, p. 74; *Chicago Broad Ax*, February 6, 1915.

68. Gosnell, *Negro Politicians*, pp. 38, 50, 74-75; Wells, *Crusade for Justice*, pp. 349-352.

CHAPTER EIGHT

1. *New York Freeman*, November 7, 1885.
2. *New York Age*, August 11, 1888; Thornbrough, *T. Thomas Fortune*, pp. 93-94.
3. Charles W. Puttkammer and Ruth Worthy "William Monroe Trotter, 1872-1934," *Journal of Negro History* 43 (October 1958): 306.
4. Interview with Alfreda Duster, Chicago, Illinois, March 30, 1977.
5. Ginger, *Altgeld's America*, p. 139.
6. Wells, *Crusade for Justice*, p. 255.
7. Stella Reed Garnett to Alfreda Duster, April 25, 1951, Ida B. Wells Papers.
8. Kreiling, "The Rise of the Black Press in Chicago," p. 6.
9. Stella Reed Garnett to Alfreda Duster, April 25, 1951, Ida B. Wells Papers.
10. Charles Branham, "Black Chicago: Accommodationist Politics before the Great Migration," in *The Ethnic Frontier*, ed. Melvin G. Holli and Peter d'A. Jones (Grand Rapids: Wm. B. Eerdmans Pub. Co., 1977), pp. 241-243.
11. Wells, *Crusade for Justice*, pp. 241, 243-244.
12. *Indianapolis Freeman*, July 13, 1895; Kreiling, "The Rise of The Black Press," p. 9.
13. Wells, *Crusade for Justice*, pp. xxiii, 249; Ida B. Wells-Barnett to her family, 30 [October,] 1920, Ida B. Wells Papers.
14. Gosnell, *Negro Politicians*, p. 85.
15. Drake and Cayton, *Black Metropolis*, p. 346.
16. *Chicago Chronicle*, November 7, 1906.
17. Interview with Alfreda Duster, Chicago, Illinois, March 27, 1978; Wells, *Crusade for Justice*, pp. 289-290, 294; Spear, *Black Chicago*, p. 76; Carter G. Woodson, *The History of the Negro Church* (Washington: Associated Publishers, 1972), p. 298.
18. *Chicago Chronicle*, November 7, 1906.
19. Aptheker, *A Documentary History of the Negro People in the United States*, Vol. 2, p. 862.
20. Wells, *Crusade for Justice*, pp. 283-285.
21. *Springfield Forum*, September 5, 1908.
22. *Chicago Broad Ax*, January 1, 1910.
23. Illinois, *Laws of the State of Illinois Enacted by the Forty-Fourth General Assembly* (Springfield: Illinois State Journal Co., State Printers, 1906), pp. 190-192.
24. Illinois, Chicago Commission on Race Relations, *The Negro in Chicago: A Study of Race Relations and a Race Riot in 1919* (Chicago Press, 1922; reprint ed., New York: Arno Press and *The New York Times*, 1968), pp. 67-70.
25. Illinois, *In the Matter of the Petition of Frank E. Davis for Reinstatement as Sheriff of Alexander County, Illinois*, by Charles S. Deneen, Executive Order, Springfield, December 6, 1909, pp. 1-3. This mimeographed copy is housed at the State Archives in Springfield, Illinois.
26. Wells, *Crusade for Justice*, pp. 310-312, 314.
27. Ibid., pp. 312-315.

28. Ibid., pp. 315-317. In *Black Chicago*, p. 60, Allan Spear states that Wells-Barnett went to Springfield in support of Sheriff Davis's reinstatement. This was the opposite of her purpose.

29. *Springfield Forum*, December 5, 1909; December 11, 1909.

30. Illinois, Executive Department, *In the Matter of the Petition of Frank E. Davis for Reinstatement as Sheriff of Alexander County, Illinois*, pp. 3-7; Wells, *Crusade for Justice*, p. 319; Wells-Barnett, "How Enfranchisement Stops Lynchings," pp. 51-52 [page 274 in the present volume].

31. *Springfield Forum*, December 5, 1909.

32. *Chicago Defender*, January 1, 1910.

33. "The Burden," *Crisis*, November 1900, p. 14.

34. Wells-Barnett, "How Enfranchisement Stops Lynchings," pp. 46, 51-52 [pages 270, 275].

35. *Springfield Forum*, January 15, 1910.

36. *Chicago Defender*, September 24, 1910; Kellogg, *NAACP: A History*, pp. 62-63; Ida B. Wells-Barnett to Joel E. Spingarn, April 21, 1911, Joel E. Spingarn Papers; Wells, *Crusade for Justice*, pp. 335-336.

37. Kellogg, *NAACP: A History of the National Association for the Advancement of Colored People*, p. 63; Oswald G. Villard to Joel E. Spingarn, October 10, 1910, Joel E. Spingarn Papers.

38. Ida B. Wells, "Mob Rule in New Orleans," reprinted in *On Lynchings*, pp. 5-6, 18, 22-24, 47.

39. Ida B. Wells-Barnett, "Our Country's Lynching Record," *Survey*, February 1, 1913, p. 574 [page 279 in the present volume].

40. Ida B. Wells-Barnett to Joel E. Spingarn, July 29, 1913, Joel E. Spingarn Papers.

41. Ida B. Wells-Barnett to Judge Harry Olson, April 23, 1914, Municipal Court Papers, Chicago Historical Society, Chicago, Illinois.

42. Illinois, *Report of the Labor Committee of the State Council of Defense of Illinois upon the Inquiry into the Recent Influx of Southern Negro Laborers into East St. Louis and Race Riot in Connection Therewith*, Chicago, June 2, 1917.

43. Illinois, *The Negro in Chicago: A Study of Race Relations and a Race Riot by the Chicago Commission on Race Relations* (Chicago: University of Chicago Press, 1922), pp. 71-73, 75.

44. Wells, *Crusade for Justice*, pp. 384-386, 388-389.

45. Illinois, *The Negro in Chicago*, pp. 73, 75.

46. *Chicago Broad Ax*, July 21, 1917.

47. Wells, *Crusade for Justice*, p. 389-390; *Chicago Defender*, November 3, 1917.

48. *Chicago Defender*, November 3, 1917; Wells, *Crusade for Justice*, pp. 391-392.

49. *Chicago Broad Ax*, October 27, 1917.

50. *Chicago Defender*, October 27, 1917; November 3, 1917.

51. Ibid., November 3, 1917.

52. Ibid., December 22, 1917; Wells, *Crusade for Justice*, p. 395.

53. John Hope Franklin, *From Slavery to Freedom*, 3rd ed. (New York: Alfred A. Knopf, Inc., 1967), pp. 480-481.

54. *Chicago Tribune*, July 7, 1919.

55. Illinois, *The Negro in Chicago*, pp. xv-xvii, 1-3.
56. Wells, *Crusade for Justice*, pp. xxvii, 414.
57. Ida B. Wells-Barnett to Illinois Negro Women Voters, September 11, 1928, Claude A. Barnett Papers, Chicago Historical Society, Chicago, Illinois.
58. Ida B. Wells-Barnett to Claude A. Barnett, October 19, 1928, Claude A. Barnett Papers; Ida B. Wells-Barnett, "Why I Am for Hoover," speech presented at Illinois Colored Women's Republican League mass meeting, Chicago, September 20, 1928, Claude A. Barnett Papers.
59. Ida B. Wells-Barnett to Claude A. Barnett, October 21, 1928, Claude A. Barnett Papers.
60. Ida B. Wells-Barnett to Claude A. Barnett, n.d., Claude A. Barnett Papers.
61. Gosnell, *Negro Politicians*, pp. 11, 15-16, 19.
62. Ida B. Wells-Barnett to Claude A. Barnett, October 21, 1928, Claude A. Barnett Papers.
63. Wells-Barnett, Diary 1930, passim.
64. Illinois, *Tabulated Statement of Canvass of Returns*, Cook County, April 8, 1930.
65. Wells, *Crusade for Justice*, p. xxix; Gosnell, *Negro Politicians*, pp. 68, 71.
66. Wells-Barnett, Diary, May 19, 1930; *Chicago Tribune*, April 9, 1930.
67. Interview with Alfreda Duster, Chicago, Illinois, February 25, 1976.
68. W. E. B. Du Bois, "Postscript," *Crisis* 40 (June 1931): 207.

CONCLUSION

1. Fortune, "Ida B. Wells, A.M.," p. 39.
2. *New York Age*, August 11, 1888.
3. Fortune, "Ida B. Wells, A.M.," p, 39.
4. *New York Age*, December 21, 1889.
5. Ida B. Wells-Barnett to Joel E. Spingarn, April 21, 1911, Joel E. Spingarn Papers.
6. Ibid.

Bibliography

WRITINGS BY IDA B. WELLS-BARNETT

Books

Wells, Ida B. *Crusade for Justice: The Autobiography of Ida B. Wells*. Edited by Alfreda M. Duster. Chicago: University of Chicago Press, 1970.

————; Douglass, Frederick; Penn, I. Garland; Barnett, Ferdinand L. *The Reason Why the Colored American Is Not in the World's Columbian Exposition*. Chicago: Ida B. Wells, 1893.

Wells-Barnett, Ida B. *On Lynchings: Southern Horrors [1892], A Red Record [1895], Mob Rule in New Orleans [1900]*. Preface by August Meier. New York: Arno Press and *The New York Times*, 1969.

Articles

Wells, Ida B. "Afro-Americans and Africa." *A.M.E. Church Review*, July 1892, pp. 40-44.

————. "Lynch Law in All Its Phases." *Our Day*, May 1893, pp. 333-347.

Wells-Barnett, Ida B. "Booker T. Washington and His Critics." *World Today*, April 1904, pp. 518-521.

————. "How Enfranchisement Stops Lynchings." *Original Rights Magazine*, June 1910, pp 42-53.

————. "Lynching and the Excuse for It." *Independent*, May 16, 1901, pp. 1133-1336.

————. "Lynch Law in America." *Arena*, January 1900, pp. 15-24.

————. "The Negro's Case in Equity." *Independent*, April 26, 1900, pp. 1010-1011.

————. "Our Country's Lynching Record." *Survey*, February 1, 1913, pp. 573-574.

MANUSCRIPT COLLECTIONS

Chicago, Ill. Chicago Historical Society. Claude A. Barnett Papers; George Washington Ellis Papers; Municipal Court Papers; Bertha Palmer Board of Lady Managers Records.

Chicago, Ill. University of Chicago. Julius Rosenwald Papers; Ida B. Wells Papers.

Chicago, Ill. University of Illinois, Chicago. Circle Campus. Illinois League of Women Voters File.

Springfield, Ill. Illinois State Historical Library. Charles S. Deneen Newspaper Scrapbooks.

Tuskegee, Ala. Tuskegee Institute Archives. Margaret Murray Washington Papers.

Washington, D.C. Howard University. Joel E. Spingarn Papers.

Washington, D.C. Library of Congress. Frederick Douglass Papers; Mary Church Terrell Papers.

Westfield, N.Y. Chautauqua County Historical Society. Albion W. Tourgee Papers.

PUBLIC DOCUMENTS

Illinois. Election Board. *Tabulated Canvass of Returns*. Cook County, April 1930.

Illinois. Executive Department. *In the Matter of the Petition of Frank E. Davis for Reinstatement as Sheriff of Alexander County, Illinois*, by Charles S. Deneen, December 6, 1909.

Illinois. Labor Committee. *Report of the Labor Committee of the State Council of Defense of Illinois Upon the Inquiry into the Recent Influx of Southern Negro Laborers into East St. Louis and Race Riot in Connection Therewith*. 1917.

Illinois. Legislative Body. *Laws of the State of Illinois Enacted by the Forty-Fourth General Assembly at the Regular Biennial Session*. 1906.

Illinois. *The Negro in Chicago: A Study of Race Relations and a Race Riot in 1909*, by the Commission on Race Relations. Chicago: University of Chicago Press, 1922; reprint ed., New York: Arno Press and *The New York Times*.

Tennessee. Court. *Reports of Cases Argued and Determined in the Supreme Court of Tennessee*, by George Wesley Pickle. Nashville: Marshall and Bruce Stationers & Printers, 1887.

NEWSPAPERS

Chicago Broad Ax, June 30, 1906–November 30, 1917.
Chicago Chronicle, November 7, 1906.
Chicago Defender, January 1, 1910–December 22, 1917; April 12, 1930; March 28, 1931; April 4, 1931.
Chicago Herald, July 31, 1894.
Chicago Inter-Ocean, October 1, 1892–July 17, 1897.
Chicago Tribune, June 28, 1895; August 18, 19, 20, 1899; July 7, 1919; April 9, 1930.
Chicago Whip, June 24, 1919–October 9, 1920.
Cleveland Gazette, January 17, 1885–April 9, 1898.
Detroit Plaindealer, October 18, 1889–May 27, 1892.
Indianapolis Freeman, January 5, 1889–January 30,1897.
Memphis Appeal Avalanche, June 30, 1892.
Memphis Commercial Appeal, June 30, 1969.
Memphis Daily Appeal, December 25, 1884.
Nashville Daily American, May 26, 1892.
Negro Fellowship Herald, June 22, 1911.
New York Age, February 12, 1888–February 6, 1892.
New York Freeman, January 10, 1885–February 2, 1888.
New York Globe, January 19, 1884–May 24, 1884.
New York Times, July 30, 1894; September 4, 1894.
Springfield Forum, February 3, 1906–December 28, 1911; July 12, 17, 1917.
Springfield Illinois Record, October 29, 1898–April 1, 1899.
Topeka Call, April 15, 1893.
Topeka Weekly Call, January 3, 1893–May 25, 1895.
Washington Bee, August 20, 1887.

OTHER PERIODICALS

American Law Review, November–December 1894.
Crisis, January, February, May, July 1911; March, September 1912; February 1914; May 1919; January 1930; May 1931; May 1934; February 1957.
Cyclopedic Review of Current History, fall 1894.
Forum, October 1893.
Freeman, June 1921.
Literary Digest, July 14, 28, 1894.

Outlook, October 1903.
Public, April 25, May 16; June 6, 13, 27 1903; April 4, 1913.
Review of Reviews, March 1892; June 1, 1894.

INTERVIEWS

Duster, Alfreda. Chicago, Illinois, July 1975; February 23, 25, 1976; March 30, 1977; March 27, 1978.
Mundy, James A. Olivet Baptist Church, Chicago, Illinois, July 14, 1975.

BOOKS

Addams, Jane. *Twenty Years at Hull House*. New York: Macmillan Co,, 1910; Signet Classic, 1961.
———, and Wells, Ida B. *Lynching and Rape: An Exchange of Views*. Edited by Bettina Aptheker. New York: American Institute for Marxist Studies, 1977.
Ames, Jesse Daniels. *The Changing Character of Lynching*. Atlanta: Commission on Interracial Cooperation, 1942; reprint ed., New York AMS Press, 1973.
Aptheker, Herbert, ed. *A Documentary History of the Negro People in the United States*. 2 vols., 4th ed. New York: Citadel Press, 1951.
Baker, Ray Stannard. *Following the Color Line*. New York: Doubleday, Page & Co., 1908; reprint ed., Williamstown, Mass.: Corner House Pub., 1973.
Bennett, Lerone. *Before the Mayflower*. Chicago: Johnson Pub. Co., 1961.
The Birth of the Afro-American National League—Proceedings. Chicago: J. C. Battles and R. B. Cabbell, 1890.
Blaustein, Albert P., and Zangrando, Robert L., eds. *Civil Rights and the American Negro: A Documentary History*. New York: Washington Square Press, 1968.
Block, Ford I. *Blacks' Blue Book*. Chicago: Block Pub., 1917.
Bontemps, Arna, and Conroy, Jack. *They Seek a City*. Garden City, N.Y.: Doubleday, Doran & Co., 1945.
Boulware, Marcus Hanna. *The Oratory of Negro Leaders*. Westport, Conn.: Negro Universities Press, 1969.
Breckinridge, Sophonisba P. *Women in the Twentieth Century*. New York: McGraw-Hill Book Co., 1933.

Broderick, Francis L. *W. E. B. Du Bois: Leader in a Time of Crisis*. Stanford: Stanford University Press, 1959.

Caughey, John Walton. *Their Majesties the Mob*. Chicago: University of Chicago Press, 1960.

Church, Annette E., and Church, Roberta. *The Robert R. Churches of Memphis*. Ann Arbor: Edward Bros., 1974.

Common, John R. *Races and Immigrants in America*. New York: Macmillan Pub. Co., 1913.

Conference of Colored Men of the United States. *Proceedings, Nashville, Tennessee*, May 6-9, 1879. Washington, D.C.: Rufus H. Darby, 1879.

Cronon, Edmund David. *Black Moses, the Story of Marcus Garvey and the Universal Negro Improvement Association*. Madison: University of Wisconsin Press, 1968.

Cutler, James Elbert. *Lynch Law: An Investigation into the History of Lynching in the United States*, New York: Longmans, Green & Co., 1905; reprint ed., Montclair, N.J.: Patterson Smith Pub. Corp., 1969.

Daniels, Sadie Iola. *Women Builders*. Rev. and enl. Edited by Charles H. Wesley and Thelma D. Perry. Washington, D.C.: Associated Publishers, 1970.

Davis, Allen. *American Heroine: The Life and Legend of Jane Addams*. New York: Oxford University Press, 1973.

———. *Spearheads for Reform: The Social Settlements and the Progressive Movement, 1890-1914*. New York: Oxford University Press, 1967.

Davis, Elizabeth Lindsay. *Lifting As They Climb: History of the National Association of Colored Women*. Washington, D.C.: National Association of Colored Women's Clubs, 1933.

———. *The Story of the Illinois Federation of Colored Women's Clubs*. N.p., n.d.

Detweiler, Frederick G. *The Negro Press in the United States*. Chicago: University of Chicago Press, 1922.

Dillon, Mary Earhart. *Frances Willard, from Prayers to Politics*. Chicago: University of Chicago Press, 1944.

Douglass, Frederick. *Address of Hon. Frederick Douglass Delivered in Metropolitan A.M.E. Church, Washington, D.C.* Baltimore: Press of Thomas & Evans, 1894.

———. *Why Is the Negro Lynched?* Bridgwater, England: John Whitby & Sons, 1895.

Drake, St. Clair, and Cayton, Horace R. *Black Metropolis: A Study of Negro Life in a Northern City*. 2 vols. Introduction by Richard Wright. New York: Harper & Row, Pub., 1945; Harper Torchbooks, 1962.

Du Bois, W. E. B. *The Autobiography of W. E. B. Du Bois: A Soliloquy on Viewing My Life from the Last Decade of Its First Century.* Edited by Herbert Aptheker. New York: International Pub. Co., 1968.

———. *The Correspondence of W. E. B. Du Bois.* 2 vols. Edited by Herbert Aptheker. Amherst: University of Massachusetts Press, 1973-1976.

———. *Dusk of Dawn.* New York: Harcourt, Brace & Co., 1940.

———. *Souls of Black Folk.* Chicago: A. C. McClurg & Co., 1903; reprint ed., New York: Kraus-Thompson, 1973.

———, and Dill, Granville. *The College-Bred Negro American.* Atlanta University Publications, No. 15. Atlanta: Atlanta University Press, 1910; reprint ed., Arno Press & *The New York Times,* 1968.

Duncan, Otis D., and Duncan, Beverly. *The Negro Population of Chicago.* Chicago: University of Chicago Press, 1957.

Factor, Robert L. *The Black Response to America: Men, Ideals, and Organizations from Frederick Douglass to the NAACP.* Reading, Mass.: Addison-Wesley Pub. Co., 1970.

Flexner, Eleanor. *Century of Struggle.* Cambridge: Harvard University Press, 1959; reprint ed., New York: Atheneum, 1970.

Foner, Philip S. *Frederick Douglass: A Biography.* New York: Citadel Press, 1964.

———, ed. *The Life and Writings of Frederick Douglass,* vol. 4. New York: International Pub., 1955.

———, ed. *The Voice of Black America: Major Speeches of Negroes in the United States, 1797-1971.* New York: Simon & Schuster, 1972.

Fox, Stephen. *The Guardian of Boston: William Monroe Trotter.* New York: Atheneum, 1970.

Franklin, John Hope. *From Slavery to Freedom.* 3rd ed. New York: Alfred A. Knopf, 1967.

———. *Reconstruction after the Civil War.* Chicago: University of Chicago Press, 1961.

Frazier, E. Franklin. *Black Bourgeoisie.* Glencoe, Ill.: Free Press, 1957; Collier Books, 1962.

———. *The Negro Family in the United States.* Rev. and abr. Dryden Press, 1948. Foreword by Nathan Glazer. Chicago: University of Chicago Press, 1966.

Fullinwider, S. P. *The Mood and Mind of Black America.* Homewood, Ill.: Dorsey Press, 1969.

Ginger, Ray. *Altgeld's America: The Lincoln Ideal versus Changing Realities.* New York: Funk & Wagnalls Co., 1958.

Goldbeck, J. Helen, ed. *A Survey of the Blacks' Response to Lynching.* Las Vegas: New Mexico Highlands University Media Materials Center, 1973.

Gosnell, Harold F. *Negro Politicians: The Rise of Negro Politics in Chicago*. Chicago: University of Chicago Press, 1953; Phoenix Books, 1967.

Grant, Donald Lee. *The Anti-Lynching Movement, 1883-1932*. San Francisco: R and E Associates, 1975.

Green, Constance. *The Secret City: A History of Race Relations in the Nation's Capitol*. Princeton: Princeton University Press, 1967.

Gutman, Herbert. *Black Families in Slavery and Freedom, 1750-1925*. New York: Pantheon Books, 1976.

Harlan, Louis. *Booker T. Washington: The Making of a Black Leader, 1856-1901*. New York: Oxford University Press, 1972.

———. ed. *The Booker T. Washington Papers*, vols. 3 and 4. Urbana: University of Illinois Press, 1974 and 1975.

Hawkins, Hugh, ed. *Booker T. Washington and His Critics: The Problems of Negro Leadership*. Boston: D. C. Heath & Co., 1962.

Hofstadter, Richard. *The American Political Tradition*. New York: Alfred A. Knopf, 1949.

———, and Wallace, Michael, eds. *American Violence*. New York: Alfred A. Knopf, 1970.

Holt, Rackham. *Mary McLeod Bethune*. Garden City, N.Y.: Doubleday and Co., 1964.

Kellogg, Charles Flint. *NAACP: A History of the National Association of Colored People*. Baltimore: Johns Hopkins Press, 1967.

Kraditor, Aileen I. *The Ideas of the Woman Suffrage Movement, 1890-1920*. New York: Columbia University Press, 1965.

Lerner, Gerda. *Black Women in White America*. New York: Pantheon Books, 1972; Vintage Books, 1973.

Lewinson, Paul. *Race, Class, and Party*. 2nd ed. New York: Grosset & Dunlap, Universal Library, 1965.

Loewenberg, Bert James, and Bogin, Ruth, eds. *Black Women in Nineteenth Century American Life*. University Park, Pa.: State University Press, 1976.

Logan, Rayford W. *The Betrayal of the Negro: From Rutherford B. Hayes to Woodrow Wilson*. Original title: *The Negro in American Life and Thought: The Nadir, 1877-1901*. New York: Macmillan, 1954; Collier Books, 1965.

———. *The Negro in the United States*. Princeton: D. Van Nostrand Co., 1957.

Lowden, Frank O. *Law Supreme in a Republic*. Springfield, Ill.: Journal Co., Printers, 1918.

Lynch, Hollis R. *The Black Urban Condition*. New York: Thomas Y. Crowell Co., 1973.

Majors, Monroe A. *Noted Negro Women, Their Triumphs and Activities*. Chicago: Donohue and Henneberry, 1893; reprint ed., Freeport, N.Y.: Books for Libraries Press, 1971.

Marquis, Albert Nelson, ed. *The Book of Chicagoans*. Chicago: By the Author, 1917.

Meier, August. *Negro Thought in America, 1880-1915*. Ann Arbor: University of Michigan Press, 1963; Ann Arbor Paperbacks, 1968.

Mossell, Mrs. N. F. *The Work of the Afro-American Women*. Philadelphia: G. S. Ferguson, 1894; reprint ed., Freeport, N.Y.: Books for Libraries Press, 1971.

National Association for the Advancement of Colored People, *Thirty Years of Lynching in the United States, 1889-1918*. New York: NAACP, 1919; reprint ed., New York: Negro Universities Press, 1969.

Newby, I[dus] A. *Jim Crow's Defense: Anti-Negro Thought in America 1900-1930*. Baton Rouge: Louisiana State University Press, 1965.

Northrop, Henry Davenport; Gay, Joseph R.; and Penn, I. Garland. *The College of Life; or, Practical Self-Educator: A Manual of Self-Improvement of the Colored Race*. Chicago: Publication & Lithograph Co., 1895.

Osofsky, Gilbert, ed. *The Burden of Race: A Documentary History of Negro-White Relations in America*. New York: Harper & Row, Pub., 1967; Harper Torchbooks, 1968.

————. *Harlem: The Making of a Ghetto*. 2nd ed. New York: Harper & Row, Pub., 1971.

Ottley, Roi. *The Lonely Warrior*. Chicago: Henry Regnery Co., 1955.

Ovington, Mary White. *The Walls Came Tumbling Down*. New York: Harcourt, Brace & Co., 1947.

Parris, Guichard, and Brooks, Lester. *Blacks in the City: A History of the National Urban League*. Boston: Little, Brown & Co., 1971.

Penn, Irving Garland. *The Afro-American Press and Its Editors*. Springfield, Mass.: Wiley and Co., 1891; reprint ed., New York: Arno Press and *The New York Times*, 1969.

Proceedings of the National Negro Conference, 1909. New York: n.p., 1909.

Ransom, Reverdy C. *The Pilgrimage of Harriet Ransom's Son*. Nashville: Sunday School Union, n.d.

Raper, Arthur F. *The Tragedy of Lynching*. Chapel Hill: University of North Carolina Press, 1933; reprint ed., New York: Negro Universities Press, 1969.

Robb, Frederick H., ed. *Intercollegiate Wonder Book or The Negro in Chicago, 1779-1927*. Chicago: Washington Intercollegiate Club of Chicago, 1929.

Ross, B. Joyce. *J. E. Spingarn and the Rise of the NAACP.* New York: Atheneum, 1972.

Rudwick, Elliott M. *Race Riot at East St. Louis, July 2, 1917.* Carbondale: Southern Illinois University Press, 1964.

————. *W. E. B. Du Bois: A Study in Minority Group Leadership.* Philadelphia: University of Pennsylvania Press, 1961.

————. *W. E. B. Du Bois: Propagandist of the Negro Protest.* New York: Atheneum, 1969.

Sandburg, Carl. *The Chicago Race Riots, July 1919.* 2nd ed. Preface by Ralph McGill. New York: Harcourt, Brace & Howe, 1969.

Scott, Anne Firor. *The Southern Lady: From Pedestal to Politics, 1830-1930.* Chicago: University of Chicago Press, 1970.

A Southern Society for the Promotion of the Study of Race and Conditions and Problems in the South. *Race Problems of the South, Report of the Proceedings of the Annual Conference, at Montgomery, Ala., May 8-10, 1900.* Richmond, Va.: B. F. Johnson Pub. Co., 1900; reprint ed., New York: Negro Universities Press, 1969.

Spear, Allan H. *Black Chicago: The Making of a Negro Ghetto, 1890-1920.* Chicago: University of Chicago Press, 1967.

Strickland, Arvarh E. *History of the Chicago Urban League.* Urbana: University of Illinois Press, 1966.

Terrell, Mary Church. *A Colored Woman in a White World.* Washington, D.C.: National Association of Colored Women's Clubs, 1968.

Thompson, John W. *An Authentic History of the Douglass Monument.* Rochester: By the Author, 1903; reprint ed., Freeport, N.Y.: Books for Libraries Press, 1971.

Thornbrough, Emma Lou. *T. Thomas Fortune, Militant Journalist.* Chicago: University of Chicago Press, 1972.

Truman, Margaret. *Women of Courage.* New York: William Morrow & Co., 1976.

Tucker, David M. *Black Pastors and Leaders: Memphis, 1819-1972.* Memphis: Memphis State University Press, 1975.

Tuttle, William M., Jr. *Race Riot.* New York: Atheneum, 1970.

————, ed. *W. E. B. Du Bois.* Englewood Cliffs, N.J.: Prentice-Hall, 1973.

Warner, W. Lloyd; Junker, Buford H.; and Adams, Walter A. *Color and Human Nature: Negro Personality in a Northern City.* Washington, D.C.: American Council on Education, 1941.

Washington, Booker T.; Wood, Norman B.; and Williams, Fannie Barrier. *A New Negro for a New Century.* Chicago: American Publishing House, 1900; reprint ed., New York: Arno Press and *The New York Times*, 1969.

Washington, E. Davidson, ed. *Selected Speeches of Booker T. Washington*. Garden City, N.J.: Doubleday, Doran & Co., 1932.

White, Walter. *Rope and Faggot*. New York: Alfred A. Knopf, 1929; reprint ed., New York: Arno Press and *The New York Times*, 1969.

Wolseley, Robert E. *The Black Press, U.S.A.* Ames, Iowa: Iowa State University Press, 1971.

Wood, Norman B. *The White Side of a Black Subject*. Chicago: American Publishing House, 1897; reprint ed., New York: Negro Universities Press, 1969.

Woodson, Carter G. *The History of the Negro Church*. 3rd ed. Washington, D.C.: Associated Publishers, 1972.

————, and Wesley, Charles H. *The Negro in Our History*. 11th ed., rev. Washington: Associated Publishers, 1966.

Woodward, C. Vann. *The Strange Career of Jim Crow*. 3rd ed., rev. New York: Oxford University Press, 1955.

Work, Monroe N. *Negro Year Book: An Annual Encyclopedia of the Negro, 1931-1932*. Tuskegee: Negro Year Book Pub. Co., 1931.

ARTICLES

Addams, Jane. "Has the Emancipation Act Been Nullified by National Indifference?" *Survey*, February 1, 1913, pp. 365-366.

————. "Respect for Law." *Independent*, January 3, 1903, pp. 18-20.

Aked, Charles V. "The Race Problem in America." *Contemporary Review*, June 1897, pp. 818-827.

Belles, A. Gilbert. "Black Press in Illinois." *Journal of the Illinois State Historical Society* 68 (September 1975): 344-352.

Bleckley, L. E. "Negro Outrage No Excuse for Lynching." *Forum*, November 1893, pp. 300-302.

Branham, Charles. "Black Chicago: Accommodationist Politics before the Great Migration." In *The Ethnic Frontier*, edited by Melvin G. Holli and Peter d'A. Jones, pp. 211-62. Grand Rapids: Wm. B. Eerdmans Pub. Co., 1977.

Carter, Hodding. "A Proud Struggle for Grace." In *A Vanishing America*, Edited by Thomas C. Wheeler, pp. 56-78. New York: Holt, Rinehart & Winston, 1964.

Crowe, Mary Davis. "Fannie Barrier Williams." *Negro History Bulletin* 5 (May 1942): 190-191.

Diner, Steven J. "Chicago Social Workers and Blacks in the Progressive Era." *Social Service Review* 44 (December 1970): 393-410.

Douglass, Frederick. "Lynching Black People Because They Are Black." *Our Day*, July-August 1894, pp. 298-306.

Drake, Donald E. "Militancy in Fortune's *New York Age.*" *Journal of Negro History* 55 (October 1970): 307-322.

Du Bois, W. E. B. "Postscript." *Crisis*, June 1931, p. 207.

Ewing, Quincy. "The Heart of the Race Problem." *Atlantic Monthly*, March 1909, pp. 389-397.

Fortune, T. Thomas. "Ida B. Wells, A.M." In *Women of Distinction*, edited by Lawson A. Scruggs, pp. 33-39. Raleigh: L. A. Scruggs, Pub., 1893.

Godkin, E. L. "Judge Lynch as an Educator," *Nation*, 28 September 1893, pp, 222-223.

Gross, Theodore L. "The Fool's Errand of Albion W. Tourgee. *Phylon* 24 (Fall 1963): 240-254,

Hackney, Sheldon. "Southern Violence." In *The History of Violence in America*, edited by Hugh D. Graham and Ted R. Gurr. New York: Frederick A. Praeger, Pub., 1969.

Haygood, Atticus G. "The Black Shadow in the South." *Forum*, October 1893, pp. 167-175.

Horowitz, Helen. "Varieties of Cultural Experience in Jane Addams' Chicago." *History of Education Quarterly* 14 (Spring 1974): 69-86.

Ladner, Joyce A. "Racism and Tradition: Black Womanhood in Historical Perspective." In *Liberating Women's History: Theoretical and Critical Essays*, edited by Berenice A. Carroll, pp. 179-193. Urbana: University of Illinois Press, 1976.

Lerner, Gerda. "Community Work of Black Club Women." *Journal of Negro History* 59 (April 1974): 158-167.

Massa, Ann. "Black Women in the 'White City.' " *Journal of American Studies* 8 (December 1974): 319-337.

McPherson, James M. "The Antislavery Legacy: From Reconstruction to the NAACP." In *Towards a New Past*, edited by Barton J. Bernstein, pp 126-157. New York: Pantheon Books, 1968.

Meier, August. "Negro Class Structure and Ideology in the Age of Booker T. Washington." *Phylon* 23 (Fall 1962): 258-266.

———, and Rudwick, Elliott. "Black Violence in the 20th Century: A Study in Rhetoric and Retaliation." In *The History of Violence in America*, edited by Hugh Davis Graham and Ted Robert Gurr, pp. 399-412. New York: Frederick A. Praeger, Pub., 1969.

Miller, Kelly. "Problems of the City Negro." *World Today*, April 1904, pp. 511-514.

Murray, Pauli. "Constitutional Law and Black Women." Afro-American Studies Program, Boston University Occasional Paper Number one.

———. "The Liberation of Black Women." In *Voices of the New Feminism*, edited by Mary Lou Thompson, pp. 87-102. Boston: Beacon Press, 1970.

Newby, I[dus] A. "Introduction: Segregationist Thought since 1890." In *The Development of Segregationist Thought*, edited by I[dus] A. Newby, pp. 1-20. Homewood, Ill.: Dorsey Press, 1968.

Page, Walter H. "The Last Hold of the Southern Bully." *Forum*, November 1893, pp. 303-314.

Pierce, Bessie L. "The Women of Illinois." *Chicago Tribune Supplement*. Chicago: Sesquicentennial Commission, 1968.

Puttkammer, Charles W., and Worthy, Ruth. "William Monroe Trotter, 1872-1934." *Journal of Negro History* 43 (October 1958): 298-316.

Reed, John Shelton. "An Evaluation of an Anti-Lynching Organization." *Social Problems* 16 (Fall 1968): 72-182.

Rudwick, Elliott M. "The Niagara Movement." *Journal of Negro History* 42 (October 1957): 177-200.

———, and Meier, August. "Black Man in the 'White City': Negroes and the Columbian Exposition, 1893." *Phylon* 26 (Winter 1965): 354-361.

Shils, Edward. "Charisma, Order, and Status." *American Sociological Review* 30 (April 1965): 199-213.

Tate, Inez. "Ida B. Wells-Barnett." *Negro History Bulletin* 5 (May 1942): 179.

Thornbrough, Emma Lou. "The National Afro-American League, 1887-1908." *Journal of Southern History* 27 (February 1961): 494-512.

Tucker, David M. "Miss Ida B. Wells and Memphis Lynching." *Phylon* 32 (Summer 1971): 112-122.

Tuttle, William M., Jr. "Contested Neighborhoods and Racial Violence: Prelude to the Chicago Riot of 1919." *Journal of Negro History* 55 (October 1970): 266-288.

———. "Views of a Negro during 'The Red Summer' of 1919." *Journal of Negro History* 61 (July 1966): 209-218.

Washington, Booker T. "The Tuskegee Idea." *World Today*, April 1904, pp. 511-514.

White, Walter F. "The Race Conflict in Arkansas." *Survey*, December 1919, pp. 233-234.

Williams, Katherine E. "The Alpha Suffrage Club." *Half Century*, September 1916, p. 12.

UNPUBLISHED MATERIALS

"The Book of the Chicago Woman's Club, Paris Souvenir Edition, 1900."

Boulware, Marcus H. "Ida B. Wells Barnett, 'Anti-Lynching Crusader.' " Chapter in unpublished book manuscript "The Afro-American Woman Speaks, 1830-1973."

Bowen, Louise DeKoven. "The Colored People of Chicago: An Investigation Made for the Juvenile Protective Association by A. P. Drucker, Sophia Boaz, A. L. Harris, Miriam Schaffer, 1913."

"Chicago Political Equality League Annual." Vol. 1895-1911.

"Chicago Urban League Folder." Chicago Historical Society Library.

Chicago Urban League. "Two Decades of Service, 1916-1936."

Crawford, Lloyd W. "Ida B. Wells: Her Anti-Lynching Crusades in Britain and Repercussions from Them in the United States." Paper presented at the meeting of the Association for the Study of Negro Life and History, Xenia, Ohio, October 1962.

––––––. "Ida B. Wells: Some American Reactions to Her Anti-Lynching Crusades in Britain." Paper presented at the meeting of the Association for the Study of Negro Life and History, Richmond, Virginia, October 1958.

Davis, Ralph N. "The Negro Newspaper in Chicago." M.A. thesis, University of Chicago, 1939.

"Ferdinand L. Barnett Scrapbook." Personal File, Alfreda Duster, Chicago.

Fields, Emma L. "Woman's Club Movement in the United States, 1877-1900." M.A. thesis, Howard University, 1948.

"Fortieth Annual Session of the Illinois Association of Colored Women, Carbondale, Illinois, June 18-20, 1940."

"Historical Souvenir, Quinn Chapel A.M.E. Church, Chicago, Illinois, 1847-40."

Hutton, Mary M. B. "The Rhetoric of Ida B. Wells: The Genesis of the Anti-Lynch Movement." Ph.D. dissertation, University of Indiana, 1975.

"Illinois Federation of Colored Women's Clubs. Proceedings of the 26th Annual Session, Brooklyn, Illinois, August 18-21, 1925."

Kreiling, Albert. "The Making of Racial Identities in the Black Press: A Cultural Analysis of Race Journalism in Chicago, 1878-1929." Ph.D. dissertation, University of Illinois, 1973.

Logsdon, Joseph A. "The Rev. Archibald J. Carey and the Negro in Chicago Politics." M.A. thesis, University of Chicago, 1961.

Pride, Armistead Scott. "A Register and History of Negro Newspapers in the United States: 1827-1950." Ph.D. dissertation, Northwestern University, 1950.

"Program of the 86th Session of the Chicago Annual Conference Celebrating the 106th Anniversary of Bethel A.M.E. Church, 1968."

"Quinn Chapel African Methodist Episcopal Church 120th Anniversary Record, 1847-1967." Chicago.

Ransom, Reverdy C. "Deborah and Jael." Sermon delivered at Bethel A.M.E. Church, Chicago, Illinois, June 6, 1897.

Walker, Eunice Rivers. "Ida B. Wells-Barnett: Her Contribution to the Field of Social Welfare." M.S.W. thesis, Loyola University, 1941.

Ida B. Wells-Barnett:

Selected Essays

Publisher's Note

We are pleased to present here nine of Ida B. Wells-Barnett's forceful essays, her only known short story, and F. L. Barnett's contribution to her pamphlet, *The Reason Why the Colored American is not in the World's Columbian Exposition*. This material includes, to our knowledge, all of her contributions to periodicals. It does not include any of her journalism or her pamphlets (with the exception of *The Reason Why*). The most important of the latter have been reprinted and the former await a bibliographical sleuth to ferret them out.

The reader will note that several of the essays on lynching repeat each other, sometimes virtually verbatium, and for this we apologize. These essays were written for different audiences and approach the argument from different angles and we decided it would be useful to the reader to have the entire spectrum of her writing available.

Afro-Americans
and Africa

The April number of THE REVIEW, which had Bishop H. M. Turner's letters on his recent visit to Africa, contained also a paper, "Will the Afro-American Return to Africa?" by that brilliant and forceful journalist, T. Thos. Fortune.

Mr. Fortune seems to think it is the white man only who wishes our race variety to return in a body to the home of its ancestors, whether the Afro-American himself will or no. Viewing the question from that standpoint the editor of the *Age* would not be the faithful watchman on the walls he is credited with being, if he had given any other reply than the emphatic and decided, "He will not!"

The Afro-American, as a race, would not return to Africa if he could, and could not if he would. We would not be true to the race if we conceded for a moment that any other race, the Anglo-Saxon not excepted, had more right to claim this country as home than the Afro-American race. The blood he has shed for liberty's sake, the toil he has given for improvement's sake, and the sacrifices he has made for the cause of progress, give him the supreme right of American citizenship. There will always be to the end of the chapter Afro-Americans here to enforce this claim and wrest from this government its tardy acknowledgment and concession of the same. Afro-Americans have no desire and cannot be forced to go to Africa.

But the entire race is not sanguine over our possessions in this country, and the object of this paper is to maintain that the right of those who wish to go to Africa should be as inviolate as that of those who wish to stay. That there are Afro-Americans who would return to Africa is proved by the presence in New York City last winter of three hundred who had managed

Originally published in the *A.M.E. Church Review*, July 1892, pp. 40-45.

to get that far on their journey. Somebody had told them they would be carried free if they got to New York. They were of course disappointed and returned to the South. The mistake these people made was not in wanting to go to Africa, but in being so poorly prepared in intelligence and finance. There are hundreds of others besides these poverty-stricken and ignorant people, all over the country, who chafe under the knowledge that what is the opportunity for the European and Chinese emigrant in this country is his disadvantage. In no other country but the vaunted "land of the free and home of the brave" is a man despised because of his color. As the Irish, Swede, Dutch, Italian and other foreigners find this the "sweet land of liberty," the Afro-American finds it the land of oppression, outrage and persecution. In the freest and most unprejudiced sections, in every walk of life, no matter how well dressed, courteous or intellectual, he never knows when he may not meet with and be humiliated by this distinctively American prejudice. He is becoming restless and discontented. He wishes to enjoy the full freedom of manhood and aspiration. Where shall he go?

Why should not they turn to Africa, the land of their forefathers, the most fertile of its kind, and the only one which the rapacious and ubiquitous Anglo-Saxon has not entirely gobbled—where they would be welcomed by their race, and given opportunities to assist in the development of Africa, such as are not possessed by any other nation waiting for a foothold?

That more Afro-Americans do not go to Africa is because the objectors say Africa is a death-trap, that we are not Africans, and that it is a country "without organized government, accepted religion or uniform language."

Everybody who goes to Africa does not die. Everybody knows of the African or acclimating fevers, and all travelers or explorers agree that with care and attention to diet, changes of weather and care of the system, the African fever is no more deadly than our Southern malaria; yet nobody thinks of staying away from the South because of it. The cause of death-rate is carelessness rather than the fever. All writers again agree that it is only along the low, marshy coast that this prevails. Back in the interior it is more healthy.

The recent contributions to African literature are instructive as to the obstacles to be met, the dangers to be overcome, and the way to accomplish it. No man who does not inform himself on any undertaking, and decide on the steps he will take, is a fit contribution to the citizenship of any country. He is not only liable, but will fall a victim to his own ignorance in any country.

The argument that Afro-Americans should not go to Africa because "it is a country without organized government, accepted religion or uniform language," is the very weakest that could be offered. No better reinforcement of the position of southern whites could be deduced than to concede the Afro-American incapable of self-government or the government of others. Children, or inherently weak persons, wait for the path to be blazed out in which they should walk. The Romans who invaded Britain, nor yet the Puritans who came over in the "Mayflower," waited for "organized government, uniform language or established religion." They brought their own customs, language and religion with them, few in number though they were, and engrafted them into the warp and woof of the body politic. Is the Afro-American incapable of doing this?

It may be argued that it is not the intelligent class who wish to go to Africa. If this is true it is discreditable alike to their intelligence and desire for gain that they do not. The resources of Africa are boundless. White men of every nationality are braving "the white man's grave," and growing rich off the simple natives. They go home every three years to recover health, then go back to the work of making a fortune. They endure all things in their young manhood for the hope of affluence in their declining years. And if they die, as die they do, will not their children reap the benefit?

The Afro-American can better stand the climate than the European, because of his kinship with the natives; his opportunities would be better, because the Republic of Liberia is already a threshold from whence the enterprising and intelligent Afro-American could enter and possess the land. The need of Liberia is the development of her resources; for this it takes capital, skilled labor, and intelligent direction. Bishop Turner says, "A man with three hundred dollars could make a fortune in a few years." The captain of the ship which took him over to Africa, and which only made ten miles an hour, made this significant remark: "The colored people of the United States throw away enough money for whisky every year to build fifty ships that could run twenty miles an hour," and that he (Bishop Turner) "had better get them to save their money and build a faster ship. The United States had no steamers at all, fast or slow." A native African also said to him: "If our brethren will not come from America and make themselves immensely rich by traffic, as they might do in a few years, we natives will do it ourselves; white men shall not always be getting rich off us." Again, "If our rich colored men in the States would come here and open up the coal mines at Carrysburg they would be worth millions in a few years."

What a grand opportunity for the many wealthy colored men in our country! They could build ships and grow wealthy off the trade, or they could form a syndicate and transport and maintain those who will go, and whose brawn and muscle will assist in the development of the country and the greater increase of wealth to themselves. Our rich men are educating their sons in the best schools of the country every year, but furnish no outlet for the exercise of their talents. Is it any wonder that being thrown back on themselves they lose ambition and become anything else than an honor to their race?

The King of Belgium sent to this country for twenty young colored men, skilled in the different trades, to go to Africa and become instructors. Africa abounds in unskilled laborers. What is needed for her development and what she would welcome is the intelligence and skill of young Afro-America; the capacity for work and physical endurance which has drained the swamps, cleared the forests and cultivated the fields of the Southland. It is a cheering sign that there are those who wish to go, and so far from dissuading those who have physical strength, energy and strong common sense, the general government, or the race at large, should assist them to get there and maintain them till they get a foothold; for, after all, it is the sturdy yeomanry—the middle classes—who develop any country.

From what can be gleaned from current history, the great need of Liberia is a strong, intelligent citizenship, to develop her resources and evolve a government which shall command the attention and respect of the civilized world. For any fraction of our eight millions of Afro-Americans to devote its talents to the work with measurable success would be an example and inspiration for Afro-Americans the world over. The greater the obstacles the more pronounced the victory, and in the years to come their success would be the theme of song and story, as is to-day the perseverance of the Puritans, whose indomitable will and energy gave to the world the greatest country of the age. A handful of them, for no greater reason than have Afro-Americans to-day, and without ceding their rights as citizens of the countries whence they came, landed on what was then the bleak, barren and inhospitable coast of Massachusetts. Their effort then seemed a visionary and impracticable one; to-day their descendants, in song and story, laud them for it. They and the Virginia settlements were but little better prepared to meet the exigencies of a foreign country than the poor three hundred Afro-Americans who made such an ill-starred start.

Finally, I quote from a letter written to one who opposed the going of those men and women to Africa: "What though they are going from the white man's civilization? Surely, with what they have they can evolve and keep alive a civilization of their own! To argue that they cannot argues the inherent weakness of the race. That's the white man's argument.

"Encourage them to work for money to pay their passage and have a little money over, if only to discover what is in them; we will never know otherwise. It is far better to die *trying* to live than drag along at such an uncertain rate, raising children under such restrictive and oppressive conditions; and these poor people show by their actions that they think so.

"I have never heard any but blessings poured out on the heads of the Puritans for their perseverance and endurance. Indeed, I think the hardships and trials brought out the energy and pluck which have been transmitted to their posterity and make the name of New England synonymous with thrift, advancement and prosperity. To me it seems an instructive effort in the right direction, and should be nurtured with hope."

Lynch Law
in all Its Phases

Address at Tremont Temple in the Boston Monday Lectureship, Feb. 13, 1893, by Miss Ida B. Wells, formerly editor of the *Free Speech*, Memphis, Tenn.

I am before the American people to-day through no inclination of my own, but because of a deep-seated conviction that the country at large does not know the extent to which lynch law prevails in parts of the Republic, nor the conditions which force into exile those who speak the truth. I cannot believe that the apathy and indifference which so largely obtains regarding mob rule is other than the result of ignorance of the true situation. And yet, the observing and thoughtful must know that in one section, at least, of our common country, a government of the people, by the people, and for the people, means a government by the mob; where the land of the free and home of the brave means a land of lawlessness, murder and outrage; and where liberty of speech means the license of might to destroy the business and drive from home those who exercise this privilege contrary to the will of the mob. Repeated attacks on the life, liberty and happiness of any citizen or class of citizens are attacks on distinctive American institutions; such attacks imperiling as they do the foundation of government, law and order, merit the thoughtful consideration of far-sighted Americans; not from a standpoint of sentiment, not even so much from a standpoint of justice to a weak race, as from a desire to preserve our institutions.

The race problem or negro question, as it has been called, has been omnipresent and all-pervading since long before the Afro-American was raised from the degradation of the slave to the dignity of the citizen. It has never

Originally published in *Our Day*, May 1893, pp. 333-337.

been settled because the right methods have not been employed in the solution. It is the Banquo's ghost of politics, religion, and sociology which will not down at the bidding of those who are tormented with its ubiquitous appearance on every occasion. Times without number, since invested with citizenship, the race has been indicted for ignorance, immorality and general worthlessness—declared guilty and executed by its self-constituted judges. The operations of law do not dispose of negroes fast enough, and lynching bees have become the favorite pastime of the South. As excuse for the same, a new cry, as false as it is foul, is raised in an effort to blast race character, a cry which has proclaimed to the world that virtue and innocence are violated by Afro-Americans who must be killed like wild beasts to protect womanhood and childhood.

Born and reared in the South, I had never expected to live elsewhere. Until this past year I was one among those who believed the condition of the masses gave large excuse for the humiliations and proscriptions under which we labored; that when wealth, education and character became more general among us,—the cause being removed—the effect would cease, and justice be accorded to all alike. I shared the general belief that good newspapers entering regularly the homes of our people in every state could do more to bring about this result than any agency. Preaching the doctrine of self-help, thrift and economy every week, they would be the teachers to those who had been deprived of school advantages, yet were making history every day—and train to think for themselves our mental children of a larger growth. And so, three years ago last June, I became editor and part owner of the *Memphis Free Speech*. As editor, I had occasion to criticize the city School Board's employment of inefficient teachers and poor school-buildings for Afro-American children. I was in the employ of that board at the time, and at the close of that school-term one year ago, was not re-elected to a position I had held in the city schools for seven years. Accepting the decision of the Board of Education, I set out to make a race newspaper pay—a thing which older and wiser heads said could not be done. But there were enough of our people in Memphis and surrounding territory to support a paper, and I believed they would do so. With nine months hard work the circulation increased from 1,500 to 3,500; in twelve months it was on a good paying basis. Throughout the Mississippi Valley in Arkansas, Tennessee and Mississippi—on plantations and in towns, the demand for and interest in the paper increased among the masses. The newsboys who would not sell it on the trains, voluntarily testified that they had never known colored people to demand a paper so eagerly.

To make the paper a paying business I became advertising agent, solicitor, as well as editor, and was continually on the go. Wherever I went among the people, I gave them in church, school, public gatherings, and home, the benefit of my honest conviction that maintenance of character, money getting and education would finally solve our problem and that it depended on us to say how soon this would be brought about. This sentiment bore good fruit in Memphis. We had nice homes, representatives in almost every branch of business and profession, and refined society. We had learned that helping each other helped all, and every well-conducted business by Afro-Americans prospered. With all our proscription in theatres, hotels and on railroads, we had never had a lynching and did not believe we could have one. There had been lynchings and brutal outrages of all sorts in our own state and those adjoining us, but we had confidence and pride in our city and the majesty of its laws. So far in advance of other Southern cities was ours, we were content to endure the evils we had, to labor and to wait.

But there was a rude awakening. On the morning of March 9, the bodies of three of our best young men were found in an old field horribly shot to pieces. These young men had owned and operated the "People's Grocery," situated at what was known as the Curve—a suburb made up almost entirely of colored people—about a mile from city limits. Thomas Moss, one of the oldest letter-carriers in the city, was president of the company, Calvin McDowell was manager and Will Stewart was a clerk. There were about ten other stockholders, all colored men. The young men were well known and popular and their business flourished, and that of Barrett, a white grocer who kept store there before the "People's Grocery" was established, went down. One day an officer came to the "People's Grocery" and inquired for a colored man who lived in the neighborhood, and for whom the officer had a warrant. Barrett was with him and when McDowell said he knew nothing as to the whereabouts of the man for whom they were searching, Barrett, not the officer, then accused McDowell of harboring the man, and McDowell gave the lie. Barrett drew his pistol and struck McDowell with it; thereupon McDowell, who was a tall, fine-looking six-footer, took Barrett's pistol from him, knocked him down and gave him a good thrashing, while Will Stewart, the clerk, kept the special officer at bay. Barrett went to town, swore out a warrant for their arrest on a charge of assault and battery. McDowell went before the Criminal Court, immediately gave bond

173

and returned to his store. Barrett then threatened (to use his own words) that he was going to clean out the whole store. Knowing how anxious he was to destroy their business, these young men consulted a lawyer who told them they were justified in defending themselves if attacked, as they were a mile beyond city limits and police protection. They accordingly armed several of their friends—not to assail, but to resist the threatened Saturday night attack.

When they saw Barrett enter the front door and a half dozen men at the rear door at 11 o'clock that night, they supposed the attack was on and immediately fired into the crowd, wounding three men. These men, dressed in citizen's clothes, turned out to be deputies who claimed to be hunting another man for whom they had a warrant, and whom any one of them could have arrested without trouble. When these men found they had fired upon officers of the law, they threw away their firearms and submitted to arrest, confident they should establish their innocence of intent to fire upon officers of the law. The daily papers in flaming headlines roused the evil passions of the whites, denounced these poor boys in unmeasured terms, nor permitted them a word in their own defense.

The neighborhood of the Curve was searched next day, and about thirty persons were thrown into jail, charged with conspiracy. No communication was to be had with friends any of the three days these men were in jail; bail was refused and Thomas Moss was not allowed to eat the food his wife prepared for him. The judge is reported to have said, "Any one can see them after three days." They were seen after three days, but they were no longer able to respond to the greetings of friends. On Tuesday following the shooting at the grocery, the papers which had made much of the sufferings of the wounded deputies, and promised it would go hard with those who did the shooting, if they died, announced that the officers were all out of danger, and would recover. The friends of the prisoners breathed more easily and relaxed their vigilance. They felt that as the officers would not die, there was no danger that in the heat of passion the prisoners would meet violent death at the hands of the mob. Besides, we had such confidence in the law. But the law did not provide capital punishment for shooting which did not kill. So the mob did what the law could not be made to do, as a lesson to the Afro-American that he must not shoot a white man,—no matter what the provocation. The same night after the announcement was made in the papers that the officers would get well, the mob, in obedience to a plan know to every prominent white man in the city, went to the jail between two and three o'clock in the morning, dragged out these young men, hatless and shoeless, put them on the yard engine of the railroad which was in waiting just behind the jail, carried them a mile north of city limits and horribly shot them to death while the locomotive at a given signal let off steam and blew the whistle to deaden the sound of the firing.

"It was done by unknown men," said the jury, yet the *Appeal-Avalanche*, which goes to press at 3 a.m., had a two-column account of the lynching. The papers also told how McDowell got hold of the guns of the mob, and as his grasp could not be loosened, his hand was shattered with a pistol ball and all the lower part of his face was torn away. There were four pools of blood found and only three bodies. It was whispered that he, McDowell, killed one of the lynchers with his gun, and it is well known that a policeman who was seen on the street a few days previous to the lynching, died very suddenly the next day after.

"It was done by unknown parties," said the jury, yet the papers told how Tom Moss begged for his life, for the sake of his wife, his little daughter and his unborn infant. They also told us that his last words were, "If you will kill us, turn our faces to the West."

All this we learned too late to save these men, even if the law had not been in the hands of their murderers. When the colored people realized that the flower of our young manhood had been stolen away at night and murdered, there was a rush for firearms to avenge the wrong, but no house would sell a colored man a gun; the armory of the Tennessee Rifles, our only colored military company, and of which McDowell was a member, was broken into by order of the Criminal Court judge, and its guns taken. One hundred men and irresponsible boys from fifteen years and up were armed by order of the authorities and rushed out to the Curve, where it was reported that the colored people were massing, and at point of the bayonet dispersed these men who could do nothing but talk. The cigars, wines, etc., of the grocery stock were freely used by the mob, who possessed the place on pretence of dispersing the conspiracy. The money drawer was broken into and contents taken. The trunk of Calvin McDowell, who had a room in the store, was broken open, and his clothing, which was not good enough to take away, was thrown out and trampled on the floor.

These men were murdered, their stock was attached by creditors and sold for less than one-eighth of its cost to that same man Barrett, who is to-day running his grocery in the same place. He had indeed kept his word, and by aid of the authorities destroyed the People's Grocery Company root and branch. The relatives of Will Stewart and Calvin McDowell are bereft of their protectors. The baby daughter of Tom Moss, too young to express how she misses her father, toddles to the wardrobe, seizes the legs of the trousers of his letter-carrier uniform, hugs and kisses them with evident delight and stretches up her little hands to be taken up into the arms which will nevermore clasp his daughter's form. His wife holds Thomas Moss, Jr., in her arms, upon whose unconscious baby face the tears fall thick and fast when she is thinking of the sad fate of the father he will never see, and of the two helpless children who cling to her for the support she cannot give. Although these men were peaceable, law-abiding citizens of this country, we are told there can be no punishment for their murderers nor indemnity for their relatives.

I have no power to describe the feeling of horror that possessed every member of the race in Memphis when the truth dawned upon us that the protection of the law which we had so long enjoyed was no longer ours; all this had been destroyed in a night, and the barriers of the law had been thrown down, and the guardians of the public peace and confidence scoffed away into the shadows, and all authority given into the hands of the mob, and innocent men cut down as if they were brutes—the first feeling was one of utter dismay, then intense indignation. Vengeance was whispered from ear to ear, but sober reflection brought the conviction that it would be extreme folly to seek vengeance when such action meant certain death for the men, and horrible slaughter for the women and children, as one of the evening papers took care to remind us. The power of the State, country and city, the civil authorities and the strong arm of the military power were all on the side of the mob and of lawlessness. Few of our men possessed firearms, our only company's guns were confiscated, and the only white man who would sell a colored man a gun, was himself jailed, and his store closed. We were helpless in our great strength. It was our first object lesson in the doctrine of white supremacy; an illustration of the South's cardinal principle that no matter what the attainments, character or standing of an Afro-American, the laws of the South will not protect him against a white man.

There was only one thing we could do, and a great determination seized upon the people to follow the advice of the martyred Moss, and "turn our faces to the West," whose laws protect all alike. The *Free Speech* supported by our ministers and leading business men advised the people to leave a community whose laws did not protect them. Hundreds left on foot to walk four hundred miles between Memphis and Oklahoma. A Baptist minister went to the territory, built a church, and took his entire congregation out in less than a month. Another minister sold his church and took his flock to California, and still another has settled in Kansas. In two months, six thousand persons had left the city and every branch of business began to feel this silent resentment of the outrage, and failure of the authorities to punish the lynchers. There were a number of business failures and blocks of houses were for rent. The superintendent and treasurer of the street railway company called at the office of the *Free Speech*, to have us urge the colored people to ride again on the street cars. A real estate dealer said to a colored man who returned some property he had been buying on the installment plan: "I don't see what you 'niggers' are cutting up about. You got off light. We first intended to kill every one of those thirty-one 'niggers' in jail, but concluded to let all go but the 'leaders.' " They did let all go to the penitentiary. These so-called rioters have since been tried in the Criminal Court for the conspiracy of defending their property, and are now serving terms of three, eight, and fifteen years each in the Tennessee State prison.

To restore the equilibrium and put a stop to the great financial loss, the next move was to get rid of the *Free Speech*,—the disturbing element which kept the waters troubled; which would not let the people forget, and in obedience to whose advice nearly six thousand persons had left the city. In casting about for an excuse, the mob found it in the following editorial which appeared in the Memphis *Free Speech*,—May 21, 1892: "Eight negroes lynched in one week. Since last issue of the *Free Speech* one was lynched at Little Rock, Ark., where the citizens broke into the penitentiary and got their man; three near Anniston, Ala., and one in New Orleans, all on the same charge, the new alarm of assaulting white women—and three near Clarksville, Ga., for killing a white man. The same program of hanging—then shooting bullets into the lifeless bodies was carried out to the letter. Nobody in this section of the country believes the old threadbare lie that negro men rape white women. If Southern white men are not careful they will overreach themselves, and public sentiment will have a reaction. A conclusion will then be reached which will be very damaging to the moral reputation of their women." Commenting on this, *The Daily Commercial* of Wednesday following said: "Those negroes who are attempting to make lynching of individuals of their race a means for arousing the worst passions of their kind, are playing with a dangerous sentiment. The negroes may as well understand that there is no mercy for the negro rapist, and little patience with his defenders. A negro organ printed in this city in a recent issue published the following atrocious paragraph: 'Nobody in this section believes the old threadbare lie that negro men rape white women. If Southern white men are not careful they will overreach themselves and public sentiment will have a reaction. A conclusion will be reached which will be very damaging to the moral reputation of their women.' The fact that a black scoundrel is allowed to live and utter such loathsome and repulsive calumnies is a volume of evidence as to the wonderful patience of Southern whites. There are some things the Southern white man will not tolerate, and the obscene intimidation of the foregoing has brought the writer to the very uttermost limit of public patience. We hope we have said enough."

The Evening *Scimitar* of the same day copied this leading editorial and added this comment: "Patience under such circumstances is not a virtue. If the negroes themselves do not apply the remedy without delay, it will be the duty of those he has attacked, to tie the wretch who utters these calumnies to a stake at the intersection of Main and Madison streets, brand him in the forehead with a hot iron and—"

Such open suggestions by the leading daily papers of the progressive city of Memphis were acted upon by the leading citizens and a meeting was held at the Cotton Exchange that evening. *The Commercial* two days later had the following account of it:

ATROCIOUS BLACKGUARDISM.

There will be no Lynching and no Repetition of the Offense.

In its issue of Wednesday *The Commercial* reproduced and commented upon an editorial which appeared a day or two before in a negro organ known as the *Free Speech*. The article was so insufferably and indecently slanderous that the whole city awoke to a feeling of intense resentment which came within an ace of culminating in one of those occurrences whose details are so eagerly seized and so prominently published by Northern newspapers. Conservative counsels, however, prevailed, and no extreme measures were resorted to. On Wednesday afternoon a meeting of citizens was held. It was not an assemblage of hoodlums or irresponsible fire-eaters, but solid, substantial business men who knew exactly what they were doing and who were far more indignant at the villainous insult to the women of the South than they would have been at any injury done themselves. This meeting appointed a committee to seek the author of the infamous editorial and warn him quietly that upon repetition of the offense he would find some other part of the country a good deal safer and pleasanter place of residence than this. The committee called a negro preacher named Nightingale, but he disclaimed responsibility and convinced the gentlemen that he had really sold out his paper to a woman named Wells. This woman is not in Memphis at present. It was finally learned that one Fleming, a negro who was driven out of Crittenden Co. during the trouble there a few years ago, wrote the paragraph. He had, however, heard of the meeting, and fled from a fate which he feared was in store for him, and which he knew he deserved. His whereabouts could not be ascertained, and the committee so reported. Later on, a communication from Fleming to a prominent Republican politician, and that politician's reply were shown to one or two gentlemen. The former was an inquiry as to whether the writer might safely return to Memphis, the latter was an emphatic answer in the negative, and Fleming is still in hiding. Nothing further will be done in the matter. There will be no lynching, and it is very certain there will be no repetition of the outrage. If there should be—Friday, May 25.

The only reason there was no lynching of Mr. Fleming who was business manager and half owner of the *Free Speech*, and who did not write the editorial, was because this same white Republican told him the committee was coming, and warned him not to trust them, but get out of the way. The committee scoured the city hunting him, and had to be content with Mr. Nightingale who was dragged to the meeting, shamefully abused (although it was known he had sold out his interest in the paper six months before). He was struck in the face and forced at the pistol's point to sign a letter which was written by them, in which he denied all knowledge of the editorial, denounced and condemned it as slander on white women. I do not censure Mr. Nightingale for his action because, having never been at the pistol's point myself, I do not feel that I am competent to sit in judgment on him, or say what I would do under such circumstances.

I had written that editorial with other matter for the week's paper before leaving home the Friday previous for the General Conference of the A.M.E. Church in Philadelphia. Conference adjourned Tuesday, and Thursday, May 25, at 3 p.m., I landed in New York City for a few days' stay before returning home, and there learned from the papers that my business manager had been driven away and the paper suspended. Telegraphing for news, I received telegrams and letters in return informing me that the trains were being watched, that I was to be dumped into the river and beaten, if not killed; it had been learned that I wrote the editorial and I was to be hanged in front of the court-house and my face bled if I returned, and I was implored by my friends to remain away. The creditors attached the office in the meantime and the outfit was sold without more ado, thus destroying effectually that which it had taken years to build. One prominent insurance agent publicly declares he will make it his business to shoot me down on sight if I return to Memphis in twenty years, while a leading white lady had remarked that she was opposed to the lynching of those three men in March, but she did wish there was some way by which I could be gotten back and lynched.

I have been censured for writing that editorial, but when I think of the five men who were lynched that week for assault on white women and that not a week passes but some poor soul is violently ushered into eternity on this trumped-up charge, knowing the many things I do, and part of which I tried to tell in the *New York Age* of June 25, (and in the pamphlets I have with me) seeing that the whole race in the South was injured in the estimation of the world because of these false reports, I could no longer hold my peace, and I feel, yes, I am sure, that if it had to be done over again (provided no one else was the loser save myself) I would do and say the very same again.

The lawlessness here described is not confined to one locality. In the past ten years over a thousand colored men, women and children have been butchered, murdered and burnt in all parts of the South. The details of these horrible outrages seldom reach beyond the narrow world where they occur. Those who commit the murders write the reports, and hence these lasting blots upon the honor of a nation cause but a faint ripple on the outside world. They arouse no great indignation and call forth no adequate demand for justice. The victims were black, and the reports are so written as to make it appear that the helpless creatures deserved the fate which overtook them.

Not so with the Italian lynching of 1891. They were not black men, and three of them were not citizens of the Republic, but subjects of the King of Italy. The chief of police of New Orleans was shot and eleven Italians were arrested charged with the murder; they were tried and the jury disagreed; the good, law-abiding citizens of New Orleans thereupon took them from the jail and lynched them at high noon. A feeling of horror ran through the nation at this outrage. All Europe was amazed. The Italian government demanded thorough investigation and redress, and the Federal Government promised to give the matter the consideration which was its due. The diplomatic relations between the two countries became very much strained and for a while war talk was freely indulged. Here was a case where the power of the Federal Government to protect its own citizens and redeem its pledges to a friendly power was put to the test. When our State Department called upon the authorities of Louisiana for investigation of the crime and punishment of the criminals, the United States government was told that the crime was strictly within the authority of the State of Louisiana, and

Louisiana would attend to it. After a farcical investigation, the usual verdict in such cases was rendered: "Death at the hand of parties unknown to the jury," the same verdict which has been pronounced over the bodies of over 1,000 colored persons! Our general government has thus admitted that it has no jurisdiction over the crimes committed at New Orleans upon citizens of the country, nor upon those citizens of a friendly power to whom the general government and not the State government has pledged protection. Not only has our general government made the confession that one of the states is greater than the Union, but the general government has paid $25,000 of the people's money to the King of Italy for the lynching of those three subjects, the evil-doing of one State, over which it has no control, but for whose lawlessness the whole country must pay. The principle involved in the treaty power of the government has not yet been settled to the satisfaction of foreign powers; but the principle involved in the right of State jurisdiction in such matters, was settled long ago by the decision of the United States Supreme Court.

I beg your patience while we look at another phase of the lynching mania. We have turned heretofore to the pages of ancient and medieval history, to Roman tyranny, the Jesuitical Inquisition of Spain for the spectacle of a human being burnt to death. In the past ten years three instances, at least, have been furnished where men have literally been roasted to death to appease the fury of Southern mobs. The Texarkana instance of last year and the Paris, Texas, case of this month are the most recent as they are the most shocking and repulsive. Both were charged with crimes from which the laws provide adequate punishment. The Texarkana man, Ed Coy, was charge with assaulting a white woman. A mob pronounced him guilty, strapped him to a tree, chipped the flesh from his body, poured coal oil over him and the woman in the case set fire to him. The country looked on and in many cases applauded, because it was published that this man had violated the honor of the white woman, although he protested his innocence to the last. Judge Tourjee in the Chicago *Inter-Ocean* of recent date says investigation has shown that Ed Coy had supported this woman, (who was known to be of bad character,) and her drunken husband for over a year previous to the burning.

The Paris, Texas, burning of Henry Smith, February 1st, has exceeded all the others in its horrible details. The man was drawn through the streets on a float, as the Roman generals used to parade their trophies of war, while the scaffold ten feet high, was being built, and irons were heated in the fire.

181

He was bound on it, and red-hot irons began at his feet and slowly branded his body, while the mob howled with delight at his shrieks. Red hot irons were run down his throat and cooked his tongue; his eyes were burned out, and when he was at last unconscious, cotton seed hulls were placed under him, coal oil poured all over him, and a torch applied to the mass. When the flames burned away the ropes which bound Smith and scorched his flesh, he was brought back to sensibility—and burned and maimed and sightless as he was, he rolled off the platform and away from the fire. His half-cooked body was seized and trampled and thrown back into the flames while a mob of twenty thousand persons who came from all over the country howled with delight, and gathered up some buttons and ashes after all was over to preserve for relics. This man was charged with outraging and murdering a four-year-old white child, covering her body with brush, sleeping beside her through the night, then making his escape. If true, it was the deed of a madman, and should have been clearly proven so. The fact that no time for verification of the newspaper reports was given, is suspicious, especially when I remember that a negro was lynched in Indianola, Sharkey Co., Miss., last summer. The dispatches said it was because he had assaulted the sheriff's eight-year-old daughter. The girl was more than eighteen years old and was found by her father in this man's room, who was a servant on the place.

These incidents have been made the basis of this terrible story because they overshadow all others of a like nature in cruelty and represent the legal phases of the whole question. They could be multiplied without number—and each outrival the other in the fiendish cruelty exercised, and the frequent awful lawlessness exhibited. The following table shows the number of black men lynched from January 1, 1882, to January 1, 1892: In 1882, 52; 1883, 39; 1884, 53; 1885, 77; 1886, 73; 1887, 70; 1888, 72; 1889, 95; 1890, 100; 1891, 169. Of these 728 black men who were murdered, 269 were charged with rape, 253 with murder, 44 with robbery, 37 with incendiarism, 32 with reasons unstated (it was not necessary to have a reason), 27 with race prejudice, 13 with quarreling with white men, 10 with making threats, 7 with rioting, 5 with miscegenation, 4 with burglary. One of the men lynched in 1891 was Will Lewis, who was lynched because "he was drunk and saucy to white folks." A woman who was one of the 73 victims in 1886, was hung in Jackson, Tenn., because the white woman for whom she cooked, died suddenly of poisoning. An examination showed arsenical poisoning. A search in the cook's room found rat poison. She was thrown into jail, and when the mob had worked itself up to the lynching pitch, she was dragged out, every stitch of clothing torn from her body, and was hung in the public court house square in sight of everybody. That white woman's husband has since died, in the insane asylum, a raving maniac, and his ravings have led to the conclusion that he and not the cook, was the poisoner of his wife. A fifteen-year-old colored girl was lynched last spring, at Rayville, La., on the same charge of poisoning. A woman was also lynched at Hollendale, Miss., last spring, charged with being an accomplice in the murder of her white paramour who had abused her. These were only two of the 159 persons lynched in the South from January 1, 1892, to January 1, 1893. Over a dozen black men have been lynched already since this new year set in, and the year is not yet two months old.

It will thus be seen that neither age, sex nor decency are spared. Although the impression has gone abroad that most of the lynchings take place because of assaults on white women only one-third of the number lynched in the past ten years have been charged with that offense, to say nothing of those who were not guilty of the charge. And according to law none of them were guilty until proven so. But the unsupported word of any white person for any cause is sufficient to cause a lynching. So bold have the lynchers become, masks are laid aside, the temples of justice and strongholds of law are invaded in broad daylight and prisoners taken out and lynched, while governors of states and officers of law stand by and see the work well done.

And yet this Christian nation, the flower of the nineteenth century civilization, says it can do nothing to stop this inhuman slaughter. The general government is willingly powerless to send troops to protect the lives of its black citizens, but the state governments are free to use state troops to shoot them down like cattle, when in desperation the black men attempt to defend themselves, and then tell the world that it was necessary to put down a "race war."

Persons unfamiliar with the condition of affairs in the Southern States do not credit the truth when it is told them. They cannot conceive how such a condition of affairs prevails so near them with steam power, telegraph wires and printing presses in daily and hourly touch with the localities where such disorder reigns. In a former generation the ancestors of these same people refused to believe that slavery was the "league with death and the covenant with hell." Wm. Lloyd Garrison declared it to be, until he was thrown into a dungeon in Baltimore, until the signal lights of Nat Turner lit the dull skies of Northampton County, and until sturdy old John Brown made his attach on Harper's Ferry. When freedom of speech was martyred in the person of Elijah Lovejoy at Alton, when the liberty of free-discussion in Senate of the Nation's Congress was struck down in the person of the fearless Charles Sumner, the Nation was at last convinced that slavery was not only a monster by a tyrant. That same tyrant is at work under a new name and guise. The lawlessness which has been here described is like unto that which prevailed under slavery. *The very same forces are at work now as then.* The attempt is being made to subject to a condition of civil and industrial dependence, those whom the Constitution declares to be free men. The events which have led up to the present wide-spread lawlessness in the South can be traced to the very first year Lee's conquered veterans marched from Appomattox to their homes in the Southland. They were conquered in war, but not in spirit. They believed as firmly as ever that it was their right to rule black men and dictate to the National Government. The Knights of White Liners, and the Ku Klux Klans were composed of veterans of the Confederate army who were determined to destroy the effect of all the slave had gained by the war. They finally accomplished their purpose in 1876. The right of the Afro-American to vote and hold office remains in the Federal Constitution, but is destroyed in the constitution of the Southern states. Having destroyed the citizenship of the man, they are now trying to destroy the manhood of the citizen. All their laws are shaped to this end,—school laws, railroad car regulations, those governing labor liens on crops,—every device is adopted to make slaves of free men and rob them of their wages. Whenever a malicious law is violated in any of its parts, any farmer, any railroad conductor, or merchant can call together a posse of his neighbors and punish even with death the black man who resists and the legal authorities sanction what is done by failing to prosecute and punish the murders. The Repeal of the Civil Rights Law removed their last barrier and the black man's last bulwark and refuge. The rule of the mob is absolute.

Those who know this recital to be true, say there is nothing they can do—they cannot interfere and vainly hope by further concession to placate the imperious and dominating part of our country in which this lawlessness prevails. Because this country has been almost rent in twain by internal dissension, the other sections seem virtually to have agreed that the best way to heal the breach is to permit the taking away of civil, political, and even human rights, to stand by in silence and utter indifference while the South continues to wreak fiendish vengeance on the irresponsible cause. They pretend to believe that with all the machinery of law and government in its hands; with the jails and penitentiaries and convict farms filled with petty race criminals; with the well-known fact that no negro has ever been known to escape conviction and punishment for any crime in the South—still there are those who try to justify and condone the lynching of over a thousand black men in less than ten years—an average of one hundred a year. The public sentiment of the country, by its silence in press, pulpit and in public meetings has encouraged this state of affairs, and public sentiment is stronger than law. With all the country's disposition to condone and temporize with the South and its methods; with its many instances of sacrificing principle to prejudice for the sake of making friends and healing the breach made by the late war; of going into the lawless country with capital to build up its waste places and remaining silent in the presence of outrage and wrong—the South is as vindictive and bitter as ever. She is willing to make friends as long as she is permitted to pursue unmolested and uncensured, her course of proscription, injustice, outrage and vituperation. The malignant misrepresentation of General Butler, the uniformly indecent and abusive assault of this dead man whose only crime was a defence of his country, is a recent proof that the South has lost none of its bitterness. The *Nashville American*, one of the leading papers of one of the leading southern cities, gleefully announced editorially that " 'The Beast is dead.' Early yesterday morning, acting under the devil's orders, the angel of Death took Ben Butler and landed him in the lowest depths of hell, and we pity even the devil the possession he has secured." The men who wrote these editorials are without exception young men who know nothing of slavery and scarcely anything of the war. The bitterness and hatred have been instilled in and taught them by their parents, and they are men who make and reflect the sentiment of their section. The South spares nobody else's feelings, and it seems a queer logic that when it comes to a question of right, involving lives of citizens and the honor of the government, the South's feelings must be respected and spared.

Do you ask the remedy? A public sentiment strong against lawlessness must be aroused. Every individual can contribute to this awakening. When a sentiment against lynch law as strong, deep and mighty as that roused against slavery prevails, I have no fear of the result. It should be already established as a fact and not as a theory, that every human being must have a fair trial for his life and liberty, no matter what the charge against him. When a demand goes up from fearless and persistent reformers from press and pulpit, from industrial and moral associations that this shall be so from Maine to Texas and from ocean to ocean, a way will be found to make it so.

In deference to the few words of condemnation uttered at the M.E. General Conference last year, and by other organizations, Governors Hogg of Texas, Northern of Georgia, and Tillman of South Carolina, have issued proclamations offering rewards for the apprehension of lynchers. These rewards have never been claimed, and these governors knew they would not be when offered. In many cases they knew the ringleaders of the mobs. The prosecuting attorney of Shelby County, Tenn., wrote Governor Buchanan to offer a reward for the arrest of the lynchers of three young men murdered in Memphis. Everybody in that city and state knew well that the letter was written for the sake of effect and the governor did not even offer the reward. But the country at large deluded itself with the belief that the officials of the South and the leading citizens condemned lynching. The lynchings go on in spite of offered rewards, and in face of Governor Hogg's vigorous talk, the second man was burnt alive in his state with the utmost deliberation and publicity. Since he sent a message to the legislature the mob found and hung Henry Smith's stepson, because he refused to tell where Smith was when they were hunting for him. Public sentiment which shall denounce these crimes in season and out; public sentiment which turns capital and immigration from a section given over to lawlessness; public sentiment which insists on the punishment of criminals and lynchers by law must be aroused.

It is no wonder in my mind that the party which stood for thirty years as the champion of human liberty and human rights, the party of great moral ideas, should suffer overwhelming defeat when it has proven recreant to its professions and abandoned a position it created; when although its followers were being outraged in every sense, it was afraid to stand for the right, and appeal to the American people to sustain them in it. It put aside the question of a free ballot and fair count of every citizen and gave its voice and influence for the protection of the coat instead of the man who wore it, for the product of labor instead of the laborer; for the seal of citizenship rather than the citizen, and insisted upon the evils of free trade instead of the sacredness of free speech. I am no politician but I believe if the Republican party had met the issues squarely for human rights instead of the tariff it would have occupied a different position to-day. The voice of the people is the voice of God, and I long with all the intensity of my soul for the Garrison, Douglas, Sumner, Wittier, and Phillips who shall rouse this nation to a demand that from Greenland's icy mountains to the coral reefs of the Southern seas, mob rule shall be put down and equal and exact justice be accorded to every citizen of whatever race, who finds a home within the borders of the land of the free and the home of the brave.

Then no longer will our national hymn be sounding brass and a tinkling cymbal, but every member of this great composite nation will be a living, harmonious illustration of the words, and all can honestly and gladly join in singing:

> My country! 'tis of thee,
> Sweet land of liberty
> Of thee I sing.
> Land where our fathers died,
> Land of the Pilgrim's pride,
> From every mountain side
> Freedom does ring.

The Reason Why

The Colored American is not in the World's Columbian Exposition.

The Afro-American's Contribution to Columbian Literature

Copies sent to any address on receipt of three cents for
postage. Address MISS IDA B. WELLS, 128
S. Clark Street, Chicago, Ill., U.S.A.

TO THE PUBLIC.

This pamphlet is published by contribution from colored people of the United States. The haste necessary for the press, prevents the incorporation of interesting data showing the progress of the colored people in commercial lines.

Besides the cuts of a school and hospital it was desired to have a cut of the Capital Savings Bank, a flourishing institution conducted by the colored people of Washington, D.C. The cut, however, did not arrive in time for the press.

Twenty thousand copies of THE REASON WHY are now ready for gratuitous distribution. Applications by mail will enclose three cents for postage. All orders addressed to the undersigned will be promptly acknowledged.

Ida B. Wells
Room 9, 128 Clark St.
Chicago, Ill.

August 30, 1893.

Preface

Columbia has bidden the civilized world to join with her in celebrating the four-hundredth anniversary of the discovery of America, and the invitation has been accepted. At Jackson Park are displayed exhibits of her natural resources, and her progress in the arts and sciences, but that which would best illustrate her moral grandeur has been ignored.

The exhibit of the progress made by a race in 25 years of freedom as against 250 years of slavery, would have been the greatest tribute to the greatness and progressiveness of American institutions which could have been shown the world. The colored people of this great Republic number eight millions—more than one-tenth the whole population of the United States. They were among the earliest settlers of this continent, landing at Jamestown, Virginia in 1619 in a slave ship, before the Puritans, who landed at Plymouth in 1620. They have contributed a large share to American prosperity and civilization. The labor of one-half of this country has always been, and is still being done by them. The first credit this country had in its commerce with foreign nations was created by productions resulting from their labor. The wealth created by their industry has afforded to the white people of this country the leisure essential to their great progress in education, art, science, industry and invention.

Those visitors to the World's Columbian Exposition who know these facts, especially foreigners will naturally ask: Why are not the colored people, who constitute so large an element of the American population, and who have contributed so large a share to American greatness,—more visibly present and better represented in this World's Exposition? Why are they not taking part in this glorious celebration of the four-hundredth anniversary of the discovery of their country? Are they so dull and stupid as to feel no interest in this great event? It is to answer these questions and supply as far as possible our lack of representation at the Exposition that the Afro-American has published this volume.

CHAPTER IV

Lynch Law

BY IDA B. WELLS

"Lynch Law," says the *Virginia Lancet*, "as known by that appellation, had its origin in 1780 in a combination of citizens of Pittsylvania County, Virginia, entered into for the purpose of suppressing a trained band of horse-thieves and counterfeiters whose well concocted schemes had bidden defiance to the ordinary laws of the land, and whose success encouraged and emboldened them in their outrages upon the community. Col. Wm. Lynch drafted the constitution for this combination of citizens, and thence "Lynch Law" has ever since been the name given to the summary infliction of punishment by private and unauthorized citizens."

This law continues in force to-day in some of the oldest states of the Union, where courts of justice have long been established, whose laws are executed by white Americans. It flourishes most largely in the states which foster the convict lease system, and is brought to bear mainly, against the Negro. The first fifteen years of his freedom he was murdered by masked mobs for trying to vote. Public opinion having made lynching for that cause unpopular, a new reason is given to justify the murders of the past 15 years. The Negro was first charged with attempting to rule white people, and hundreds were murdered on that pretended supposition. He is now charged with assaulting or attempting to assault white women. This charge, as false as it is foul, robs us of the sympathy of the world and is blasting the race's good name.

The men who make these charges encourage or lead the mobs which do the lynching. They belong to the race which holds Negro life cheap, which owns the telegraph wires, newspapers, and all other communication with the outside world. They write the reports which justify lynching by painting the Negro as black as possible, and those reports are accepted by the press associations and the world without question or investigation. The mob spirit has increased with alarming frequency and violence. Over a thousand black men, women and children have been thus sacrificed the past ten years. Masks have long since been thrown aside and the lynchings of the present day take place in broad daylight. The sheriffs, police and state officials stand by and see the work well done. The coroner's jury is often formed among those who took part in the lynchings and a verdict, "Death at the hands of parties unknown to the jury" is rendered. As the number of lynchings have increased, so has the cruelty and barbarism of the lynchers. Three human beings was burned alive in civilized America during the first six months of this year (1893). Over one hundred have been lynched in this half year. They were hanged, then cut, shot and burned.

The following table published by the Chicago *Tribune* January, 1892, is submitted for thoughtful consideration.

1882, 52	Negroes murdered by mobs
1883, 39	Negroes murdered by mobs
1884, 53	Negroes murdered by mobs
1885, 77	Negroes murdered by mobs
1886, 73	Negroes murdered by mobs
1887, 70	Negroes murdered by mobs
1888, 72	Negroes murdered by mobs
1889, 95	Negroes murdered by mobs
1890, 100	Negroes murdered by mobs
1891, 169	Negroes murdered by mobs

Of this number

269	were charged with rape.
253	were charged with murder.
44	were charged with robbery.
37	were charged with incendiarism.
4	were charged with burglary.
27	were charged with race prejudice.
13	were charged with quarreling with white men.
10	were charged with making threats.
7	were charged with rioting.
5	were charged with miscegenation.
32	were charged with no reasons given.

This table shows (1) that only one-third of nearly a thousand murdered black persons have been even charged with the crime of outrage. This crime is only so punished when white women accuse black men, which accusation is never proven. The same crime committed by Negroes against Negroes, or by white men against black women is ignored even in the law courts.

(2) That nearly as many were lynched for murder as for the above crime, which the world believes is the cause of all the lynchings. The world affects to believe that *white* womanhood and childhood, surrounded by their lawful protectors, are not safe in the neighborhood of the black man, who protected and cared for them during the four years of civil war. The husband, fathers and brothers of those white women were away for four years, fighting to keep the Negro in slavery, yet not one case of assault has ever been reported!

(3) That "robbery, incendiarism, race prejudice, quarreling with white men, making threats, rioting, miscegenation (marrying a white person), and burglary," are capital offenses punishable by death when committed by a black against a white person. Nearly as many blacks were lynched for these charges (and unproven) as for the crime of rape.

(4) That for nearly fifty of these lynchings no reason is given. There is no demand for reasons, or need of concealment for what no one is held responsible. The simple word of any white person against a Negro is sufficient to get a crowd of white men to lynch a Negro. Investigation as to the guilt or innocence of the accused is never made. Under these conditions, white men have only to blacken their faces, commit crimes against the peace of the community, accuse some Negro, nor rest till he is killed by a mob. Will Lewis, an 18 year old Negro youth was lynched at Tullahoma, Tennessee, August 1891, for being "drunk and saucy to white folks."

The women of the race have not escaped the fury of the mob. In Jackson, Tennessee, in the summer of 1886, a white woman died of poisoning. Her black cook was suspected, and as a box of rat poison was found in her room, she was hurried away to jail. When the mob had worked itself into the lynching pitch, she was dragged out of jail, every stitch of clothing torn from her body, and she was hung in the public court-house square in sight of everybody. Jackson is one of the oldest towns in the State, and the State Supreme Court holds its sittings there; but no one was arrested for the deed—not even a protest was uttered. The husband of the poisoned woman has since died a raving maniac, and his ravings showed that he, and not the poor black cook, was the poisoner of his wife. A fifteen year old Negro girl was hanged in Rayville, Louisiana, in the spring of 1892, on the same charge of poisoning white persons. There was no more proof or investigation of this case than the one in Jackson. A Negro woman, Lou Stevens, was hanged from a railway bridge in Hollendale, Mississippi, in 1892. She was charged with being accessory to the murder of her white paramour, who had shamefully abused her.

In 1892 there were 241 persons lynched. The entire number is divided among the following states.

Alabama	22	Montana	4
Arkansas	25	New York	1
California	3	North Carolina	5
Florida	11	North Dakota	1
Georgia	17	Ohio	3
Idaho	8	South Carolina	5
Illinois	1	Tennessee	28
Kansas	3	Texas	15
Kentucky	9	Virginia	7
Louisiana	29	West Virginia	5
Maryland	1	Wyoming	9
Mississippi	16	Arizona Ter.	3
Missouri	6	Oklahoma	2

Of this number 160 were of Negro descent. Four of them were lynched in New York, Ohio and Kansas; the remainder were murdered in the south. Five of this number were females. The charges for which they were lynched cover a wide range. They are as follows:

Rape	46	Attempted Rape	11
Murder	58	Suspected Robbery	4
Rioting	3	Larceny	1
Race prejudice	6	Self-defense	1
No cause given	4	Insulting women	2
Incendiarism	6	Desperadoes	6
Robbery	6	Fraud	1
Assault and		Attempted murder	2
Battery	1		
	No offense stated, boy and girl	2	

In the case of the boy and girl above referred to, their father, named Hastings, was accused of the murder of a white man; his fourteen year old daughter and sixteen year old son were hanged and their bodies filled with bullets, then the father was also lynched. This was in November, 1892, at Jonesville, Louisiana.

A lynching equally as cold-blooded took place in Memphis, Tennessee, March, 1892. Three young colored men in an altercation at their place of business, fired on white men in self-defense. They were imprisoned for three days, then taken out by a mob and horribly shot to death. Thomas Moss, Will Stewart and Calvin McDowell, were energetic business men who had built up a flourishing grocery business. This business had prospered and that of a rival white grocer named Barrett had declined. Barrett let the attack on their grocery which resulted in the wounding of three white men. For this cause were three innocent men barbarously lynched, and their families left without protectors. Memphis is one of the leading cities of Tennessee, a town of seventy-five thousand inhabitants! No effort whatever was made to punish the murderers of these three men. It counted for nothing that the victims of this outrage were three of the best known young men of a population of thirty thousand colored people of Memphis. They were the officers of the company which conducted the grocery. Moss being the President, Stewart the Secretary of the Company and McDowell the Manager. Moss was in the Civil Service of the United States as letter carrier, and all three men were of splendid reputation for honesty, integrity and sobriety. But their murderers, though well known, have never been indicted, were not even troubled with a preliminary examination.

With law held in such contempt, it is not a matter of surprise that the same city—one of the so-called queen cities of the South, should again give itself over to a display of almost indescribable barbarism. This time the mob made no attempt to conceal its identity, but reveled in the contemplation of its feast of crime. Lee Walker, a colored man was the victim. Two white women complained that while driving to town, a colored man jumped from a place of concealment and dragged one of the two women from the wagon, but their screams frightened him away. Alarm was given that a Negro had made an attempted assault upon the women and bands of men set out to run him down. They shot a colored man who refused to stop when called. It was fully ten days before Walker was caught. He admitted that he did attack the women, but that he made no attempt to assault them; that he offered them no indecency whatever, of which as a matter of fact, they never accused him. He said he was hungry and he was determined to have something to eat, but after throwing one of the women out of the wagon, became frightened and ran away. He was duly arrested and taken to the Memphis jail. The fact that he was in prison and could be promptly tried and punished did not prevent the good citizens of Memphis from taking the law in their own hands, and Walker was lynched.

The *Memphis Commercial* of Sunday, July 23, contains a full account of the tragedy from which the following extracts are made.

At 12 o'clock last night, Lee Walker, who attempted to outrage Miss Mollie McCadden, last Tuesday morning, was taken from the country jail and hanged to a telegraph pole just north of the prison. All day rumors were afloat that with nightfall an attack would be made upon the jail, and as everyone anticipated that a vigorous resistance would be made, a conflict between the mob and the authorities was feared.

At 10 o'clock Capt. O'Haver, Sergt. Horan and several patrol men were on hand, but they could do nothing with the crowd. An attack by the mob was made on the door in the south wall and it yielded. Sheriff McLendon and several of his men threw themselves into the breach, but two or three of the storming party shoved by. They were seized by the police but were not subdued, the officers refraining from using their clubs. The entire mob might at first have been dispersed by ten policemen who would use their clubs, but the sheriff insisted that no violence be done.

The mob got an iron rail and used it as a battering ram against the lobby doors. Sheriff McLendon tried to stop them, and some one of the mob knocked him down with a chair. Still he counseled moderation and would not order his deputies and the police to disperse the crowd by force. The pacific policy of the sheriff impressed the mob with the idea that the officers were afraid, or at least would do them no harm, and they redoubled their efforts, urged on by a big switchman. At 12 o'clock the door of the prison was broken in with a rail.

As soon as the rapist was brought out of the door, calls were heard for a rope; then some one shouted "Burn him!" But there was no time to make a fire. When Walker got into the lobby a dozen of the men began beaten and stabbing him. He was half dragged, half carried to the corner of Front street and the alley between Sycamore and Mill, and hung to a telephone pole.

Walker made a desperate resistance. Two men entered his cell first and ordered him to come forth. He refused and they failing to drag him out, others entered. He scratched and bit his assailants, wounding several of them severely with his teeth. The mob retaliated by striking and cutting him with fists and knives. When he reached the steps leading down to the door he made another stand and was stabbed again and again. By the time he reached the lobby his power to resist was gone, and he was shoved along through the mob of yelling, cursing men and boys, who beat, spat upon and slashed the wretch-like demon. One of the leaders of the mob fell, and the crowd walked ruthlessly over him. He was badly hurt—a jawbone fractured and internal injuries inflicted. After the lynching friends took charge of him.

The mob proceeded north to Front street with the victim, stopping at Sycamore street to get a rope from a grocery. "Take him to the iron bridge on Main street," yelled several men. The men who had hold of the Negro were in a hurry to finish the job, however, and when they reached the telephone pole at the corner of Front street and the first alley north of Sycamore they stopped. A hastily improvised noose was slipped over the Negro's head and several young men mounted a pile of lumber near the pole and threw the rope over one of the iron stepping pins. The Negro was lifted up until his feet were three feet above the ground, the rope was made taut, and a corpse dangled in midair. A big fellow who helped lead the mob pulled the Negro's legs until his neck cracked. The wretch's clothes had been torn off, and, as he swung, the man who pulled his legs mutilated the corpse.

One or two knife cuts, more or less, made little difference in the appearance of the dead rapist, however, for before the rope was around his neck his skin was cut almost to ribbons. One pistol shot was fired while the corpse was hanging. A dozen voices protested against the use of firearms, and there was no more shooting. The body was permitted to hang for half an hour, then it was cut down and the rope divided among those who lingered around the scene of the tragedy. Then it was suggested that the corpse be burned, and it was done. The entire performance, from the assault on the jail to the burning of the dead Negro was witnessed by a score or so of policemen and as many deputy sheriffs, but not a hand was lifted to stop the proceedings after the jail door yielded.

As the body hung to the telegraph pole, blood steaming down from the knife wounds in his neck, his hips and lower part of his legs also slashed with knives, the crowd hurled expletives at him, swung the body so that it was dashed against the pole, and, so far from the ghastly sight proving trying to the nerves, the crowd looked on with complaisance, if not with real pleasure. The Negro died hard. The neck was not broken, as the body was drawn up without being given a fall, and death came by strangulation. For fully ten minutes after he was strung up the chest heaved occasionally and there were convulsive movements of the limbs. Finally he was pronounced dead, and a few minutes later Detective Richardson climbed on a pile of staves and cut the rope. The body fell in a ghastly heap, and the crowed laughed at the sound and crowded around the prostrate body, a few kicking the inanimate carcass.

Detective Richardson, who is also a deputy coroner, then proceeded to impanel the following jury of inquest J. S. Moody, A. C. Waldran, B. J. Childs, J. N. House, Nelson Bills, T. L. Smith, and A. Newhouse. After viewing the body the inquest was adjourned without any testimony being taken until 9 o'clock this morning. The jury will meet at the coroner's office, 51 Beale street, upstairs, and decide on a verdict. If no witnesses are forthcoming, the jury will be able to arrive at a verdict just the same, as all members of it saw the lynching. Then some one raised the cry of, "Burn him!" It was quickly taken up and soon resounded from a hundred throats. Detective Richardson for a long time, single handed, stood the crowd off. He talked and begged the men not to bring disgrace on the city by burning the body, arguing that all the vengeance possible had been wrought.

While this was going on a small crowd was busy starting a fire in [the] middle of the street. The material was handy. Some bundles of staves were taken from the adjoining lumber yard for kindling. Heavier wood was obtained from the same source, and coal oil from a neighboring grocery. Then the cries of "Burn him! Burn him!" were redoubled.

Half a dozen men seized the naked body. The crowd cheered. They marched to the fire, and giving the body a swing, it was landed in the middle of the fire. There was a cry for more wood, as the fire had begun to die owing to the long delay. Willing hands procured the wood, and it was piled up on the Negro, almost, for a time, obscuring him from view. The head was in plain view, as also were the limbs, and one arm which stood out high above the body, the elbow crooked, held in that position by a stick of wood. In a few moments the hands began to swell, then came great blisters over all the exposed parts of the body; then in places the flesh was burned away and the bones began to show through. It was a horrible sight, one which perhaps none there had ever witnessed before. It proved too much for a large part of the crowd and the majority of the mob left very shortly after the burning began.

But a large number stayed, and were not a bit set back by the sight of a human body being burned to ashes. Two or three white women, accompanied by their escorts, pushed to the front to obtain an unobstructed view, and looked on the with astonishing coolness and nonchalance. One man and woman brought a little girl, not over 12 years old, apparently their daughter, to view a scene which was calculated to drive sleep from the child's eyes for many nights, if not to produce a permanent injury to her nervous system. The comments of the crowd were varied. Some remarked on the efficacy of this style of cure for rapists, others rejoiced that men's wives and daughters were now safe from this wretch. Some laughed as the flesh cracked and blistered, and while a large number pronounced the burning of a dead body as an useless episode, not in all that throng was a word of sympathy heard for the wretch himself.

The rope that was used to hang the Negro, and also that which was used to lead him from the jail, were eagerly sought by relic hunters. They almost fought for a chance to cut off a piece of rope, and in an incredibly short time both ropes had disappeared and were scattered in the pockets of the crowd in sections of from an inch to six inches long. Others of the relic hunters remained until the ashes cooled to obtain such ghastly relics as the teeth, nails and bits of charred skin of the immolated victim of his own lust. After burning the body the mob tied a rope around the charred trunk and dragged it down Main street to the court house, where it was hanged to a center pole. The rope broke and the corpse dropped with a thud, but it was again hoisted, the charred legs barely touching the ground. The teeth were knocked out and the finger nails cut off as souvenirs. The crowd made so much noise that the police interfered. Undertaker Walsh was telephoned for, who took charge of the body and carried it to his establishment, where it will be prepared for burial in the potter's field today.

A prelude to this exhibition of 19th century barbarism was the following telegram received by the Chicago *Inter-Ocean* at 2 o'clock, Saturday afternoon—ten hours before the lynching:

"Memphis, Tenn, July 22, to *Inter-Ocean*, Chicago.

Lee Walker, colored man, accused of raping white women, in jail here, will be taken out and burned by whites to-night. Can you send Miss Ida Wells to write it up? Answer. R. M. Martin, with Public Ledger."

The *Public Ledger* is one of the oldest evening daily papers in Memphis, and this telegram shows that the intentions of the mob were well known long before they were executed. The personnel of the mob is given by the Memphis *Appeal-Avalanche*. It says, "At first it seemed as if a crowd of roughs were the principals, but as it increased in size, men in all walks of life figured as leaders, although the majority were young men."

This was the punishment meted out to a Negro, charged, not with rape, but attempted assault, and without any proof as to his guilt, for the women were not given a chance to identify him. It was only a little less horrible than the burning alive of Henry Smith, at Paris, Texas, February 1st, 1893, or that of Edward Coy, in Texarkana, Texas, February 20, 1892. Both were charged with assault on white women, and both were tied to the stake and burned while yet alive, in the presence of ten thousand persons. In the case of Coy, the white woman in the case, applied the match, even while the victim protested his innocence.

The cut which is here given is the exact reproduction of the photograph taken at the scene of the lynching at Clanton, Alabama, August, 1891. The cause for which the man was hanged is given in the words of the mob which were written on the back of the photograph, and they are also given. This photograph was sent to Judge A. W. Tourgee, of Mayville, N.Y.

In some of these cases the mob affects to believe in the Negro's guilt. The world is told that the white woman in the case identifies him, or the prisoner "confesses." But in the lynching which took place in Barnwell County, South Carolina, April 24, 1893, the mob's victim, John Peterson escaped and placed himself under Governor Tillman's protection; not only did he declare his innocence, but offered to prove an alibi, by white witnesses. Before his witnesses could be brought, the mob arrived at the Governor's mansion and demanded the prisoner. He was given up, and although the white woman in the case said he was *not* the man, he was hanged 24 hours after, and over a thousand bullets fired into his body, on the declaration that "a crime had been committed and some one had to hang for it."

The lynching of C. J. Miller, at Bardwell, Kentucky, July 7, 1893, was on the same principle. Two white girls were found murdered near their home on the morning of July 5th; their bodies were horribly mutilated. Although their father had been instrumental in the prosecution and conviction of one of his white neighbors for murder, that was not considered as a motive. A hue and cry was raised that some Negro had committed rape and murder, and a search was immediately begun for a Negro. A bloodhound was put on the trail which he followed to the river and into the boat of a fisherman named Gordon. This fisherman said he had rowed a white man, or a very fair mulatto across the river at six o'clock the evening before. The bloodhound was carried across the river, took up the trail on the Missouri side, and ran about two hundred yards to the cottage of a white farmer, and there lay down refusing to go further.

Meanwhile a strange Negro had been arrested in Sikeston, Missouri, and the authorities telegraphed that fact to Bardwell, Kentucky. The sheriff, without requisition, escorted the prisoner to the Kentucky side and turned him over to the authorities who accompanied the mob. The prisoner was a man with dark brown skin; he said his name was Miller and that he had never been in Kentucky. The fisherman who had said the man he rowed over was white, when told by the sheriff that he would be held responsible as knowing the guilty man, if he failed to identify the prisoner, said Miller was the man. The mob wished to burn him then, about ten o'clock in the morning, but Mr. Ray, the father of the girls, with great difficulty urged them to wait till three o'clock that afternoon. Confident of his innocence, Miller remained cool, while hundreds of drunken, heavily armed men raged about him. He said: "My name is C. J. Miller, I am from Springfield, Ill., my wife lives at 716 North Second Street. I am here among you to-day looked upon as one of the most brutal men before the people. I stand here surrounded by men who are excited; men who are not willing to let the law take its course, and as far as the law is concerned, I have committed no crime, and certainly no crime gross enough to deprive me of my life or liberty to walk upon the green earth. I had some rings which I bought in Bismarck of a Jew peddler. I paid him $4.50 for them. I left Springfield on the first day of July and came to Alton. From Alton I went to East St. Louis, from there to Jefferson Barracks, thence to Desota, thence to Bismarck; and to Piedmont, thence to Poplar Bluff, thence to Hoxie, to Jonesboro, and then on a local freight to Malden, from there to Sikeston. On the 5th day of July, the day I was supposed to have committed the offense, I was at Bismarck."

Failing in any way to connect Miller with the crime, the mob decided to give him the benefit of the doubt and *hang, instead of burn him*, as was first

SCENE OF LYNCHING AT CLANTON, ALABAMA, AUG 1891.

205

FAC-SIMILE OF BACK OF PHOTOGRAPH.

intended. At 3 o'clock, the hour set for the execution, the mob rushed into the jail, tore off Miller's clothing and tied his shirt around his loins. Some one said the rope was "a white man's death," and a long-chain nearly a hundred feet in length, weighing nearly a hundred pounds was placed about his neck. He was led through the street in that condition and hanged to a telegraph pole. After a photograph of him was taken as he hung, his fingers and toes cut off, and his body otherwise horribly mutilated, it was burned to ashes. This was done within twelve hours after Miller was taken prisoner. Since his death, his assertions regarding his movements have been proven true. But the mob refused the necessary time for investigation.

No more appropriate close for this chapter can be given than an editorial quotation from that most consistent and outspoken journal the *Inter-Ocean.* Commenting on the many barbarous lynchings of these two months (June and July) in its issue of August 5th, 1893, it says:

"So long as it is known that there is one charge against a man which calls for no investigation before taking his life there will be mean men seeking revenge ready to make that charge. Such a condition would soon destroy all law. It would not be tolerated for a day by white men. But the Negroes have been so patient under all their trials that men who no longer feel that they can safely shoot a Negro for attempting to exercise his right as a citizen at the polls are ready to trump up any other charge that will give them the excuse for their crime. It is a singular coincidence that as public sentiment has been hurled against political murders there has been a corresponding increase in lynchings on the charge of attacking white women. The lynchings are conducted in much the same way that they were by the Ku-Klux Klans when Negroes were mobbed for attempting to vote. The one great difference is in the cause which the mob assigns for its action.

"The real need is for a public sentiment in favor of enforcing the law and giving every man, white and black, a fair hearing before the lawful tribunals. If the plan suggested by the Charleston *News and Courier* will do this let it be done at once. No one wants to shield a fiend guilty of these brutal attacks upon unprotected women. But the Negro has as good a right to a fair trial as the white man, and the South will not be free from these horrible crimes of mob law so long as the better class of citizens try to find excuse for recognizing Judge Lynch."

CHAPTER VI

The Reason Why

BY F. L. BARNETT.

The celebration of the four hundredth anniversary of the discovery of America is acknowledged to be our greatest National enterprise of the century. From the inception of the plan down to the magnificent demonstration of the opening day, every feature has had for its ultimate attainment the highest possible degree of success. The best minds were called upon to plan a work which should not only exceed all others in the magnitude of its scope, but which should at the same time surpass all former efforts in the excellence and completion of every detail.

No such enthusiasm ever inspired the American people to any work. From the humblest citizen to the Chief Magistrate of the Nation, the one all absorbing question seemed to be, "How shall America best present its greatness to the civilized world?" Selfishness abated its conflicting interest, rivalry merged itself into emulation and envy lost its tongue. An "era of good feeling" again dawned upon the land and with "Malice towards none and charity to all" the Nation moved to the work of preparing for the greatest Exposition the world has ever known.

The enthusiasm for the work which permeated every phase of our National life, especially inspired the colored people who saw in this great event their first opportunity to show what freedom and citizenship can do for a slave. Less than thirty years have elapsed since "Grim visaged war smoothed its wrinkled front," and left as a heritage of its short but eventful existence four millions of freedmen, now the Nation's wards. In its accounting to the world, none felt more keenly than the colored men, that America could not omit from the record the status of the former slave. He hoped that the American people with their never failing protestation of justice and fair play, would gladly respond to this call, and side by side with the magnificence of its industry, intelligence and wealth give evidence of its broad charity and splendid humane impulses. He recognized that during the twenty-five years past the United States in the field of politics and economics has had a work peculiar to itself. He knew that achievements of his country would interest the world, since no event of the century occurred in the life of any nation, of greater importance than the freedom and enfranchisement of the American slaves. He was anxious to respond to this interest by showing to the world, not only what America has done for the Negro, but what the Negro has done for himself.

It had been asserted that slavery was a divine institution, that the Negro, in the economy of nature, was predestinated to be a slave, and that he was so indolent and ignorant that his highest good could be attained only under the influence of a white master. The Negro wanted to show by his years of freedom, that his industry did not need the incentive of a master's whip, and that his intelligence was capable of successful self direction. It had been said that he was improvident and devoid of ambition, and that he would gradually lapse into barbarism. He wanted to show that in a quarter of a century, he had accumulated property to the value of two hundred million dollars, that his ambition had led him into every field of industry, and that capable men of his race had served his Nation well in the legislatures of a dozen states in both Houses of the Nation's Congress and as National Representatives abroad.

It had been said that the Negro was fit only for a "hewer of wood and a drawer of water" and that he could not be educated. In answer to this, the Negro wanted to show, that in a quarter of a century after emancipation, nearly one half of the race had learned to read and that in schools of higher education colored scholars had repeatedly won highest honors in contest with scholars of the dominant race. In a word, the Negro wanted to avail himself of the opportunity to prove to his friends that their years of unselfish work for him, as a slave, had been appreciated by him in his freedom, and that he was making every possible effort to gratify the sanguine expectations of his friends and incidentally to confound the wisdom of those who justified his oppression on the ground that God cursed Ham.

But herein he was doomed to be disappointed. In the very first steps of the Exposition work, the colored people were given to understand that they were *persona non grata*, so far as any participation in the directive energy of the Exposition was concerned. In order to Nationalize the Exposition the

United States Congress by legislation in its behalf, provided for the appointment of a National Board of Commissioners, which Board should be constituted by the appointment of two Commissioners from each state, one from each territory and ten Commissioners at large. It was further provided that one alternate should be named for every commissioner. These appointments were made by the President of the United States (Benjamin Harrison) who thus had the appointment of a Board of National Commissioners numbering two hundred and eight members to represent the sixty millions of our population.

The colored people of our country number over seven and one half millions. In two of the states of the south the colored population exceeds the white population, and so far as the productive energy of the southern states is concerned, almost the entire output of agricultural products is the work of Negro labor. The colored people therefore thought that their numbers, more than one eighth of the entire population of the country, would entitle them to one Commissioner at Large, and that their importance as a labor factor in the South would secure for them fair representation among the Commissioners appointed from the states. But it was not so. President Harrison appointed his entire list of Commissioners, and their alternates, and refused to name one colored man. The President willfully ignored the millions of colored people in the country and thus established a precedent which remained inviolate through the entire term of Exposition work.

Finding themselves with no representation on the National Board, a number of applications were made to the direct management of the Exposition through the Director General, Hon. George S. Davis, for the appointment of some capable colored person, in some representative capacity to the end that the intelligent and enthusiastic co-operation of the colored people might be secured. The Director General declined to make any such appointment.

Prominent colored men suggested the establishment of a Department of Colored Exhibits in the Exposition. It was urged by them that nothing would so well evidence the progress of the colored people as an exhibit made entirely of the products of skill and industry of the race since emancipation. This suggestion was considered by the National Directors and it was decided that no separate exhibit for the colored people be permitted.

Recognizing that there was not much hope for successful work under authority of the Board of Directors, there was still a hope that in the work undertaken by the women there would be sympathy and a helpful influence for colored women. Unprecedented importance had been given to woman's work by the Congress of the United States, which in its World's Fair legislation provided for a Board of Lady Managers and set aside for their exclusive use sufficient money to make a most creditable exhibit of women's work. It was hoped that this Board would take especial interest in helping all aspiring womankind to show their best possible evidence of thrift and intelligent labor. It was therefore decided by colored women in various parts of the country to secure, if possible, means for making an exhibit that would partly compensate for the failure made in the attempt with the National Board of Directors. An idea of the plan of work suggested by these colored organizations can be had from one petition, addressed to the Lady Managers, from Chicago. It is as follows:

> *To the Board of Lady Managers,*
> *World's Columbian Exposition,*
> *Chicago, Illinois.*

The Women's Columbian Auxiliary Association desires to bring its work properly before your honorable body, with a few suggestions which we hope may be of assistance in promoting the cause of woman's work among our colored citizens.

The above organization is working under a charter granted by the State of Illinois, and has perfected plans upon which it is working with the most gratifying success. Our membership in Chicago numbers nearly one hundred active, earnest workers, who have at heart the success of the women's department, and a creditable display of the skill and energy of the colored people.

Besides our city organization, the work has had the endorsement of two National Orders of a benevolent nature, and its work is being especially urged in that direction.

Much more will be done when we find that our plan of work meets the approval and has the endorsement of the Board of Lady Managers. To that end we desire to be accorded an audience with this body, or some representative of this body, who will give our work the consideration we believe it merits.

In the prosecution of our work, we have consulted some of the best minds of our race. We do not in any way suggest a separate department in the coming exposition, for colored people, but we do believe there is a field of labor among the colored people, in which members of the race can serve with special effectiveness and success.

Our ideas and plans in this connection are carefully outlined in a published prospectus for use of societies co-operating with us. We enclose a copy for your consideration.

Hoping to render you a service, in which we will gladly engage, We remain, respectfully,

Women's Columbian Auxiliary Association,
Mrs. R.D. Boone, Pres.

Prior to this movement, another society, by name the Woman's Columbian Association had filed a similar petition, through Mrs. Lettie Trent, its president. The two associations suggested work on nearly the same general plan, and contemplated work through various channels, such as secret societies, private schools and church organizations, which particularly reach the colored people. Naturally the two organizations had different leaders whom they endorsed and supported for the work, with more or less earnestness, fidelity and sometimes acerbity of temper, each of course, desiring its plans to succeed through the success of its representative. But both failed as the Board of Lady Managers eagerly availed itself of the opportunity to say that the colored people were divided into factions and it would be impolitic to recognize either faction.

The promptness which marked their assumption of this position, is fairly indicative of the hypocrisy and duplicity which the colored people met in every effort made. In refusing to give the colored people any representation whatever, upon the ground that they were not united, the Board made an excuse which was wholly unworthy of itself. The failure of the few colored people of Chicago to agree, could not by any kind of logic, justify the Board in ignoring the seven and one half millions outside of the city. A number of colored women in other sections of the country were highly endorsed and commended to the Board as capable, earnest and efficient representatives of the race. Because the few people here in Chicago did not agree upon the same person for their support the Board of Lady Managers ignored the plea of the entire race.

If in a reflective mood, the Lady Managers had read the minutes of their own organization, punctured as they are with points of order, cries of "shame," "shame," enlivened frequently with hysterics and bathed at times in tears, their sisterly love and sweetness of temper, marking a rose wreathed way through the law courts into Congress itself, possibly they would have been better able to realize that all people are liable to differ and that colored people are not alone in their failure to agree upon the same person, to do a designated work.

But they never thought of such a possibility at that time. They dismissed the entire matter by referring the petitions of the colored people to the various State Boards.

With but a single exception the State Boards refused to take any action calculated to enlist the interest of the colored people. The State of New York, the exception referred to, appointed a capable and worthy colored woman, Miss Imogene Howard, as a member of the Board of Lady Managers. In the short period of her service she worked earnestly in behalf of her race, but met only with indifferent success.

The relegation of the interests of the colored people to the State Boards plainly proved that the Board of Lady Managers did not desire to have anything to do with the colored people. Still something was needed to be done and thousands of capable and conscientious colored men and women were waiting patiently for some suggestion of the work they might attempt to do. No suggestions came however, and renewed efforts were exerted.

Miss Hallie Q. Brown, a teacher of Wilberforce College, Ohio, concluded to secure, if possible, from the several Lady Managers an expression of their views upon the subject of enlisting the interest and co-operation of the colored people in the formative work of the Fair. In pursuance of her plans, Miss Brown sent a letter of inquiry to each member of the Board of Lady Managers asking the personal consideration of her plan of appointing some colored person who would make this work a special care. The letter of Miss Brown reads as follows:

Chicago, Illinois, April 8, 1892.

Mrs._____

Lady Manager of the Columbian Exposition for _____
Dear Madam:

It seems to be a settled conviction among the colored people, that no adequate opportunity is to be offered them for proper representation in the World's Fair. A circular recently issued and widely distributed makes that charge direct. That there is an element of truth in it seems apparent, since neither recognition has been granted, nor opportunity offered.

And further it is shown that the intercourse between the two races, particularly in the southern states, is so limited that the interchange of ideas is hardly seriously considered. If, therefore, the object of the Woman's Department of the Columbian Exposition is to present to the world the industrial and educational progress of the breadwinners—the wage women—how immeasurably incomplete will that work be without the exhibit of the thousands of the colored women of this country.

The question naturally arises, who is awakening an interest among our colored women, especially in the South where the masses are, and how many auxiliaries have been formed through which they may be advised of the movement that is intended to be so comprehensive and all inclusive? Considering the peculiar relation that the Negro sustains in this country, is it less than fair to request for him a special representation?

Presuming that such action would be had, several colored men and women, including the writer, have endorsements of unquestionable strength from all classes of American citizens. These endorsements are on file in the President's office of the Woman's Commission in this city.

It is urged at headquarters that the Lady Managers would seriously object to the appointment of a special representative to canvass the various states. Permit me to emphasize the fact, that this matter is in earnest discussion, among the representatives of eight millions of the population of the United States.

I address this circular to you, kindly requesting your opinion upon the suggestions made herein, and solicit a reply at your earliest convenience.

Yours respectfully,

4440 Langley Ave.,   (Miss) Hallie Q. Brown
Chicago, Illinois.

The inquiry of Miss Brown received answers from less than one-half of the Lady Mangers and in not more than three cases was any endorsement given to her suggestion to appoint some colored person to give especial attention to the work of securing exhibits from the colored people. In most of the answers received, the writers said that the appointment of a colored person could not be made without interfering with the work already assigned to the respective states. Several members excused the action of the Exposition Managers in refusing representation to the colored people among the promoters of the Exposition, by stating that the colored people themselves were divided upon the character of the exhibit which should be made; some declaring in favor of a separate colored exhibit, and others opposing it. Great emphasis was placed upon this statement and the further specious argument that colored people are citizens, and that it was against the policy of the Exposition to draw any distinction between different classes of American citizens. These arguments upon the first thought appear reasonable, but a slight consideration shows that they were made only as a subterfuge to compass the discrimination already planned.

The majority of the Lady Managers ignored the letters of inquiry entirely, while some were frank enough to speak their pronounced opposition to any plan which would bring them in contact with a colored representative and to emphasize the opposition by a declaration that they would resign in case such an appointment was made.

So far as the character of the exhibit was concerned there was an honest difference of opinion among both white and colored people, as to the manner of making the exhibit, some declaring in favor of a separate exhibit to be composed exclusively of products of the skill, ingenuity and industry of the colored people, others quite as earnestly opposed to any colored line exhibit and insisted upon placing exhibits furnished by colored people in the classes to which they respectively belonged.

In support of the plan for the separate exhibit it was urged:

First: That the exhibits by the colored people would be so few in number, that when installed in their places as classified they would be almost unnoticed and as there would be no way of ascertaining that they were products of our skill and industry, the race would lose the credit of their production.

Second: That while the exhibits made by colored people would not compare favorably with the general exhibit of the white people, still in number, variety and excellence they would give most gratifying evidence of the capacity, industry and ambition of the race, showing what it had accomplished in the first third of a century of freedom.

The opponents to the separate exhibit, both colored and white, based their opposition upon the broad principle that merit knows no color line, and that colored people should be willing to be measured by the same rule which was applied to other people. The colored people asked that no special grade of merit be established for them; but held that the race was willing to accept whatever place was accorded it by virtue of the measure of merit shown. They asked that colored persons specially interested in the cause be appointed to promote the work among colored people, but that the exhibits when received, should be impartially judged and assigned to their places as classified.

But this was a question of method rather than action. The colored people were untiring in their demands for some responsible work, and were perfectly willing to allow the arrangement of details with the exposition management. But they earnestly maintained that whether the colored exhibits be installed in bulk or placed as properly classified, there was no doubt that the existing condition of public sentiment warranted the active assistance of colored representatives in promoting the work among colored people.

The fact patent to all thinking people that, in the first steps of exposition work they had been purposely ignored together with the equally apparent fact that the various State Boards, with one exception, had emphasized this slight by refusing to give any representation whatever to colored people, gave good ground for the belief that colored people were not wanted in any responsible connection with the Exposition work. But the demands for a separate exhibit and for the appointment of colored persons to assist in promoting the work of the exposition were all fruitless. They were met always with the statement that the exposition authorities had considered it best to act entirely without reference to any color line, that all citizens of all classes stood on the same plane, that no distinctions should be drawn between any classes and special work extended to none. This position which has every indication of justice would still be inequitable even if fairly maintained.

It may have been strictly just but it was certainly not equitable to compel the colored people who have been emancipated but thirty years to stand on the same plane with their masters who for two and one half centuries had enslaved them. Had the colored people of America enjoyed equal opportunities with the white people they would have asked in the Exposition no favor of any kind. But when it is remembered that only a few years ago the statutes of many of the states made it a misdemeanor to teach a colored person to read, it must be conceded that in no competition with the white man is it possible for the former slave to stand upon the same plane.

But the position taken was not only inequitable but was a false and shallow pretense. If no distinctions were to be drawn in favor of the colored man, then it was only fair that none should be drawn against him. Yet the whole history of the exposition is a record of discrimination against the colored people. President Harrison began it when with the appointment of more than two hundred and eight national commissioners and their alternates to represent the several states, he refused to appoint a single representative of seven and one half millions of colored people, more than one-eighth of the entire population of the United States.

When it was ascertained that the seals and glaciers of Alaska had been overlooked in the appointment of National Commissioners, it was a comparatively easy task for the President to manipulate matters so that he could give that far away land a representative on the National Board. It was entirely different, however, with the colored people. When the fact was laid before the President that they had been ignored and were entirely unrepresented, he found his hands tied and the best he was ever willing to do thereafter to remedy the matter, was to appoint a colored man, Mr. Hale G. Parker, as an alternate commissioner from the State of Missouri.

In the appointments made on the Board of Lady Managers the discrimination was equally apparent, not a single colored woman being named on the Board proper and only one named on the entire list of members of the State Boards of managements.

Taking these precedents for aid and comfort, the management of the Exposition found it easy to refuse to employ colored men or women in places of honor or emolument. Hundreds of clerks were necessary to carry on the work of preparation for the Exposition but all applications by colored men or women for clerical positions were politely received and tenderly pigeon-holed. Of the entire clerical force of the Exposition, only one colored man, Mr. J. E. Johnson ever received a clerical appointment. A clerical position was filled for a few months by Mrs. A. M. Curtis and soon after her resignation a similar place was filled by Mrs. Fannie B. Williams who was appointed only two months before the Exposition opened. These three clerical places constitute the best representation accorded the colored people during the entire Exposition period. This in spite of the fact that the propriety and justice of their employment was freely recognized and admitted. By vote of the Board of Reference and Control, the Director General was requested to report on the expediency of giving colored people a place in the great work. The minutes of the above Board show, that after a clear and forceful presentation of the claims of the colored people by Mrs. F. B. Williams the following resolution was adopted:

"*Resolved*: That the Director General be requested to lay before the Local Directory the expediency of having the department of Publicity and Promotion employ a colored man and a colored woman to promote the interests of the World's Columbian Exposition throughout the United States."

Whether the Board really meant anything by the resolution or not it is difficult to say, but certain it is that nothing was done. The expediency of the appointments was not questioned, but claim was made that there was not money to pay for the service. In fact a standing reply to suggestions for the employment of colored persons was the assertion that the Exposition had no fund which it could use for that purpose. It had no funds to meet the expenses contemplated in the suggestion made in the above quoted resolution of the Board of Control, yet it had actually and wantonly wasted nearly ninety thousand dollars in the construction of floats for use on opening day; which floats were discarded before they were finished and never used at all, their entire cost being an absolute and total loss of the entire sum of money used in their construction. The management readily found ninety thousand dollars to waste in this child's play, but could not find a fraction of that sum to meet a demand which was just, urgent and plainly apparent.

A final effort was made to secure the service of good statistician whose duty it would be to prepare a statistical exhibit of the Negro since emancipation. The work mentioned could be done by colored people and would have contributed helpfully to the effort of proving our ability in all lines of thought and action. The appropriation asked for was only two thousand dollars, but the Board refused to allow that sum, and the plan was abandoned.

This unwritten law of discrimination was felt not only in higher places but its effects were seen in the employment of persons of positions of no more importance than the Columbian Guards. These were selected for duty on the Exposition grounds. The Commander, Col. Rice, requested a blank to be used in making applications, the questions asked being as carefully framed as those found upon the application blanks of an insurance company. It was noted that all colored applicants had some defect which disqualified them for service. This was more marked when so many colored persons were rejected who appeared to be eligible from every point of view, and from the further fact that many of the guards who were chosen clearly failed to meet the printed requirements, and a number of them could scarcely speak English. The rumor soon ripened into conviction, and it was generally understood that so far as the Columbian Guards were concerned, "No Negro need apply."

A sample of the treatment accorded colored applicants will serve to show that discrimination was undoubtedly practiced and was plainly intentional. The applicant in this case was Wm. J. Crawford of Chicago. He filled out his application blank and was soon ordered for examination. He reported and the examiner deliberately falsified the record and returned his report rejecting the applicant upon the ground that his chest measurement was only thirty-four inches (the requirement being thirty-six inches), a report which he knew to be false. This action of the medical examiner was so clearly unjust that the applicant concluded to appeal to the Commander for a redress of the wrong. He prepared his appeal of which the following is a copy.

Chicago, Ill., March 5, 1893.

Col. Edward Rice,
    Commander Columbian Guards,
    World's Columbian Exposition.

Dear Sir:

I desire to ask your consideration of a matter, which I think belongs to your department of the World's Fair. On the first day of the present month, I made an application for appointment on the force of guards for the exposition. My application was made on a blank furnished by Capt. Farnham, and I was ordered for examination.

The physician who examined me gave my height five feet eleven and one eighth inches; my weight one hundred and sixty-five and one half pounds, which was declared satisfactory. Upon examination for chest measurement, however, the examiner said that I measured thirty-four inches. He then said that this was too small and that I could not be accepted. He wrote on my application—"Rejected," adding "not on account of color, but because chest measurement not thirty six inches."

I knew at the time that his mark was incorrect and as soon as I left the grounds, went to a reputable physician, who gave me a certificate of measurement of thirty-six and one half inches. As I was rejected because the examiner made my measurement thirty-four inches, I respectfully appeal to you for a reversal of that finding and an appointment upon the force of the Columbian Guards.

Obediently Yours,
W.J. Crawford.

This appeal was sent by registered letter to Commander Rice, and was receipted for by G. N. Farnham, his chief assistant. But the Commander gave no reply whatever to the appeal. Still determined to have a hearing, the applicant, after waiting ten days for an answer made an appeal to the President of the Board of Control. This second appeal was as follows:

Chicago, Ill., March 15, 1893.

To the President of the
    Board of Control of the
        World's Columbian Exposition,
Chicago, Illinois.

Dear Sir:

I have the honor to appeal to you for a consideration of my rejected application for a position as one of the Columbian Guards of the World's Columbian Exposition.

I have been a resident of Chicago for seven years and on the first day of March, 1893, I made a formal application and was subjected to the required examination by the medical examiner. At the conclusion of my examination, I was told by the examining surgeon that I had met every requirement and was in every way qualified except in the single point of chest measurement; the rule of the department requires a chest measurement of thirty-six inches, but the said medical examiner stated in his certificate of examination that my chest measurement was less than thirty-five inches, and further marked on said certificate the gratuitous information "not rejected on account of color."

I appeal to your honorable board for a reopening of my application for appointment as a Columbian Guard on the following grounds:

I am satisfied that my application was rejected solely on account of my color. I have been especially convinced that it is a case of mean and unjust discrimination against me, because, after leaving the World's Fair Grounds and the regular medical examiner in the employment of the Columbian Guard authority, I went to no less eminent physician than Dr. S. N. Davis of this city, and requested him to give me a careful and impartial examination as to my chest. I would respectfully refer you to Dr. Davis' certificate attached hereto. It will be seen that the finding of Dr. Davis' examination is in direct contradiction to the alleged measurement of the medical examiner at the World's Fair Grounds.

Although the said medical examiner at the World's Fair grounds laboriously stretched his tape measure and compressed my chest in every possible way, so as to force a short measurement, and in other ways aroused my suspicions as to his willingness to give me a fair examination, I did not feel justified in questioning his findings and appealing to you, until I had obtained an impartial examination from a physician, who could have no interest in me and my plans.

A further reason for this appeal to you is to call your attention to the fact that it is the settled policy on the part of the authorities in charge to make it impossible for any American Negro, however well qualified, to become a member of the force of Columbian Guards. It is a significant fact that every colored applicant, thus far, has been rejected for causes more or less trivial, or, as in my case, false.

I would respectfully state that before submitting this appeal to your Honorable Board, I duly applied to Colonel Rice, Commander in Chief of said Columbian Guards. Attached hereto please find a copy of the letter sent to Colonel Rice, but from which I received no reply. I also appealed to the Council of Administration and Control for a consideration of my claim, but I was refused a hearing.

It is believed by many of our people that this fixed policy of discrimination against us, is without the sanction and knowledge of the Board of Control, and as I have no means of redress from the injustice done me, as above set forth, I have determined to lay the matter before you, hoping that my appeal will be justly considered, and that I will be given a chance to win the position for which I have made due application, if I am qualified therefor.

Obediently yours,

No. 400 27th street.   W. J. Crawford.

It was merely an indication of the plan and policy of the Exposition Management that no notice whatever was taken of the respectful but, at the same time, convincing appeal made by Mr. Crawford. It has been determined that no colored man should be employed on the force of the Columbian Guards and that determination was not to be varied. The fact that one colored man had succeeded in discovering the contemptible duplicity and falsehood used to compass that purpose, made no difference in the plan, nor affected in any way its promoters. Theoretically open to all Americans, the Exposition practically is, literally and figuratively, a "White City," in the building of which the Colored American was allowed no helping hand, and in this glorious success he has no share.

Recognizing that the spirit and purpose of the local management of the Exposition were inimical to the interests of the colored people, leaders of the race made effective appeals to Congress and asked that the general government reserve out of its appropriation to the Exposition a sum of money to be used in making a Statistical Exhibit which should show the moral, educational and financial growth of the American Negro since his emancipation. The colored people recognized that the discrimination which prevented their active participation in the Exposition work could not be remedied, but they hoped that the Nation would take enough interest in its former slaves to spend a few thousand dollars in making an exhibit which would tell to the world what they as freedmen had done.

But here they were disappointed again. Congress refused to act. One appropriation bill passed the Senate and at another time an appropriation was made by the House of Representatives, but at no time did both bodies agree upon the same measure. The help that was expected from Congress failed and having failed in every other quarter to secure some worthy place in this great National undertaking the Colored American recognized the inevitable and accepted with the best grace possible one of the severest disappointments which has fallen to his lot.

In consideration of the color proof character of the Exposition Management it was the refinement of irony to set aside August 25th to be observed as "Colored People's Day." In this wonderful hive of National industry, representing an outlay of thirty million dollars, and numbering its employees by the thousands, only two colored persons could be found whose occupations were of a higher grade than that of janitor, laborer, and porter, and these two only clerkships. Only as a menial is the Colored American to be seen—the Nation's deliberate and cowardly tribute to the Southern demand "to keep the Negro in his place." And yet in spite of this fact, the Colored Americans were expected to observe a designated day as their day—to rejoice and be exceeding glad. A few accepted the invitation, the majority did not. Those who were present, by the faultless character of their service showed the splendid talent which prejudice had led the

Exposition to ignore; those who remained away evinced a spirit of manly independence which could but command respect. They saw no reason for rejoicing when they knew that America could find no representative place for a colored man, in all its work, and that it remained for the Republic of Hayti to give the only acceptable representation enjoyed by us in the Fair. That republic chose Frederick Douglass to represent it as Commissioner through which courtesy the Colored American received from a foreign power the place denied to him at home.

That we are not alone in the conviction that our country should have accorded an equal measure of recognition to one of its greatest citizens is evidenced by the following editorial in the Chicago *Herald* of Sunday, August 27th, 1893: "That a colored man, Douglass, Langston or Bruce, should have been named a National Commissioner, will be admitted by fair-minded Americans of all political parties. That President Harrision should have omitted to name one of them is apparently inexplicable. That the race has made extraordinary progress will also be conceded."

The World's Columbian Exposition draws to a close and that which has been done is without remedy. The colored people have no vindictiveness actuating them in this presentation of their side of this question, our only desire being to tell the reason why we have no part nor lot in the Exposition. Our failure to be represented is not of our own working and we can only hope that the spirit of freedom and fair play of which some Americans so loudly boast, will so inspire the Nation that in another great National endeavor the Colored American shall not plead for a place in vain.

Two Christmas Days: A Holiday Story

"Going out to Wilson's this afternoon, George?"

"For what," asks George.

"To the croquet party. You surely haven't forgotten it."

"By George, Harry, I just had. It's too confoundedly hot to do what you have to, much less play croquet. But Mrs. Wilson would never forgive me if I didn't go. This affair is in honor of her guest, I believe; Miss ——— what's her name?"

"Minton. Well if you are going, it's time you're getting a move on you. Its past five now," said Harry, rising.

"Guess I'll have to, as I haven't even called on the young lady yet. It's too bad to have to play the agreeable when you don't want to. Wait a minute, I'll go up with you." And George Harris leisurely put away his law papers, and was soon on the way with his friend, Harry Brown.

Arriving at the home of Mrs. Wilson they found the spacious green lawn alive with young girls in cool summer dresses, who with obliging partners were playing croquet.

Mrs. Wilson and her son, Clarence, rallied the young men on being late and introduced Harris, who knew of but had never met Miss Minton until now.

"What do you think of the visitor, George?" asked his friend as they rested on one of the rustic settees watching the players.

"Don't know," drawled George. "You can't tell much about girls at first sight. One thing she doesn't seem to put on airs. I take it also, that she goes in to win in everything she attempts. She is the only one of all those

Originally published in the *A.M.E. Zion Church Quarterly*, January 1894, pp. 129-140.

girls who cares a pin about being beaten. See how hard she works in this heat, and with what precision she makes her shots. The other girls are so taken up flirting with their partners they neither know nor care when their turn comes to play."

"Ah, George, at your old professional habit of dissecting every character you meet in that cold analytic fashion. Don't you see anything to admire in the woman?"

"Yes, I see she is charmingly and becomingly dressed—a thing so few girls have the good taste to do."

Harry laughed. "You're a hard critic, my fastidious friend. You'll meet your match yet some day, old fellow; then you'll rave, too, over your lady's charms without stopping to analyze her."

The conversation was ended, as with a peal of laughter Miss Minton and her partner won. Flushed with excitement and victory she seated herself in the place vacated by Harry Brown, who went to take a hand in another game just beginning. She and George exchanged a few words, and as she rested he looked at her more closely. She was a tall, slender, graceful girl, olive complexion, black hair and eyes. She was not strictly beautiful, but the features were regular and there was a nobility of expression which betokened the thinker; a clear open countenance, with wonderful eyes, a sweet yet dignified manner. Her dress of pink muslin fitted her figure to perfection and suited her complexion admirably. She was twenty-three years old and was a college graduate from one of the American Missionary Colleges in the South. She has made so enviable a record that she was appointed teacher in her Alma Mater—the first Afro-American teacher they had ever employed. She was in high spirits over her victory and her sallies of wit interested the young man beside her; he mentally decided to see more of her.

Meanwhile twilight had fallen and it was too dark to see the wickets. Mrs. Wilson called and the guests gathered round the dining room table, a laughing, happy group. While they discussed melons and ices, they chatted of everything in general and nothing in particular, as young folks will.

"So you have really decided to go to Oklahoma, Will," asked Mrs. Wilson, during a lull in the gay badinage.

"Yes, ma'am," replied Will Bramlette, a tall brown-skinned young fellow of twenty-five. "I leave next week."

"But I can't see what you want to go away out there for; you are doing well here at your trade. Mr. Wilson says you have all the work you can do."

"Yes, but I want to do better. I want to live where I can have something, and a man is as free as anybody else, once in my life. If Uncle Sam will give me one hundred and sixty acres of land to go and get it, I'm going after it sure."

"Oklahoma will never see me," laughed one of the young men. "Nor me," echoed another.

"I admire your spirit and determination, Mr. Bramlette," said Emily Minton, speaking very quickly.

"What, you an Oklahoma convert too?" chorused a number of voices.

"Yes, I am. I have long thought our young men have not enough ambition and get-up, or they couldn't be content to drift along here in the South the way things are going every day. For the last half dozen years, ever since I've been able to see clearly the causes of so much race trouble, everybody has said education would solve the problem. I have watched the young men who have left school when I was a pupil and since I became a teacher. They gave signs of the brightest promise, but the majority soon fall into a soft easy position which affords them a living and there they vegetate, until they lose all the manhood they ever possessed. If I could have my way with them, I'd transplant them all to Oklahoma or some place else where they would have to work and that would develop character and strengthen manhood in them."

"Thank you, Miss Emily, for your endorsement," said Will Bramlette. "It has given me a better determination, as the Methodist sisters say."

"Are you not rather hard on the young men, Miss Minton?" asked George Harris.

"I think not," answered she; "the race needs their services so much. Indeed, I think the most discouraging feature of it all, is the seeming contentment under conditions which ought to stir all the manhood's blood in them. So whenever I do meet one who thinks as I do and is ambitious to be somebody, I cannot help wishing him God-speed. If I were a man, I would join him only too quick."

"You might join some 'him' anyway Emily," said one of the young girls.

"Yes, indeed, and be far more acceptable as a companion—a helpmeet," Miss Wilson teasingly rejoined.

Everybody laughed, and even Emily, who had grown very earnest, was forced to smile at this clever turning of the tables on herself.

The party broke up, but George and Harry lingered in the moonlight on the veranda talking to the homefolks. George felt strangely attracted to this

227

girl, and walking over to where she sat, he said, watching her out of the corners of his eyes: "Bramlette was delighted with your approval of his course, Miss Minton. You have made a conquest of him already. That's the way with you girls—you have no mercy on a fellow's heart. How many scalps have you dangling at your belt already?"

Emily turned on him with a grieved, reproachful expression: "You do not mean to say you think me a flirt, Mr. Harris?"

"No, indeed," said he, quickly dropping his jesting tone, "I think you are too noble a girl for that." George spoke so gravely and respectfully that Emily knew he meant it.

"Thank you," she said simply. He bade them good-night and left shortly after.

"She is a remarkable girl," mused George as he went home. He called the next afternoon and the next. Very soon it so happened that there was no day after the Sun-god hid his face, that George Harris did not "call by" on his way home, although it was several blocks out of his way. Sometimes it was a proposed walk, oftener a drive, a few flowers, or a few minutes conversation. Mrs. Wilson's niece was a brilliant musician, and George had a fine baritone voice, and they made splendid music these long summer evenings. Emily had the soul of a musician, with none of a musician's talent.

Those evenings with the moonlight, the music and fragrance of the rose, the honeysuckle and the night-blooming jesamine, seemed the happiest of her life. She had become interested in this man as in no other, and she had met many in her short life. But this man with courtly manners, general culture and quiet, yet masterful and self-contained bearing, was unlike any she had ever met. If a day passed without his coming, she was conscious of something lacking in its pleasure. Given to self-examination, she felt that she was falling in love, and she was sure the interest was mutual. She mentally determined before yielding herself to the fascinations of her feelings, to know more about him. The opportunity came soon after.

While down town shopping one hot August day, they passed Harris's office. Mrs. Wilson teasingly asked Emily if she would like to call on him. She consented and they stepped into the office only to find him absent. The room was such a disagreeable surprise to her, that Emily was glad Harris was absent. It was a dingy apartment, with old and rickety furniture, and the atmosphere was musty with the fumes of tobacco smoke. There was absolutely nothing to harmonize with the careful, cleanly well-dressed man she had known for nearly two months. She gave no sign but was glad when Mrs. Wilson said they would not wait.

At tea-table that evening, the conversation turned on Harris, and Emily inquired of Mr. Wilson how long the young lawyer had been practicing, and was told about five years.

"Do our people patronize him very well? You know it seems our failing never to have the same confidence in our own ability that we have in the white man's," said she.

"I don't think it's our people's fault this time, Miss Emily. We've all known George every since he was a baby and were proud of his record at school. When he came home and opened an office, I sent him several cases and gave him some of my own work to do. He attended to them all right enough, but he didn't get out and 'hustle' for other work. He's either too proud to do it, or lacks energy, one or the other. We all feel that he's no woman that we should be hunting work for. He gets work enough to do around these magistrate's courts and now and then a case in the Criminal Court, and manages to make a living out of these petty cases, but he's never had a case of any special merit that has demonstrated his real ability, like that young Johnson of your town."

The conversation drifted to other topics, but Emily thought she could understand some things more clearly than before.

A day or so after, in a talk with Harris about mutual friends who had gone out into the world, he was aroused at the trenchant criticism. "How merciless you are toward us poor fellows, Miss Emily," he exclaimed.

"Yes, indeed," she quickly replied. "I have no patience with dawdlers."

"But you find fault with all. Are there none who merit your ladyship's favor?"

"If not, it is because they do not measure up to their highest possibilities," said she.

"No? Well you shouldn't expect them to do so at a bound."

"But so few seem to be even striving in that direction, Mr. Harris. That's the discouraging feature. Even Mr. Harris, who might achieve splendid success in his profession—and of course any distinction he might win, would redound to the credit of his race—does not seem ambitious to do so." She spoke gently yet regretfully.

George was silenced for the moment, but rallying immediately said: "Give us a picture of your model man, Miss Emily?"

"But where would I find a model to sit for the picture?" asked Emily playfully.

"Take me," said George, with double meaning in his tone and a tender light in his eyes.

"You?" asked Emily, striving hard to seem unconscious; "you wouldn't do at all—there's one great objection."

"What is it, Emily?" eagerly asked George. "Tell me please."

"Not to-night," said she, shaking her head, "some other time."

George's musings as he walked home that night were not of the most pleasant kind. It was not the first time since he knew this girl that he had left her presence with a faint felling of discontent with himself and surroundings. He wondered what the particular flaw this keen-eyed young woman had discovered in his make-up. The thought haunted him all next day and when wending his way homeward to dinner, he spied her in a hammock in the yard. With the liberty of a frequent visitor, he went in, and after a few words, asked her what was the fault she had found in him. She laughed musically, yet there was a tremor in her voice as she rallied him on his "woman's curiosity." He persisted, telling her he had thought of it all day.

"Have you not hit upon it yet?"

"I can think of only one thing," said he; "is it that I am not tall enough?"

Emily blushed as she saw he was thinking her objection a personal one. She felt he was on the eve of a proposal and she thought it her duty to spare him the refusal, if possible. She laughed again to cover her embarrassment and asked what height would have to do with the "model man."

"It's a question of deeds, not physical proportions, Mr. Harris," she remarked gravely.

He took her hand and in a voice trembling with emotion, besought her to tell him what it was. She thought a moment. "You promise not to be angry?"

"I promise."

"Well, Mr. Harris, I am almost sorry I spoke," said she, but since you will have it, if I were asked the principal drawback to your becoming a model man I should say it is a love of—liquor."

He dropped her hand and turned away. After a moment he said in a constrained tone: "May I ask how Miss Minton has become so wise as to my habits?"

"I have detected the smell of it on your breath," answered Emily, flushing as she rapidly continued. "I hope you won't be angry, my friend, but I have wondered that you seem to have so much leisure. I was in your office one day and was struck with the general poverty of your surroundings. Mr. Johnson, of my own town, has a fine an office as there is in the city, and has made a name for successful practice in the Criminal and Chancery courts. He has not your education, nor has he been practicing so long. For a man of such brilliant parts, I thought there must be a reason for such contentment, such a seeming lack of energy. I have concluded this is the reason, but I should not have risked your displeasure by saying so, if you had not urged me. The race needs the best service our young manhood can give it, my friend, and it seems so wrong to divert any part of it to the practice of a habit which can bring you no credit and gratify no noble ambition."

George's mind was in a conflicting whirl of emotions. He knew she spoke the truth; and yet with all his feelings of anger and mortification, he seemed to feel that this peerless girl was slipping away from him. He wanted her to think well of him and forgetful of the French proverb: "He who excuses, accuses," said eagerly:

"But this habit of mine never interferes with my business, Miss Emily. Indeed it rather helps me. I am the only Afro-American at this bar, and I must have some stimulus to help me through the difficulties the wall of prejudice throws in my way. Besides had I wished to appear other than I am, I might have kept this knowledge from you."

"But it isn't I, who is to be considered," said Emily, struggling for composure. "It is the race, Mr. Harris, and what you owe it. This habit may not have seriously interfered before, but it will if indulged, render you less ambitious to excel, if nothing more. For us as a race, in our present position, stagnation means death. The men who are best fitted for it, should be the leaders; those who lead others must be slaves to no unworthy passion or habit. The model man—*my* model man—is in deed and truth, in body and mind, master of himself."

As low earnest tones ceased to vibrate, Emily extended her hand and George pressed it warmly, saying, "Thank you, Miss Emily. No girl ever talked to me that way before."

"I have paid your common sense a compliment in that I have risked your displeasure to be your friend, and you do not know how I appreciate your manner of taking it," said she. "You know I go away to-morrow, and as you have made the summer so pleasant for me, I should like for us to part friends."

"You will let me write to you?" asked George. She gave her consent and on the morrow went home.

George wrote her before the week was out; throughout the fall he sent her letters regularly telling of his struggles. He understood as fully as if she had told him in so many words, that if he would win her he must make himself worthy, and he manfully withstood the jeers of his friends on his refusal to drink.

Emily answered promptly and rejoiced that the latent forces in him were at last roused to action. Her love for him and faith in him grew stronger with every letter. She looked forward to a promised visit during the holidays with much anticipation.

George arrived in the city New Year's Eve; was met by old friends who had arranged a "stag" for him at the home of the friend with whom he was to stop. He was tempted and yielded for the first time in four months, and drank the more for his past abstinence. In the early morning hours he was helped to bed by the "boys" who all voted him a jolly good fellow.

He arose late next day with a terrible headache and guilty conscience; he was to call on Emily that afternoon, and he knew she would discover his condition. With a mental comment on being soft enough to defer to a "woman's whim," he obeyed the craving for a "stimulant" and took several drinks during the day. When he presented himself at the house, Emily went forward to meet him and beaming face and outstretched hand, and present "Mr friend, Mr. Harris," to the several callers in the room. Catching the smell of liquor, she looked at him searchingly and as she realized his condition felt as if turned to stone. The heat and Emily's constraint, had their effect on George. He talked volubly and loudly, and the fumes of brandy were distilled throughout the room.

Emily maintained her composure till the other guests had gone; then without a word she broke down and wept convulsively. Shame, surprise, indignation and mortification each struggled for the mastery. No one had ever dared to come in her presence in such condition before, and to receive this humiliation at the hands of the man she loved; and in the presence of witnesses to whom she had spoken so highly of him. What must they think of her,—Miss Minton, the exclusive? To think that after all these years of choosing, her heart should go out to a—drunkard!

232

George came and stood before her. "Tears for me, my darling? I am not worthy of them. I came here to ask you to marry me, but after such a weak, miserable spectacle, I know it is useless. I do not deserve even your forgiveness. Farewell." He left the house, and the city that same evening. He wrote Emily a long letter of apology, telling her how dearly he loved her and that her influence could save him for his weakness and make a man of him. He told her how he came to yield to his weakness without sparing himself and cast himself on her mercy.

Emily wept over his letter. Her heart plead for the writer, but she could not get the consent of her judgment to risk her happiness in the hands of a man who she could not trust; who was not master of himself. Though it cost her a great deal to say so, she did it after a night of anguish.

Shortly after she heard that he had wound up his business suddenly and gone West, and then she heard no more for two years.

One day in November she found a letter on her return from school, in a strange hand writing. It read as follows:

Oklahoma City, O.T., Nov. 15, 1892.

Dear Miss Minton:

You may not remember me and you must pardon the liberty I take. But for the sake of a friend one risks much. I am the one you so generously encouraged when I declared my intention to come to Oklahoma nearly three years ago. I came and have never regretted it. Nearly two years ago, my friend George Harris joined me and we have been together ever since. In our lonely hours he has talked much of you and I know how dear you are to him. Since that fatal New Year's Day, (you see he has told me all,) not a drop of liquor has passed his lips. He says it lost him the only woman he ever loved and he never wants to look at it again. He thinks you have never forgiven him, and says he doesn't blame you. He has built up a fine practice in the territory by hard work, and now he is very ill with pneumonia. He has the best attention, but he does not care to get well; he has lost all hope and says nothing when he is at himself but when he is out of his mind he is always calling your name. He does not know I have written this letter, but I know a word from you would do him more good than medicine. Won't you write him a word, Miss Emily, and save the best friend I have on earth.

And Oblige, Yours,

Will Bramlette.

Emily was crying when she finished, but they were happy tears. Without a word she sat down at the desk and this is the letter she sent him:

233

My own Dear Love:

A little bird had brought me the news that you are a very sick man and that you do not get well because you do not seem to care to live. If I tell you that I wish you to live for my sake, will you try to get well? I have always loved you, and since you would neither write to me nor ask me again to marry you, I am going to make use of my leap year prerogative and ask you to marry me. As the New Year is near at hand, and I have no gift to send, now that I know where you are, I have been wondering if you would accept me as a New Year's gift, and if you will be able to come for me by the New Year. I have a fancy I would like to give myself to you on that day. Will you come?

Yours, Emily.

When Bramlette read this letter to the sick man it was Thanksgiving Day, and tears of thankfulness stole down his wasted cheeks. "Can you pray Will," he asked. "Then kneel down here and thank God for my happiness." A look of great content spread over his face. "Write her a letter, Will, and tell her I'll be there on New Year's Day if God spares my life."

He called for food and with the precious letter pressed to his heart he fell asleep with the first smile Will had seen on his face. The letter which had been more than medicine, he had Will read every day until he was able to read it himself, and having something to live for, he gradually got better. Will wrote to Emily every day and she sent loving cheerful massages in return, urging him to be careful of his health. He had never been a demonstrative man, but when he was able to write, he poured out his soul to her and consecrated the life he said she had given back to him, to renewed effort for individual and race advancement. "With you by my side," he wrote, "to cheer life's pathway and strengthen my zeal, life which has been so dreary, will indeed be enriched and ennobled."

Emily handed in her resignation, to take effect with the holidays. On New Year's Day, directly after the service, these two,—George Harris and Emily Minton,—stood before the altar, and pronounced the words which for "better or for worse" unite them "until death do us part." Then hand in hand they went out to the boundless west to make a home together, in which love and confidence reign supreme.

Lynch Law
In America

O ur country's national crime is *lynching*. It is not the creature of an hour, the sudden outburst of uncontrolled fury, or the unspeakable brutality of an insane mob. It represents the cool, calculating deliberation of intelligent people who openly avow that there is an "unwritten law" that justifies them in putting human beings to death without complaint under oath, without trial by jury, without opportunity to make defense, and without right of appeal. The "unwritten law" first found excuse with the rough, rugged, and determined man who left the civilized centers of eastern States to seek for quick returns in the gold-fields of the far West. Following in uncertain pursuit of continually eluding fortune, they dared the savagery of the Indians, the hardships of mountain travel, and the constant terror of border State outlaws. Naturally, they felt slight toleration for traitors in their own ranks. It was enough to fight the enemies from without; woe to the foe within! Far removed from and entirely without protection of the courts of civilized life, these fortune-seekers made laws to meet their varying emergencies. The thief who stole a horse, the bully who "jumped" a claim, was a common enemy. If caught he was promptly tried, and if found guilty was hanged to the tree under which the court convened.

Those were busy days of busy men. They had no time to give the prisoner a bill of exception or stay of execution. The only way a man had to secure a stay of execution was to behave himself. Judge Lynch was original in methods but exceedingly effective in procedure. He made the charge, impaneled the jurors, and directed the execution. When the court adjourned,

Originally published in *Arena*, January 1900, pp. 15-24.

the prisoner was dead. Thus lynch law held sway in the far West until civilization spread into the Territories and the orderly processes of law took its place. The emergency no longer existing, lynching gradually disappeared from the West.

But the spirit of mob procedure seemed to have fastened itself upon the lawless classes, and the grim process that at first was invoked to declare justice was made the excuse to wreak vengeance and cover crime. It next appeared in the South, where centuries of Anglo-Saxon civilization had made effective all the safeguards of court procedure. No emergency called for lynch law. It asserted its sway in defiance of law and in favor of anarchy. There it has flourished ever since, marking the thirty years of its existence with the inhuman butchery of more than ten thousand men, women, and children by shooting, drowning, hanging, and burning them alive. Not only this, but so potent is the force of example that the lynching mania has spread throughout the North and middle West. It is now no uncommon thing to read of lynchings north of Mason and Dixon's line, and those most responsible for this fashion gleefully point to these instances and assert that the North is no better than the South.

This is the work of the "unwritten law" about which so much is said, and in whose behest butchery is made a pastime and national savagery condoned. The first statute of this "unwritten law" was written in the blood of thousands of brave men who thought that a government that was good enough to create a citizenship was strong enough to protect it. Under the authority of a national law that gave every citizen the right to vote, the newly-made citizens chose to exercise their suffrage. But the reign of the national law was short-lived and illusionary. Hardly had the sentences dried upon the statute-books before one Southern State after another raised the cry against "negro domination" and proclaimed there was an "unwritten law" that justified any means to resist it.

The method then inaugurated was the outrages by the "red-shirt" bands of Louisiana, South Carolina, and other Southern States, which were succeeded by the Ku-Klux Klans. These advocates of the "unwritten law" boldly avowed their purpose to intimidate, suppress, and nullify the negro's right to vote. In support of its plans the Ku-Klux Klans, the "red-shirt" and similar organizations proceeded to beat, exile, and kill negroes until the purpose of their organization was accomplished and the supremacy of the "unwritten law" was effected. Thus lynchings began in the South, rapidly spreading into the various States until the national law was nullified and the reign of the "unwritten law" was supreme. Men were taken from their homes by "red-shirt" bands and stripped, beaten, and exiled; others were assassinated when their political prominence made them obnoxious to their political opponents; while the Ku-Klux barbarism of election days, reveling in the butchery of thousands of colored voters, furnished records in Congressional investigations that are a disgrace to civilization.

The alleged menace of universal suffrage having been avoided by the absolute suppression of the negro vote, the spirit of mob murder should have been satisfied and the butchery of negroes should have ceased. But men, women, and children were the victims of murder by individuals and murder by mobs, just as they had been when killed at the demands of the "unwritten law" to prevent "negro domination." Negroes were killed for disputing over terms of contracts with their employers. If a few barns were burned some colored man was killed to stop it. If a colored man resented the imposition of a white man and the two came to blows, the colored man had to die, either at the hands of the white man then and there or later at the hands of a mob that speedily gathered. If he showed a spirit of courageous manhood he was hanged for his pains, and the killing was justified by the declaration that he was a "saucy nigger." Colored women have been murdered because they refused to tell the mobs where relatives could be found for "lynching bees." Boys of fourteen years have been lynched by white representatives of American civilization. In fact, for all kinds of offenses—and for no offenses—from murders to misdemeanors, men and women are put to death without judge or jury; so that, although the political excuse was no longer necessary, the wholesale murder of human beings went on just the same. A new name was given to the killings and a new excuse was invented for so doing.

Again the aid of the "unwritten law" is invoked, and again it comes to the rescue. During the last ten years a new statute has been added to the "unwritten law." This statute proclaims that for certain crimes or alleged crimes no negro shall be allowed a trial; that no white woman shall be compelled to charge an assault under oath or to submit any such charge to the investigation of a court of law. The result is that many men have been put to death whose innocence was afterward established; and to-day, under this reign of the "unwritten law," no colored man, no matter what his reputation, is safe from lynching if a white woman, no matter what her standing or motive, cares to charge him with insult or assault.

It is considered a sufficient excuse and reasonable justification to put a prisoner to death under this "unwritten law" for the frequently repeated charge that these lynching horrors are necessary to prevent crimes against women. The sentiment of the country has been appealed to, in describing the isolated condition of white families in thickly populated negro districts; and the charge is made that these homes are in as great danger as if they were surrounded by wild beasts. And the world has accepted this theory without let or hindrance. In many cases there has been open expression that the fate meted out to the victim was only what he deserved. In many other instances there has been a silence that says more forcibly than words can proclaim it that it is right and proper that a human being should be seized by a mob and burned to death upon the unsworn and the uncorroborated charge of his accuser. No matter that our laws presume every man innocent until he is proved guilty; no matter that it leaves a certain class of individuals completely at the mercy of another class; no matter that it encourages those criminally disposed to blacken their faces and commit any crime in the calendar so long as they can throw suspicion on some negro, as is frequently done, and then lead a mob to take his life; no matter that mobs make a farce of the law and a mockery of justice; no matter that hundred of boys are being hardened in crime and schooled in vice by the repetition of such scenes before their eyes—if a white woman declares herself insulted or assaulted, some life must pay the penalty, with all the horrors of the Spanish Inquisition and all the barbarism of the Middle Ages. The world looks on and says it is well.

Not only are two hundred men and women put to death annually, on the average, in this country by mobs, but these lives are taken with the greatest publicity. In many instances the leading citizens aid and abet by their presence when they do not participate, and the leading journals inflame the public mind to the lynching point with scare-head articles and offers of rewards. Whenever a burning is advertised to take place, the railroads run excursions, photographs are taken, and the same jubilee is indulged in that characterized the public hangings of one hundred years ago. There is, however, this difference: in those old days the multitude that stood by was permitted only to guy or jeer. The nineteenth century lynching mob cuts off ears, toes, and fingers, strips off flesh, and distributes portions of the body as souvenirs among the crowd. If the leaders of the mob are so minded, coal-oil is poured over the body and the victim is then roasted to death. This has been done in Texarkana and Paris, Tex., in Bardswell, Ky., and in Newman,

Ga. In Paris the officers of the law delivered the prisoner to the mob. The mayor gave the school children a holiday and the railroads ran excursion trains so that the people might see a human being burned to death. In Texarkana, the year before, men and boys amused themselves by cutting off strips of flesh and thrusting knives into their helpless victim. At Newman, Ga., of the present year, the mob tried every conceivable torture to compel the victim to cry out and confess, before they set fire to the faggots that burned him. But their trouble was all in vain—he never uttered a cry, and they could not make him confess.

This condition of affairs were brutal enough and horrible enough if it were true that lynchings occurred only because of the commission of crimes against women—as is constantly declared by ministers, editors, lawyers, teachers, statesmen, and even by women themselves. It has been to the interest of those who did the lynching to blacken the good name of the helpless and defenseless victims of their hate. For this reason they publish at every possible opportunity this excuse for lynching, hoping thereby not only to palliate their own crime but at the same time to prove the negro a moral monster and unworthy of the respect and sympathy of the civilized world. But this alleged reason adds to the deliberate injustice of the mob's work. Instead of lynchings being caused by assaults upon women, the statistics show that not one-third of the victims of lynchings are even charged with such crimes. The Chicago *Tribune*, which publishes annually lynching statistics, is authority for the following:

In 1892, when lynching reached high-water mark, there were 241 persons lynched. The entire number is divided among the following States:

Alabama	22	Montana	4
Arkansas	25	New York	1
California	3	North Carolina	5
Florida	11	North Dakota	1
Georgia	17	Ohio	3
Idaho	8	South Carolina	5
Illinois	1	Tennessee	28
Kansas	3	Texas	15
Kentucky	9	Virginia	7
Louisiana	29	West Virginia	5
Maryland	1	Wyoming	9
Mississippi	16	Arizona Ter.	3
Missouri	6	Oklahoma	2

Of this number, 160 were of negro descent. Four of them were lynched in New York, Ohio, and Kansas; the remainder were murdered in the South. Five of this number were females. The charges for which they were lynched cover a wide range. They are as follows:

Rape	46	Attempted rape	11
Murder	58	Suspected robbery	4
Rioting	3	Larceny	1
Race prejudice	6	Self-defense	1
No cause given	4	Insulting women	2
Incendiarism	6	Desperadoes	6
Robbery	6	Fraud	1
Assault & battery	1	Attempted murder	2

No offense stated, boy and girl   2

In the case of the boy and girl above referred to, their father, named Hastings, was accused of the murder of a white man. His fourteen-year-old daughter and sixteen-year-old son were hanged and their bodies filled with bullets; then the father was also lynched. This occurred in November, 1892, at Jonesville, La.

Indeed, the record for the last twenty years shows exactly the same or a smaller proportion who have been charged with this horrible crime. Quite a number of the one-third alleged cases of assault that have been personally investigated by the writer have shown that there was no foundation in fact for the charges; yet the claim is not made that there were no real culprits among them. The negro has been too long associated with the white man not to have copied his vices as well as his virtues. But the negro resents and utterly repudiates the efforts to blacken his good name by asserting that assaults upon women are peculiar to his race. The negro has suffered far more from the commission of this crime against the women of his race by white men than the white race has ever suffered through *his* crimes. Very scant notice is taken of the matter when this is the condition of affairs. What becomes a crime deserving capital punishment when the tables are turned is a matter of small moment when the negro woman is the accusing party.

But since the world has accepted this false and unjust statement, and the burden of proof has been placed upon the negro to vindicate his race, he is taking steps to do so. The Anti-Lynching Bureau of the National Afro-American Council is arranging to have every lynching investigated and publish the facts to the world, as has been done in the case of Sam Hose, who was burned alive last April at Newman, Ga. The detective's report showed that Hose killed Cranford, his employer, in self-defense, and that, while a mob was organizing to hunt Hose to punish him for killing a white man, not till twenty-four hours after the murder was the charge of rape, embellished with psychological and physical impossibilities, circulated. That gave an impetus to the hunt, and the Atlanta *Constitution's* reward of $500 keyed the mob to the necessary burning and roasting pitch. Of five hundred newspaper clippings of that horrible affair, nine-tenths of them assumed Hose's guilt—simply because his murderers said so, and because it is the fashion to believe the negro peculiarly addicted to this species of crime. All the negro asks is justice—a fair and impartial trial in the courts of the country. That given, he will abide the result.

But this question affects the entire American nation, and from several points of view: First, on the ground of consistency. Our watchword has been "the land of the free and the home of the brave." Brave men do not gather by thousands to torture and murder a single individual, so gagged and bound he cannot make even feeble resistance or defense. Neither do brave men or women stand by and see such things done without compunction of conscience, nor read of them without protest. Our nation has been active and outspoken in its endeavors to right the wrongs of the Armenian Christian, the Russian Jew, and the Irish Home Ruler, the native women of India, the Siberian exile, and the Cuban patriot. Surely it should be the nation's duty to correct its own evils!

Second, on the ground of economy. To those who fail to be convinced from any other point of view touching this momentous question, a consideration of the economic phase might not be amiss. It is generally known that mobs in Louisiana, Colorado, Wyoming, and other States have lynched subjects of other countries. When their different governments demanded satisfaction, our country was forced to confess her inability to protect said subjects in the several States because of our State-rights doctrines, or in turn demand punishment of the lynchers. This confession, while humiliating in the extreme, was not satisfactory; and, while the United States cannot protect, she can pay. This she has done, and it is certain will have to do again in the case of the recent lynching of Italians in Louisiana. The United States already has paid in indemnities for lynching nearly a half million dollars, as follows:

Paid China for Rock Springs (Wyo.) massacre	$147,748.74
Paid China for outrages on Pacific Coast	276,619.75
Paid Italy for massacre of Italian prisoners at	
New Orleans	24,330.90
Paid Italy for lynchings at Walsenburg, Col.	10,000.00
Paid Great Britain for outrages on James Bain	
and Frederick Dawson	2,800.00

Third, for the honor of Anglo-Saxon civilization. No scoffer at our boasted American civilization could say anything more harsh of it than does the American white man himself who says he is unable to protect the honor of his women without resort to such brutal, inhuman, and degrading exhibitions as characterize "lynching bees." The cannibals of the South Sea Islands roast human beings alive to satisfy hunger. The red Indian of the Western plains tied his prisoner to the stake, tortured him, danced in fiendish glee while his victim writhed in the flames. His savage, untutored mind suggested no better way than that of wreaking vengeance upon those who had wronged him. These people knew nothing about Christianity and did not profess to follow its teachings; but such primary laws as they had they lived up to. No nation, savage or civilized, save only the United States of America, has confessed its inability to protect its women save by hanging, shooting, and burning alleged offenders.

Finally, for love of country. No American travels abroad without blushing for shame for his country on this subject. And whatever the excuse that passes current in the United States, it avails nothing abroad. With all the powers of government in control; with all laws made by white men, administered by white judges, jurors, prosecuting attorneys, and sheriffs; with every office of the executive department filled by white men—no excuse can be offered for exchanging the orderly administration of justice for barbarous lynchings and "unwritten laws." Our country should be placed speedily above the plane of confessing herself a failure at self-government. This cannot be until Americans of every section, of broadest patriotism and best and wisest citizenship, not only see the defect in our country's armor but take the necessary steps to remedy it. Although lynchings have steadily increased in number and barbarity during the last twenty years, there has been no single effort put forth by the many moral and philanthropic forces of the country to put a stop to this wholesale slaughter. Indeed, the silence and seeming condonation grow more marked as the years go by.

A few months ago the conscience of this country was shocked because, after a two-weeks trial, a French judicial tribunal pronounced Captain Dreyfus guilty. And yet, in our own land under our own flag, the writer can give day and detail of one thousand men, women, and children who during the last six years were put to death without trial before any tribunal on earth. Humiliating indeed, but altogether unanswerable, was the reply of the French press to our protest: "Stop your lynchings at home before you send your protests abroad."

The Negro's Case in Equity

The INDEPENDENT publishes an earnest appeal to negro editors, preachers and teachers "to tell their people to defend the laws and their own rights even to blood, but never, never to take guilty participation in lynching white man or black." This advice is given by way of comment on the double lynching in Virginia the other day. Theoretically the advice is all right, but viewed in the light of circumstances and conditions it seems like giving a stone when we ask for bread.

For twenty years past the negro has done nothing else but defend the law and appeal to public sentiment for defense *by* the law. He has seen hundreds of men of his race murdered in cold blood by connivance of officers of the law, from the governors of the States down to sheriffs of counties, as in this Virginia case, and that upon the unsupported word of some white man or woman. He has seen his women and children stripped and strung up to trees or riddled with bullets for the gratification of spite, as in the case of Postmaster Baker's family two years ago, and in that in Alabama a few weeks ago, when an entire family was wiped out of existence because a white man had been murdered.

The negro has seen scores of his race, absolutely innocent of any charge whatever, used as scapegoats for some white man's crime, as in the case of C. J. Miller, lynched in Bardwell, Ky., in 1893, and John Peterson of Denmark, S.C., the same year. Miller was stripped, hung with a log chain to a telegraph pole, riddled with bullets, then burned, since which proceeding he was found to have suffered for a crime committed by a white man. Peterson had sought protection from Governor (now Senator) Tillman, but

Originally published in the *Independent*, April 26, 1900, pp. 1010-1011.

was given over to the mob, and altho the girl in the case said he was not the man, yet the lynchers, led by a State Senator, said a crime had been committed and somebody had to hang for it; so Peterson was swung up and five hundred bullets fired into his body. Such also was the case of a negro woman in Jackson, Tenn., who was stripped and hung in the court house yard by a mob led by the woman's employer. Her mistress had died suddenly of arsenical poisoning and the negro cook was accused because a box of rat poison was found in her room. The husband of the woman who was poisoned, and who led the mob, has since been confined in the insane asylum, and his ravings prove him to have been the poisoner of his wife.

All this and more the negro has seen and suffered without taking the law into his hands for, lo, these many years. There have been no Nat Turner insurrections and San Domingan horrors in retaliation for all the wrongs he has suffered. When the negro has appealed to the Christian and moral forces of the country—asking them to create a sentiment against this lawlessness and unspeakable barbarism; demanding justice and the protection of the law for every human being regardless of color—that demand has been met with general indifference or entirely ignored. Where this is not true he has been told that these same forces upon which he confidently depends refuse to make the demand for justice, because they believe the story of the mob that negroes are lynched because they commit unspeakable crimes against white women. For this reason the Christian and moral forces are silent in the presence of the horrible barbarities alleged to be done in the name of woman.

When the negro, confident in the justice of his cause and the sincerity of the aforesaid Christian and moral forces, seeks the opportunity to disprove this slander, he is refused, except in very rare instances. The columns of the powerful dailies, religious periodicals and thoughtful magazines have printed these charges wholesale until the civilized world has accepted them, but few wish to consider the refutation of them or give space for the possible other side. The leading pulpits of the country are open to stories of the negro's degradation and ignorance, but not to his defense from slander.

Again and again, during the present session of Congress, in both the House and Senate, the negro has been attacked and this foul slander against his good name made in several speeches and sent broadcast. Except a brief rejoinder by Congressman George White, there was no attempt at refutation or rebuke in Congress or out by any of the champions of truth and justice.

Notwithstanding all this is true and has been true for twenty years past, while ten thousand men, women and children have been done to death in the same manner as in the late Virginia case; in spite of the fact that the governors of States, commanders of militia, sheriffs and police have taken part in these disgraceful exhibitions; and with absolute proof that the public sentiment of the country was with the mob—who, if not the negro preachers, editors and teachers, are to be credited with the fact that there are few, if any, instances of negroes who have had "guilty participation in lynching white men or black?"

And if all the negro preachers, editors and teachers should charge themselves with the responsibility of this one lapse after years of the greatest human provocation, should not all the white preachers, editors and teachers charge themselves with the thousands of lynchings by white men? Ought not they to tell their people over and over again that ten human beings have been burned alive in this country during the past seven years—three of them during the year 1899? For the seven years the negro has been agitating against lynching he has made this appeal to the leaders of thought and action among the white race. If they will do their duty in this respect the negroes will soon have no bad examples of the lynching kind set, which in their desperation they may be tempted to follow.

As matters now stand, the negroes down in Virginia the other day would have fared badly had they attempted to defend the law in either case. A band of negroes prevented a lynching in Jacksonville, Fla., in the summer of 1892 by guarding the jail, tho not a shot was fired. The man who led the band has been an exile from his home ever since. He was indicted for "conspiracy" and about to be sent to the penitentiary for preventing white men from lynching a negro, when he forfeited his bond by leaving home and sacrificing his property. Only last summer the same thing happened in Darien, Ga. A white woman gave birth to a negro child, and the mob prepared to lynch the father for the "usual crime." The negroes got wind of it, guarded the jail and prevented the lynching. They were all indicted for that "conspiracy" and lodged in jail. John Delegal, who helped guard his father when the mob was after him, lived in the country. The posse went after him as a "conspirator," broke open his house and entered firing. He returned the fire, killing the leader instantly. Those negroes have all been tried since by a jury of the kind of men who tried to lynch Delegal's father, found guilty of "conspiracy," and are now doing time in the penitentiary. John was sent up for life. In the present apathetic condition of public sentiment, North and South, this is what the negro gets who attempts to "defend the law and his rights." Not until the white editors, preachers and teachers of the country join with him in his fight for justice and protection by law can there be any hope of success.

Lynching and the Excuse for it

It was eminently befitting that THE INDEPENDENT's first number in the new century should contain a strong protest against lynching. The deepest dyed infamy of the nineteenth century was that which, in its supreme contempt for law, defied all constitutional guaranties of citizenship, and during the last fifteen years of the century put to death two thousand men, women and children, by shooting, hanging and burning alive. Well would it have been if every preacher in every pulpit in the land had made so earnest a plea as that which came from Miss Addams's forceful pen.

Appreciating the helpful influences of such a dispassionate and logical argument as that made by the writer referred to, I earnestly desire to say nothing to lessen the force of the appeal. At the same time an unfortunate presumption used as a basis for her argument works so serious, tho doubtless unintentional, an injury to the memory of thousands of victims of mob law, that it is only fair to call attention to this phase of the writer's plea. It is unspeakably infamous to put thousands of people to death without a trial by jury; it adds to that infamy to charge that these victims were moral monsters, when, in fact, four-fifths of them were not so accused even by the fiends who murdered them.

Almost at the beginning of her discussion, the distinguished writer says:

"Let us assume that the Southern citizens who take part in and abet the lynching of negroes honestly believe that that is the only successful method of dealing with a certain class of crimes."

It is this assumption, this absolutely unwarrantable assumption, that vitiates every suggestion which it inspires Miss Addams to make. It is the same

Originally published in the *Independent*, May 16, 1901, pp. 1133-1336.

baseless assumption which influences ninety-nine out of every one hundred persons who discuss this question. Among many thousand editorial clippings I have received in the past five years, ninety-nine per cent discuss the question upon the presumption that lynchings are the desperate effort of the Southern people to protect their women from black monsters, and while the large majority condemn lynching, the condemnation is tempered with a plea for the lyncher—that human nature gives way under such awful provocation and that the mob, insane for one moment, must be pitied as well as condemned. It is strange that an intelligent, law-abiding and fair minded people should so persistently shut their eyes to the facts in the discussion of what the civilized world now concedes to be America's national crime.

This almost universal tendency to accept as true the slander which the lynchers offer to civilization as an excuse for their crime might be explained if the true facts were difficult to obtain. But not the slightest difficulty intervenes. The Associated Press dispatches, the press clipping bureau, frequent book publications and the annual summary of a number of influential journals give the lynching record every year. This record, easily within the reach of every one who wants it, makes inexcusable the statement and cruelly unwarranted the assumption that negroes are lynched only because of their assaults upon womanhood.

For an example in point: For fifteen years past, on the first day of each year, the Chicago *Tribune* has given to the public a carefully compiled record of all the lynchings of the previous year. Space will not permit a *resume* of these fifteen years, but as fairly representing the entire time, I desire to briefly tabulate here the record of the five years last past. The statistics of the ten years preceding do not vary, they simply emphasize the record here presented.

The record gives the name and nationality of the man or woman lynched, the alleged crime, the time and place of the lynching. With this is given a *resume* of the offenses charged, with the number of persons lynched for the offenses named. That enables the reader to see at a glance the causes assigned for the lynchings, and leaves nothing to be assumed. The lynchers, at the time and place of the lynching, are the best authority for the causes which actuate them. Every presumption is in favor of this record, especially as it remains absolutely unimpeached. This record gives the following statement of the colored persons lynched and the causes of the lynchings for the years named:

1896

Murder	24	Arson	2
Attempted murder	4	Assault	3
Rape	31	Unknown cause	1
Incendiarism	2	Slapping a child	1
No cause	2	Shooting at officer	1
Alleged rape	2	Alleged murder	2
Cattle stealing	1	Threats	1
Miscegenation	2	Passing counterfeit	
		money	1
Attempted rape	4	Theft	1
Murderous assault	1		

1897

Murder	55	Writing insulting letter	1
Attempted rape	8	Cattle Thief	1
Mistaken identity	1	Felony	1
Arson	3	Train wrecking	1
Murderous assault	2	Rape	22
Running quarantine	1	Race prejudice	1
Burglary	1	Alleged arson	1
Bad reputation	1	Robbery	6
Unknown offense	3	Assault	2
Killing white cap	1	Disobeying Federal	
Attempted murder	1	regulations	1
Insulting white		Theft	2
woman	1	Elopement	1
Suspected arson	1	Concealing murderer	1
Giving evidence	2		
Refusing to give			
evidence	1		

1898

Murder	42	Theft	6
Rape	14	Miscegenation	1
Attempted rape	7	Unknown offense	2
Complicity in rape	1	Violation of contract	1
Highway robbery	1	Insults	2
Burglary	1	Race prejudice	3
Mistaken identity	1	Resisting arrest	1
Arson	1	Suspected murder	13
Murderous assault	1	Assaults upon whites	4

1899

Murder	23	Arson	8
Robbery	6	Unknown offense	4
Inflammatory language	1	Resisting arrest	1
Desperado	1	Mistaken identity	1
Complicity in murder	3	Aiding escape of	
Rape	11	murderer	3
Attempted rape	8		

1900

Murder	30	No offense	1
Rape	16	Arson	2
Attempted assault	12	Suspicion of arson	1
Race prejudice	9	Aiding escape of murderer	1
Plot to kill whites	2	Unpopularity	1
Suspected robbery	1	Making threats	1
Giving testimony	1	Informer	1
Attacking white men	3	Robbery	2
Attempted murder	4	Burglary	4
Threats to kill	1	Assault	2
Suspected murder	2		
Unknown offense	2		

With this record in view there should be no difficulty in ascertaining the alleged offenses given as justification for lynchings during the last five years. If the Southern citizens lynch negroes because "that is the only successful method of dealing with a certain class of crimes," then that class of crimes should be known unmistakably by this record. Now consider the record.

It would be supposed that the record would show that all, or nearly all, lynchings were caused by outrageous assaults upon women; certainly that this particular offense would outnumber all other causes for putting human beings to death without a trial by jury and the other safeguards of our Constitution and laws.

But the record makes no such disclosure. Instead, it shows that five women have been lynched, put to death with unspeakable savagery, during the past five years. They certainly were not under the ban of the outlawing crime. It shows that men, not a few, but hundreds, have been lynched for misdemeanors, while others have suffered death for no offense known to the law, the causes assigned being "mistaken identity," "insult," "bad reputation," "unpopularity," "violating contract," "running quarantine," "giving evidence," "frightening child by shooting at rabbits," etc. Then, strangest of all, the record shows that the sum total of lynchings for these offenses—not crimes—and for the alleged offenses which are only misdemeanors, greatly exceeds the lynchings for the very crime universally declared to be the cause of lynching.

A careful classification of the offenses which have caused lynchings during the past five years shows that contempt for law and race prejudice constitute the real cause of all lynching. During the past five years 147 white persons were lynched. It may be argued that fear of the "law's delays" was the cause of their being lynched. But this is not true. Not a single white victim of the mob was wealthy or had friends or influence to cause a miscarriage of justice. There was no such possibility—it was contempt for law which incited the mob to put so many white men to death without complaint under oath, much less a trial.

In the case of the negroes lynched the mobs' incentive was race prejudice. Few white men were lynched for any such trivial offenses as are detailed in the causes for lynching colored men. Negroes are lynched for "violating contracts," "unpopularity," "testifying in court" and "shooting at rabbits." As only negroes are lynched for "no offense," "unknown offenses," offenses not criminal, misdemeanors and crimes not capital, it must be admitted that the real cause of lynching in all such cases is race prejudice, and should be so classified. Grouping these lynchings under that classification and excluding rape, which in some States is made a capital offense, the record for the five years, so far as the negro is concerned, reads as follows:

Year	Race prejudice	Murder	Rape	Total lynchings
1896	31	24	31	86
1897	46	55	22	123
1898	39	47	16	102
1899	56	23	11	90
1900	57	30	16	103
Total	229	179	96	504

This table tells its own story, and shows how false is the excuse which lynchers offer to justify their fiendishness. Instead of being the sole cause of lynching, the crime upon which lynchers build their defense furnishes the least victims for the mob. In 1896 less than thirty-nine per cent of the negroes lynched were charged with this crime; in 1897, less than eighteen per cent; in 1898, less than sixteen per cent; in 1899, less than fourteen per cent, and in 1900, less than fifteen percent were so charged.

No good result can come from any investigation which refuses to consider the facts. A conclusion that is based upon a presumption, instead of the best evidence, is unworthy of a moment's consideration. The lynching record, as it is compiled from day to day by unbiased, reliable and responsible public journals, should be the basis of every investigation which seeks to discover the cause and suggest the remedy for lynching. The excuses of lynchers and the specious pleas of their apologists should be considered in the light of the record, which they invariably misrepresent or ignore. The Christian and moral forces of the nation should insist that misrepresentation should have no place in the discussion of this all important question, that the figures of the lynching record should be allowed to plead, trumpet tongued, in defense of the slandered dead, that the silence of concession be broken, and that truth, swift-winged and courageous, summon this nation to do its duty to exalt justice and preserve inviolate the sacredness of human life.

Booker T. Washington
and His Critics

Industrial education for the Negro is Booker T. Washington's hobby. He believes that for the masses of the Negro race an elementary education of the brain and a continuation of the education of the hand is not only the best kind, but he knows it is the most popular with the white South. He knows also that the Negro is the butt of ridicule with the average white American, and that the aforesaid American enjoys nothing so much as a joke which portrays the Negro as illiterate and improvident; a petty thief or a happy-go-lucky inferior.

The average funny paragrapher knows no other class. Ignatius Donnelly, with all his good intentions in writing "Dr. Huguet," could make no other disposition of his hero than to have him change places with a Negro chicken thief. The obvious moral was to portray a cultured white man's mental torture over the metamorphosis; and not, as the author intended, to show the mental, moral and physical anguish of the educated, Christian Negro gentleman, over the intolerable caste conditions which confront him at every step. There is no such type of Negro gentleman in Anglo-Saxon literature or art, and therefore the reader accepts, as a matter of course, the coarse swaggering Sam Johnsing of evil instinct, who is masquerading under the white skin of Dr. Huguet. That for white America is the typical Negro.

What Dr. Huguet did unintentionally Booker T. Washington has done deliberately. Yet he knows, as do all students of sociology, that the representatives which stand as the type for any race, are chosen not from the worst but from the best specimens of that race; the achievements of the few rather than the poverty, vice and ignorance of the many, are the standards

Originally published in *World Today*, April 1904, pp. 518-521, as part of a symposium entitled *The Negro Problem from the Negro Point of View.*

of any given race's ability. There is a Negro faculty at Tuskegee, some of whom came from the masses, yet have crossed lances with the best intellect of the dominant race at their best colleges. Mr. Washington knows intimately the ablest members of the race in all sections of the country and could bear testimony as to what they accomplished before the rage for industrial schools began. The Business League, of which he is founder and president, is composed of some men who were master tradesmen and business men before Tuskegee was born. He therefore knows better than any man before the public to-day that the prevailing idea of the typical Negro is false.

But some will say Mr. Washington represents the masses and seeks only to depict the life and needs of the black belt. There is a feeling that he does not do that when he will tell a cultured body of women like the Chicago Woman's Club the following story:

"Well, John, I am glad to see you are raising your own hogs."

"Yes, Mr. Washington, ebber sence you done tole us bout raisin our own hogs, we niggers round her hab resolved to quit stealing hogs and gwinter raise our own." The inference is that the Negroes of the black belt as a rule were hog thieves until the coming of Tuskegee.

There are those who resent this picture as false and misleading, in the name of the hundreds of Negroes who bought land, raised hogs and accumulated those millions of which they were defrauded by the Freedmen's Savings Bank, long before Booker Washington was out of school. The men and women of to-day who are what they are by grace of the honest toil on the part of such parents, in the black belt and out, and who are following in their footsteps, resent also the criticism of Mr. Washington on the sort of education they received and on those who gave it.

They cherish most tender memories of the northern teachers who endured ostracism, insult and martyrdom, to bring the spelling-book and Bible to educate those who had been slaves. They know that the leaders of the race, including Mr. Washington himself, are the direct product of schools of the Freedmen's Aid Society, the American Missionary Association and other such agencies which gave the Negro his first and only opportunity to secure any kind of education which his intellect and ambition craved. Without these schools our case would have been more hopeless indeed than it is; with their aid the race has made more remarkable intellectual and material progress in forty years than any other race in history. They have given us thousands of teachers for our schools in the South, physicians to heal our ailments, druggists, lawyers and ministers.

They have given us 2,000 college graduates, over half of whom own property worth over $1,000 per capita. The Negro owes a debt of gratitude which he can never repay to the hundreds of self-sacrificing teachers who gave their lives to the work of Negro education, to the end that they brought the light of knowledge, the strength of educated manhood and the example of Christian culture to those who would otherwise have been without.

That one of the most noted of their own race should join with the enemies to their highest progress in condemning the education they had received, has been to them a bitter pill. And so for a long while they keenly, though silently, resented the gibes against the college-bred youth which punctuate Mr. Washington's speeches. He proceeds to draw a moral therefrom for his entire race. The result is that the world which listens to him and which largely supports his educational institution, has almost unanimously decided that college education is a mistake for the Negro. They hail with acclaim the man who has made popular the unspoken thought of that part of the North which believes in the inherent inferiority of the Negro, and the always outspoken southern review to the same effect.

This gospel of work is no new one for the Negro. It is the South's old slavery practice in a new dress. It was the only education the South gave the Negro for two and a half centuries she had absolute control of his body and soul. The Negro knows that now, as then, the South is strongly opposed to his learning anything else but how to work.

No human agency can tell how many black diamonds lie buried in the black belt of the South, and the opportunities for discovering them become rarer every day as the schools for thorough training become more cramped and no more are being established. The president of Atlanta University and other such schools remain in the North the year round, using their personal influence to secure funds to keep those institutions running. Many are like the late Collis P. Huntington, who had given large amounts to Livingston College, Salisbury, North Carolina. Several years before his death he told the president of that institution that as he believed Booker Washington was educating Negroes in the only sensible way, henceforth his money for that purpose would go to Tuskegee. All the schools in the South have suffered as a consequence of this general attitude, and many of the oldest and best which have regarded themselves as fixtures now find it a struggle to maintain existence. As another result of this attitude of the philanthropic public, and this general acceptance of special education standards for the Negro, Tuskegee is the only endowed institution for the Negro in the South.

Admitting for argument's sake that its system is the best, Tuskegee could not accommodate one-hundredth part of the Negro youth who need education. The Board of Education of New Orleans cut the curriculum in the public schools for Negro children down to the fifth grade, giving Mr. Washington's theory as an inspiration for so doing. Mr. Washington denied in a letter that he had ever advocated such a thing, but the main point is that this is the deduction the New Orleans school board made from his frequent statement that previous systems of education were a mistake and that the Negro should be taught to work. Governor Vardaman, of Mississippi, the other day in his inaugural address, after urging the legislature to abolish the Negro public school and substitute manual training therefor, concluded that address by saying that all other education was a curse to the Negro race.

This is the gospel Mr. Washington has preached for the past decade. The results from this teaching then would seem to be first, a growing prejudice in northern institutions of learning against the admission of Negro students; second, a contracting of the number and influence of the schools of higher learning so judiciously scattered through all the southern states by the missionary associations, for the Negro's benefit; third, lack of a corresponding growth of industrial schools to take their places; and fourth, a cutting down of the curriculum for the Negro in the public schools of the large cities of the South, few of which ever have provided high schools for the race.

Mr. Washington's reply to his critics is that he does not oppose the higher education, and offers in proof of this statement his Negro faculty. But the critics observe that nowhere does he speak for it, and they can remember dozens of instances when he has condemned every system of education save that which teaches the Negro how to work. They feel that the educational opportunities of the masses, always limited enough, are being threatened by this retrogression. And it is this feeling which prompts the criticism. They are beginning to feel that if they longer keep silent, Negro educational advantages will be even more restricted in all directions.

Does some one ask a solution of the lynching evil? Mr. Washington says in substance: Give me money to educate the Negro and when he is taught how to work, he will not commit the crime for which lynching is done. Mr. Washington knows when he says this that lynching is not invoked to punish crime but color, and not even industrial education will change that.

Again he sets up the dogma that when the race becomes taxpayers, producers of something the white man wants, landowners, business, etc., the Anglo-Saxon will forget all about color and respect that race's manhood. One of the leading southern papers said editorially, in discussing the separate street car law which was to go into effect last winter in Memphis, Tennessee, that it was not the servant or working class of Negroes, who know their places, with whom the white people objected to riding, but the educated, property-owning Negro who thought himself the white man's equal.

There are many who can never be made to feel that it was a mistake thirty years ago to give the unlettered freedman the franchise, their only weapon of defense, any more than it is a mistake to have fire for cooking and heating purposes in the home, because ignorant or careless servants sometimes burn themselves. The thinking Negro knows it is still less a mistake to-day when the race has had thirty years of training for citizenship. It is indeed a bitter pill to feel that much of the unanimity with which the nation to-day agrees to Negro disfranchisement comes from the general acceptance of Mr. Washington's theories.

Does this mean that the Negro objects to industrial education? By no means. It simply means that he knows by sad experience that industrial education will not stand him in place of political, evil and intellectual liberty, and he objects to being deprived of fundamental rights of American citizenship to the end that one school for industrial training shall flourish. To him it seems like selling a race's birthright for a mess of pottage.

They believe it is possible for Mr. Washington to make Tuskegee all it should become without sacrificing or advocating the sacrifice of race manhood to do it. They know he has the ear of the American nation as no other Negro of our day has, and he is therefore molding public sentiment and securing funds for his educational theories as no other can. They know that the white South has labored ever since reconstruction to establish and maintain throughout the country a color line in politics, in civil rights and in education, and they feel that with Mr. Washington's aid the South has largely succeeded in her aim.

The demand from this class of Negroes is growing that if Mr. Washington can not use his great abilities and influence to speak in defense of and demand for the rights withheld when discussing the Negro question, for fear of injury to his school by those who are intolerant of Negro manhood, then he should be just as unwilling to injure his race for the benefit of his school. They demand that he refrain from assuming to solve a problem which is too big to be settled within the narrow confines of a single system of education.

Lynching:
Our National Crime

The lynching record for a quarter of a century merits the thoughtful study of the American people. It presents three salient facts:

First: Lynching is color line murder.

Second: Crimes against women is the excuse, not the cause.

Third: It is a national crime and requires a national remedy.

Proof that lynching follows the color line is to be found in the statistics which have been kept for the past twenty-five years. During the few years preceding this period and while frontier lynch law existed, the executions showed a majority of white victims. Later, however, as law courts and authorized judiciary extended into the far West, lynch law rapidly abated and its white victims became few and far between.

Just as the lynch law regime came to a close in the West, a new mob movement started in the South. This was wholly political, its purpose being to suppress the colored vote by intimidation and murder. Thousands of assassins banded together under the name of Ku Klux Klans, "Midnight Raiders," "Knights of the Golden Circle," etc., spread a reign of terror, by beating, shooting and killing colored people by the thousands. In a few years, the purpose was accomplished and the black vote was suppressed. But mob murder continued.

From 1882, in which year 52 were lynched, down to the present, lynching has been along the color line. Mob murder increased yearly until in 1892 more than 200 victims were lynched and statistics show that 3,284 men, women and children have been put to death in this quarter of a century. During the last ten years from 1899 to 1908 inclusive the number lynched

Originally published in *National Negro Conference: Proceedings*. New York, 1909, pp. 174-179.

was 959. Of this number 102 were white while the colored victims numbered 857. No other nation, civilized or savage, burns its criminals; only under the stars and stripes is the human holocaust possible. Twenty-eight human beings burned at the stake, one of them a woman and two of them children, is the awful indictment against American civilization—the grewsome tribute which the nation pays to the color line.

Why is the mob murder permitted by a Christian nation? What is the cause of this awful slaughter? This question is answered almost daily—always the same shameless falsehood that "Negroes are lynched to protect womanhood." Standing before a Chautauqua assemblage, John Temple Graves, at once champion of lynching and apologist for lynchers, said: "The mob stands to-day as the most potential bulwark between the women of the South and such a carnival of crime as would infuriate the world and precipitate the annihilation of the Negro race." This is the never varying answer of lynchers and their apologists. All know that it is untrue. The cowardly lyncher revels in murder, then seeks to shield himself from public execration by claiming devotion to woman. But truth is mighty and the lynching record discloses the hypocrisy of the lyncher as well as his crime.

The Springfield, Illinois, mob rioted for two days, the militia of the entire state was called out, two men were lynched, hundreds of people were driven from their homes, all because a white woman said a Negro had assaulted her. A mad mob went to the jail, tried to lynch the victim of her charge and, not being able to find him, proceeded to pillage and burn the town and to lynch two innocent men. Later, after the police had found that the woman's charge was false, she published a retraction, the indictment was dismissed and the intended victim discharged. But the lynch victims were dead. Hundreds were homeless and Illinois was disgraced.

As a final and complete refutation of the charge that lynching is occasioned by crimes against women, a partial record of lynchings is cited; 285 persons were lynched for causes as follows:

Unknown cause, 92; no cause, 10; race prejudice, 49; miscegenation, 7; informing, 12; making threats, 11; keeping saloon, 3; practicing fraud, 5; practicing voodooism, 2; bad reputation, 8; unpopularity, 3; mistaken identity, 5; using improper language, 3; violation of contract, 1; poisoning well, 2; by white caps, 9; vigilantes, 14; Indians, 1; moonshining, 1; refusing evidence, 2; political causes, 5; disputing, 1; disobeying quarantine regulations, 2; slapping a child, 1; turning state's evidence, 3; protecting a Negro, 1; to prevent giving evidence, 1; knowledge of larceny, 1; writing letter to white woman, 1; asking white woman to marry, 1; jilting girl, 1; having smallpox, 1; concealing criminal, 2; threatening political exposure, 1; self-defense, 6; cruelty, 1; insulting language to woman, 5; quarreling with white man, 2; colonizing Negroes, 1; throwing stones, 1; quarreling, 1; gambling,1.

Is there a remedy, or will the nation confess that it cannot protect its protectors at home as well as abroad? Various remedies have been suggested to abolish the lynching infamy, but year after year, the butchery of men, women and children continues in spite of plea and protest. Education is suggested as a preventive, but it is as grave a crime to murder an ignorant man as it is a scholar. True, few educated men have been lynched, but the hue and cry once started stops at no bounds, as was clearly shown by the lynchings in Atlanta, and in Springfield, Illinois.

Agitation, though helpful, will not alone stop the crime. Year after year statistics are published, meetings are held, resolutions are adopted and yet lynchings go on. Public sentiment does measurably decrease the sway of mob law, but the irresponsible blood-thirsty criminals who swept through the streets of Springfield, beating an inoffensive law-abiding citizen to death in one part of the town, and in another torturing and shooting to death a man who, for threescore years, had made a reputation for honesty, integrity and sobriety, had raised a family and had accumulated property, was not deterred from its heinous crimes by either education or agitation.

The only certain remedy is an appeal to law. Lawbreakers must be made to know that human life is sacred and that every citizen of this country is first a citizen of the United States and secondly a citizen of the state in which he belongs. This nation must assert itself and defend its federal citizenship at home as well as abroad. The strong arm of the government must reach across state lines whenever unbridled lawlessness defies state laws and must give to the individual citizen under the Stars and Stripes the same measure of protection which it gives to him when he travels in foreign lands.

Federal protection of American citizenship is the remedy for lynching. Foreigners are rarely lynched in America. If, by mistake, one is lynched, the national government quickly pays the damages. The recent agitation in California against the Japanese compelled this nation to recognize that federal power must yet assert itself to protect the nation from the treason of sovereign states. Thousands of American citizens have been put to death and no President has yet raised his hand in effective protest, but a simple insult to a native of Japan was quite sufficient to stir the government at

Washington to prevent the threatened wrong. If the government has power to protect a foreigner from insult, certainly it has power to save a citizen's life.

The practical remedy has been more than once suggested in Congress. Senator Gallinger of New Hampshire in a resolution introduced in Congress called for an investigation "with a view of ascertaining whether there is a remedy for lynching which Congress may apply." The Senate Committee has under consideration a bill drawn by A. E. Pillsbury, formerly Attorney-General of Massachusetts, providing for federal prosecution of lynchers in cases where the state fails to protect citizens or foreigners. Both of these resolutions indicate that the attention of the nation has been called to this phase of the lynching question.

As a final word, it would be a beginning in the right direction if this conference can see its way clear to establish a bureau for the investigation and publication of the details of every lynching, so that the public could know that an influential body of citizens has made it a duty to give the widest publicity to the facts in each case; that it will make an effort to secure expressions of opinion all over the country against lynching for the sake of the country's fair name; and lastly, but by no means least, to try to influence the daily papers of the country to refuse to become accessory to mobs either before or after the fact. Several of the greatest riots and most brutal burnt offerings of the mobs have been suggested and incited by the daily papers of the offending community. If the newspaper which suggests lynching in its accounts of an alleged crime, could be held legally as well as morally responsible for reporting that "threats of lynching were heard"; or, "It is feared that if the guilty one is caught, he will be lynched"; or "There were cries of 'lynch him,' and the only reason the threat was not carried out was because no leader appeared," a long step toward a remedy will have been taken.

In a multitude of counsel there is wisdom. Upon the grave question presented by the slaughter of innocent men, women and children there should be an honest courageous conference of patriotic, law-abiding citizens anxious to punish crime promptly, impartially and by due process of law, also to make life, liberty, and property secure against mob rule.

Time was when lynching appeared to be sectional, but now it is national—a blight upon our nation, mocking our laws and disgracing our Christianity. "With malice toward none but with charity for all" let us undertake the work of making the "law of the land," effective and supreme upon every foot of American soil—a shield to the innocent and to the guilty punishment swift and sure.

How Enfranchisement Stops Lynching

The Negro question has been present with the American people in one form or another since the landing of the Dutch Slaveship at Jamestown, Virginia, in 1619. For twelve years the founders of the English colony had indifferently succeeded in getting permanently established. The younger sons of the British were miserable failures as pioneers. They would not do the work necessary to wrest a livelihood from the bowels of the earth, and they could not make the Indian do it for them. One such colony perished from the face of the earth and succeeding ones lagged with indifferent success until the coming of those fourteen African slaves, who became the hewers of wood, drawers of water and tillers of the soil. They were submissive, and easily dominated, so they were harnessed to the plow and became the beasts of burden; then the Jamestown Colony began to thrive.

So successful was the first venture into slavery, that the shores of Africa were again invaded. Men, women and children were overpowered, captured, crowded into the holds of the slaveships, brought to this new country and made the slaves of the colonists. For two hundred and fifty years this condition obtained. The original fourteen slaves became four millions. Their unrequited toil had made this country blossom as a rose, created vast wealth for the masters and made the United States one of the mighty nations of the earth, ere the American people harkened to the voice which commanded, "Let my people go." When the mighty upheaval came which almost rent the American nation in twain, it struck the shackles from the Negro slave, and did not stop until he was not only a free man, but a citizen.

The flower of the nineteenth century civilization for the American people

---

Originally published in *Original Rights Magazine*, June 1910, pp. 42-53.

was the abolition of slavery, and the enfranchisement of all manhood. Here at last was squaring of practice with precept, with true democracy, with the Declaration of Independence and with the Golden Rule. The reproach and disgrace of the twentieth century is that the whole of the American people have permitted a part, to nullify this glorious achievement, and make the fourteenth and fifteenth amendments to the Constitution playthings, a mockery and a byword; an absolute dead letter in the Constitution of the United States. One-third of the states of the union have made and enforced laws which abridge the rights of American citizens. Although the Constitution specially says, no state shall do so, they *do* deprive persons of life, liberty and property without due process of law, and *do* deny equal protection of the laws to persons of Negro descent. The right of citizens to vote is denied and abridged in these states, on account of race, color and previous condition of servitude, and has been so denied ever since the withdrawal of the United States troops from the South. This in spite of the fifteenth amendment, which declares that no state shall do this.

These rights were denied first by violence and bloodshed, by ku-klux klans, who during the first years after the Civil War murdered Negroes by wholesale, for attempting to exercise the rights given by these amendments, and for trusting the government which was powerful enough to give them the ballot, to be strong enough to protect them in its exercise. Senator Tillman told how it was done in a speech on the floor of the United States Senate, when he said, that he and the people of South Carolina shot Negroes to death to keep them from voting. This they did till Congressional investigation of Ku-Klux methods turned the limelight on the unspeakable barbarism of those wholesale murders.

The South changed its tactics after that investigation, but never once let up on its aim to nullify and finally abrogate these amendments, and rob the Negro of the only protection to his citizenship—his ballot. Again we have the testimony of the United States Senator, on the floor of the Senate, as to how this was further done, when Senator Tillman defiantly told how he and his compatriots stuffed ballot boxes, and threw out those of that remnant of the black South, which still tried to register its gratitude at the polls.

When this bewildered race turned in dazed appeal to the Government which gave it freedom and the ballot, awaiting explanation and beseeching protection, it was told that the Government had made a mistake in enfranchising them; that it had offended the South by so doing, and was now busy repealing the civil rights bill, affirming Jim Crow legislation, upholding disfranchising state constitution, and removing in every way possible the constitutional guarantees to life, liberty and the pursuit of happiness, removing everything, in fact, which was offensive to those who had fired on the flag and tried to break up the union, and the Negro must now look out for himself.

This he has done for the past thirty years as best he could. He was advised that if he gave up trying to vote, minded his own business, acquired property and educated his children, he could get along in the South without molestation. But the more lands and houses he acquired, the more rapidly discriminating laws have been passed against him by those who control the ballot, and less protection is given by the lawmakers for his life, liberty and property. The Negro has been given separate and inferior schools, because he has no ballot. He therefore cannot protest against such legislation by choosing other law makers, or retiring to private life those who legislate against his interests. The more he sends his children to school the more restrictions are placed on Negro education, and he has absolutely no voice in the disposition of the school funds his taxes help to supply. His only weapon of defense has been taken from him by legal enactment in all of the old confederacy—and the United States Government, a consenting Saul, stands by holding the clothes of those who stone and burn him to death literally and politically.

With no sacredness of the ballot there can be no sacredness of human life itself. For if the strong can take the weak man's ballot, when it suits his purpose to do so, he will take his life also. Having successfully swept aside the constitutional safeguards to the ballot, it is the smallest of small matters for the South to sweep aside its own safeguards to human life. Thus "trial by jury" for the black man in that section has become a mockery, a plaything of the ruling classes and rabble alike. The mob says: "This people has no vote with which to punish us or the consenting officers of the law, therefore we indulge our brutal instincts, give free rein to race prejudice and lynch, hang, burn them when we please." Therefore, the more complete the disfranchisement, the more frequent and horrible has been the hangings, shootings, and burnings.

The records show that beginning with 1882, in which year there were fifty-two persons lynched, there was steady increase until 1892, when two hundred and fifty persons were lynched with the utmost cruelty, publicity and barbarism. Public sentiment condoned and approved this method of disposing of Negroes suspected or accused of misdemeanor or crime against white persons. The custom spread to the North, East and West and lynchings and burnings occurred in any community in which a crime was committed and suspicion put on the Negro. An effort made in 1893 to get these facts before the conscience of the world, proved by statistics based on charges made by the lynchers themselves, that less than one-fourth of the persons hanged, shot and burned by white Christians were even accused of the usual crime—that of assaulting white women.

From the year 1894 lynchings decreased year by year for the next decade. The conscience of the nation was again lulled to sleep and the record of the past ten years shows a surprising increase in lynchings and riot even in the North. No Northern state has more frequently offended in this crime than Illinois, the State of Lincoln, Grant and Logan. Since 1893 there have been sixteen lynchings within the State, including the Springfield riot. With each repetition there has been increased violence, rioting and barbarism. The last lynching, which took place November 11th of last year in Cairo, was one of the most inhuman spectacles every witnessed in this country.

The Negroes of Illinois have taken counsel together for a number of years over Illinois' increased lynching record. They elected one of their number to the State Legislature in 1904, who secured the passage of a bill which provided for the suppression of mob violence, not only by punishment of those who incited lynchings, but provided for damages against the City and County permitting lynchings. The Bill goes further and provides that if any person shall be taken from the custody of the Sheriff or his deputy and lynched, it shall be prima facie evidence of failure on the part of the Sheriff to do his duty. And upon that fact being made to appear to the Governor, he shall publish a proclamation declaring the office of Sheriff vacant, and such Sheriff shall not thereafter be eligible to either election or reappointment to the office. Provided, however, that such former Sheriff may within ten days after such lynching occurs file with the Governor his petition for reinstatement, and give ten days' notice of the filing of such petition. If the Governor upon hearing the evidence and argument, shall find that such Sheriff has done all within his power to protect the life of such prisoner then the Governor may reinstate the Sheriff and the decision of the Governor shall be final. This Bill passed both houses, was signed by Governor Deneen and became a law in 1905.

In the Springfield riot and lynching of two years later, the only parts of this law that were applicable were those providing punishment for the persons inciting rioting and lynching, and damages for the relatives of the victims of the mob. The men lynched then were not prisoners in the custody of the Sheriff, but peaceable, lawabiding citizens whom the mob lynched at their homes for the fun of it. Because of the dangerous public sentiment, which says it is all right to kill so long as the victim is a Negro, no jury has been found in Springfield to convict any of those who were tried for that lynching and murder.

On the morning of November 11th last year, a double lynching was reported from Cairo, Ill.—a white man and a Negro. A white girl had been found murdered two days before. The bloodhounds which were brought led to a Negro's house three blocks away. A Negro who had stayed in that house the night before was arrested and sweated for twenty-four hours. Although the only clew found was that the gag in the girl's mouth was the same kind of cloth as the handkerchief of the prisoner, threats of lynching him became so frequent that the Sheriff took him away from the city, back in the woods twenty-five miles away. When the mob had increased its numbers, they chartered a train, went after the Sheriff, brought him and his prisoner back to Cairo. A rope was thrown over Will James' neck, he was dragged off the train to the main business corner of the town. The rope was thrown over a steel arch, which had a double row of electric lights. The lights were turned on and the body hauled up in view of the assembled thousands of men, women and children. The rope broke before James was strangled to death and before hundreds of waiting bullets could be fired into his body. However, as many as could crowd around, emptied their revolvers into the quivering mass of flesh as it lay on the ground. Then seizing the rope the mob dragged the corpse a mile up Washington Street, the principle thoroughfare, to where the girl's body had been found. They were followed by a jeering, booting, laughing throng of all ages and of both sexes of white people. There they built a fire and placed this body on the flames. It was then dragged out of the fire, the head cut off and stuck on a nearby fence post. The trunk was cut open, the heart and other organs were cut out, sliced up and passed around as souvenirs of the ghastly orgy and our American civilization. Having tasted blood, a voice in the crowd said, "Let's get Salzner." Away went the mob to the county jail. Salzner, a white man, had been indicted for wife murder and was in jail awaiting trail. The suggestion is said to have come from the brother of Salzner's murdered wife. The mob demanded that the Sheriff, who had repaired to his office in the jail when Will James had been taken from him an hour before—get Salzner for them. He begged them to go away, but when they began battering in the doors he telephoned the Governor for troops. The lynchers got Salzner, hanged him in the court yard in front of the jail, emptied their remaining bullets in his body and went away. When troops reached the scene six hours later, they found, as the leading morning paper said next day, that "the fireworks were all over."

In mass meeting assembled the Negro citizens of Chicago called on Governor Deneen to do his duty and suspend the Sheriff. Two days later the Sheriff's office was vacated. Ten days more and Sheriff Davis had filed his petition for reinstatement, and on December 1st, argument was had before Governor Deneen both for and against the Sheriff.

The Sheriff's counsel, an ex-state Senator, and one of the leading lawyers of Southern Illinois, presented the Sheriff's petition of reinstatement, which declared he had done all in his power to protect the prisoners in his charge. He read letters and telegrams from Judges, editors, lawyers, bankers, merchants, clergymen, the Mayor of the City, Captain of Company K, of the State Militia, his political opponents and even the temporary incumbent of the Sheriff's office himself—all wrote to urge Sheriff Davis' reinstatement. The petitions were signed by hundreds of citizens in all walks of life and the Catholic Priest of Sheriff Davis' Parish was present all day and sat at the Sheriff's side.

As representing the people who had sent me to Cairo to get the facts, I told of the lynching, of visiting the scenes thereof, of the three days' interview with the colored people of Cairo, and of reading the files of every newspaper in the city published during the lynching to find some account of the steps that had been taken to protect the prisoner. I told of the mass meeting of the Negroes of Cairo in which a resolution was passed declaring that from Tuesday morning when Will James was arrested, until Thursday night when he was lynched—the Sheriff had neither sworn in deputies to aid him in defending the prisoners, nor called on the Governor for troops. We said that a reinstatement of the Sheriff would be an encouragement to mobs to hang, shoot, burn and pillage whenever they felt inclined in the future, as they had done in the past.

Governor Deneen rendered his decision a week later, removing the Sheriff. After reviewing the case he said:

> The sole question presented is, does the evidence show that the said Frank E. Davis, as Sheriff of Alexander County, did all in his power to protect the life of the prisoners and perform the duties required of him by existing laws for the protection of prisoners? The measure of the duty of the Sheriff is to be

determined from a consideration of his power. He is vested in his County with the whole executive power of the State. He wields within his jurisdiction all the power of the State for the preservation and protection of the public peace. In this capacity it is within his power to call to his aid when necessary any person or the power of the County. The law has made it a criminal offense for any person over the age of eighteen years to neglect or refuse to join the posse comitatus. In case the preservation of the peace and good order of society of any community shall require it, the Sheriff has the power to summon and enroll any number of special deputies. Such deputies when enrolled, have all the powers of deputy sheriffs and are subject absolutely to the orders of the Sheriff. It is made a criminal offense to decline to be enrolled as a special deputy. The Sheriff has the power to arm such force of special deputies to suppress riot. After having commanded the riotous persons to disperse, the Sheriff or his special deputies are justified in taking life should such riotous persons refuse to disperse.

The Sheriff is the keeper of the jail and has custody of all persons confined therein. In case of mob violence, which the Sheriff and his deputies are unable to suppress, the Sheriff may call upon the Governor for troops.

Such being the tremendous power vested in the Sheriff, what are his duties with respect to the protection of a prisoner who has been committed to his keeping?

Upon this question the Legislature has spoken in such terms as not to be misunderstood. It has cast upon the Sheriff the very highest degree of care. The Legislature in the mob violence Act of 1905, has said that in case a prisoner is taken from the Sheriff and lynched, the Sheriff after having been removed from office, must before reinstatement, show that he did all in his power to protect the life of such prisoner. The Legislature has in this Statute specifically defined the duty of the Sheriff. No part of his power can with safety be neglected. The very highest degree of care must be exercised for the protection of the prisoner. The Sheriff must take every precaution that human foresight can reasonably anticipate. In fact under the Statute, the Sheriff is practically the insurer of the safety of the prisoner.

The law guarantees to the prisoner a fair and impartial trial, not by mob violence, but by the orderly proceedings of duly constituted courts. To this the personal presence of the prisoner is necessary. To await his trial the State has deprived the prisoner of his liberty. By the Statue in question, however, the whole power of the State surrounds the prisoner and guarantees to him the protection of his life.

Measured with these standards it does not appear that Frank E. Davis, as Sheriff of Alexander County, did all in his power for the protection of the prisoners. The crime was of such a nature to excite great public indignation. Ordinary prudence would indicate that at such a time riots, turmoils and breaches of the peace might be expected. No attempt was made then, nor at any time, to summon or enroll special deputies. Not the slightest preparation was made to resist the mob. No showing is made that the jail in Alexander County would not have been safe for the confinement of the prisoner William James. The Sheriff knew some hours before taking William James into custody that mob violence was threatened. Knowing this he neither enrolled special deputies nor communicated with the Governor advising him of the fact and requesting the aid of troops, although two companies of State Militia were stationed in the City of Cairo. In the face of this the Sheriff took his prisoner almost without protection, outside the County. When the Sheriff left the train at Dongola, no attempt was made to communicate either with the Governor or with the Sheriff of Union County. While the Sheriff had the prisoner William James in custody, it does not appear from the evidence in my judgment, that reasonable precaution was taken for his protection.

After the execution of James the mob repaired to the County jail. Although cognizant of the temper of the mob, no effort whatever was made to place additional guards about the jail. Neither the Sheriff nor his deputies made any showing of force. The most that was done was to ask for volunteers. Although it must have taken some time to beat down the cell door, yet the Sheriff is unable to identify a single person composing the mob, or to identify a single person whom he asked to aid him in suppressing the mob. After Salzner was taken from his cell, no effort was made to follow up the mob and rescue Salzner.

In view of these facts only one conclusion can be reached, and that is that the Sheriff failed to take the necessary precaution for the protection of his prisoners. Mob violence has no place in Illinois. It is denounced in every line of the Constitution and in every Statute. Instead of breeding respect for the law it breeds contempt. For the suppression of mob violence our Legislature has spoken in no uncertain terms. When such mob violence threatens the life of a prisoner in the custody of the Sheriff, the law charges the Sheriff, at the penalty of the forfeiture of his office, to use the utmost human endeavor to protect the life of his prisoner. The law may be severe. Whether severe or not it must be enforced.

Believing as I do that Frank E. Davis, as Sheriff of Alexander County, did not do all within his power to protect the lives of William James and Henry Salzner, I must deny the petition of said Frank E. Davis for reinstatement as Sheriff of Alexander County, and the same is done accordingly.

Alexander County was one of the pivotal Counties, politically speaking, in the last election. Sheriff Davis belonged to the faction of the Republican party in Illinois, which gave Governor Deneen his re-election to the executive chair in 1908, by a smaller majority than four years before. It was believed that because of this the Governor was obligated to heed the wishes of Sheriff Davis' friends. But he had a higher obligation as Governor to protect the fair fame and uphold the Laws of Illinois. He had the highest obligation of protecting his friends from themselves, of enforcing their respect for the majesty of the law, and of aiding them to see beyond their passions and prejudices, "so they might rise on stepping stones of their dead selves to higher things."

It is believed that this decision with its slogan "Mob law can have no place in Illinois" has given lynching its death blow in this State. On three separate occasions since Sheriffs of other Counties in the State have checked the formation of mobs by calling at once on the Governor for troops, and in this way prevented the scheduled lynching.

But the people of Cairo were not convinced, besides they were in an ugly mood because of Sheriff Davis' retirement from office and they were determined to try the metal of the new Sheriff, who had sworn to uphold the laws. During the first week in March, two months ago, two Negroes were in jail in Cairo, having been arrested on suspicion of pocket-book snatching. Sheriff Nellis, having heard threats of lynching, immediately swore in special deputies and strengthened his guard at the jail. When the mob appeared at eleven o'clock that night, the Sheriff warned them not to cross the threshold. The warning was unheeded—a volley rang out, and one man—the leader of the mob—lay dead on the steps, and several more were wounded. No lynching took place that night and Sheriff Nellis had done what the Grand Jury of Alexander County, sitting for the whole month of December, had failed to do—found the leaders of a mob. The dead man was John Halliday, the son of a former Mayor of Cairo, and his uncle owns the leading hotel in Cairo—the Halliday House, which bears his name. The others who were wounded were men of like station. They have since been indicted by the Grand Jury and it rests with local public sentiment whether a jury can be found to convict them of attempted murder, and make their punishment so severe that the lesson will not soon be forgotten.

In this work all may aid. Individuals, organizations, press and pulpit should unite in vigorous denunciation of all forms of lawlessness and earnest, constant demand for the rigid enforcement of the law of the land. Nay, more than this, there must spring up in all sections of the country vigilant, aggressive defenders of the Constitution of our beloved land. South Carolina and her section have dominated this country to its hurt and sorrow from the beginning. When Payne wrote the Declaration of Independence, South Carolina refused to come into the Federation Colonies unless they struck out the clause abolishing slavery. She won, and slavery was fastened as an octopus upon the vitals of the land. She was responsible for the cringing, compromising, yielding attitude of Congress on the slavery question for the fifty years preceding the war. She fired on the flag of the United States and for the fifth time attempted to secede from the Union. She plunged the country into the most terrible Civil War the world has ever known. She has led in all the secession movements for the nullification of the constitution and for the abrogation of the 14th and 15th amendments. She has led in all the butcheries on the helpless Negro which makes the United States appear a more cruel government than Russia, for her deeds are not done under the guise of democracy and in the name of liberty.

Our Country's Lynching Record

The closing month of the year 1912 witnessed an incident which probably could not happen in any other civilized country. The governor of one of the oldest states of the Union in an address before the Conference of Governors defended the practice of lynching, and declared that he would willingly lead a mob to lynch a Negro who had assaulted a white woman. Twenty years ago, another governor of the same state not only made a similar statement, but while he was in office actually delivered to a mob a Negro who had merely been charged with this offense—it was unproven—and who had taken refuge with the governor for protection.

It is gratifying to know that the governors' meeting formally condemned these expressions, and that a leading Georgia citizen has undertaken to refute the sentiment expressed by Governor Blease. However, while no other official has thus officially encouraged this form of lawlessness, yet, because of the widespread acquiescence in the practice, many governors have refused to deal sternly with the leaders of mobs or to enforce the law against lynchers.

To the civilized world, which has demanded an explanation as to why human beings have been put to death in this lawless fashion, the excuse given has been the same as that voiced by Governor Blease a short month ago. Yet statistics show that in none of the thirty years of lynching has more than one-fourth of the persons hung, shot and burned to death, been even charged with this crime. During 1912, sixty-five persons were lynched.

Up to November 15 the distribution among the states was as follows:

Originally published in *Survey*, February 1, 1913, pp. 573-574.

Alabama	5	Oregon	1
Arkansas	3	Oklahoma	1
Florida	3	South Carolina	5
Georgia	11	Tennessee	5
Louisiana	4	Texas	3
Mississippi	5	Virginia	1
Montana	1	West Virginia	1
North Carolina	1	Wyoming	1
North Dakota	1		

Fifty of these were Negroes; three were Negro women. They were charged with these offenses:

Murder	26	Insults to white women	3
Rape	10	Attempted rape	2
Murderous assault	2	Assault and robbery	1
Complicity in murder	3	Race prejudice	1
Arson	3	No cause assigned	1

Because the Negro has so little chance to be heard in his own defense and because those who have participated in the lynching have written most of the stories about them, the civilized world has accepted almost without question the excuse offered.

From this table it appears that less than a sixth of these persons were lynched because the mob believed them to be guilty of assaulting white women. In some cases the causes have been trivial. And it appears that the northern states have permitted this lawless practice to develop and the lives of hapless victims to be taken with as much brutality, if not as frequently, as those of the South—witness, Springfield, Ill., a few years ago and Coatesville, Pa., only last year.

The lynching mania, so far as it affects Negroes, began in the South immediately after the Emancipation Proclamation fifty years ago. It manifested itself through what was known as the Ku Klux Klan, armed bodies of masked men, who during the period between 1865 and 1875, killed Negroes who tried to exercise the political rights conferred on them by the United States until by such terrorism the South regained political control. The aftermath of such practices is displayed in the following table giving the number of Negroes lynched in each year since 1885:

1885	184	1899	107
1886	138	1900	115
1887	122	1901	135
1888	142	1902	96
1889	176	1903	104
1890	127	1904	87
1891	192	1905	66
1892	235	1906	60
1893	200	1907	63
1894	190	1908	100
1895	171	1909	87
1896	131	1910	74
1897	106	1911	71
1898	127	1912	64

With the South in control of its political machinery, the new excuse was made that lynchings were necessary to protect the honor of white womanhood. Although black men had taken such good care of the white women of the South during the four years their masters were fighting to keep them in slavery, this calumny was published broadcast. The world believed it was necessary for white men in hundreds to lynch one defenseless Negro who had been accused of assaulting a white woman. In the thirty years in which lynching has been going on in the South, this falsehood has been universally accepted in all sections of our country, and has been offered by thousands as a reason why they do not speak out against these terrible outrages.

It is charged that a ceaseless propaganda has been going on in every northern state for years, with the result that not only is there no systematic denunciation of these horrible barbarisms, but northern cities and states have been known to follow the fashion of burning human beings alive. In no one thing is there more striking illustration of the North's surrender of its position on great moral ideas than in its lethargic attitude toward the lynching evil.

The belief is often expressed that if the North would stand as firmly for principle as the South does for prejudice, lynching and many other evils would be checked. It seems invariably true, however, that when principle and prejudice come into collision, principle retires and leaves prejudice the victor.

In the celebration of the fiftieth year of the Negro's freedom, does it seem too much to ask white civilization, Christianity and Democracy to be true to themselves on this as all other questions? They can not then be false to any man or race of men. Our democracy asserts that the people are fighting for the time when all men shall be brothers and the liberty of each shall be the concern of all. If this is true, the struggle is bound to take in the Negro. We cannot remain silent when the lives of men and women who are black are lawlessly taken, without imperiling the foundations of our government.

Civilization cannot burn human beings alive or justify others who do so; neither can it refuse a trial by jury for black men accused of crime, without making a mockery of the respect for law which is the safeguard of the liberties of white men. The nation cannot profess Christianity, which makes the golden rule its foundation stone, and continue to deny equal opportunity for life, liberty and the pursuit of happiness to the black race.

When our Christian and moral influences not only concede these principles theoretically but work for them practically, lynching will become a thing of the past, and no governor will again make a mockery of all the nation holds dear in the defense of lynching for any cause.

Index

Abbott, Robert S., 100, 122
Addams, Jane, 76, 84, 93, 101, 249
  and racial prejudice, 94
Africa
  black immigration to, 165-169
Afro-American Council
  1899 convention of, 77-78
  Anti-Lynching Bureau of, 240
  formation of, 72-74
  Washington, Booker T. dominates, 78-79
Afro-American League, 8
  formation of, 20
  reorganized as Afro-American Council, 72
Afro-American Press Association
  supports Wells-Barnett, 62-63
Aked, Reverend C.F., 52
Alpha Suffrage Club, 129
  activities of, 101-105
American Baptist, 16
American Missionary Association, 256
Anderson, Louis B., 105, 120
Anti-Caste, 37
Anti-Lynching Committee (London), 54
Aptheker, Herbert
  quoted on Wells-Barnett, 3
Arena, 5
Argyll, Duke of, 54
Astwood, H.C.C.
  quoted, 62
Atlanta Constitution, 39

Bain, James, 242
Baker, Postmaster
  murdered by mob, 245
Balgarnie, Florence, 57, 69, 70
  and 1895 World WCTU convention, 60
Barber, J. Max, 112
Barnett, Alfreda (daughter), 5
  quoted on her mother, 4
Barnett, Claude, 124

Barnett, Ferdinand L., 4, 5, 8
  his background and philosophy, 48-49
  loses race for judgeship, 110-112
  marriage to Ida B. Wells, 70, 85-86
  described, 108
  and *Memphis Commercial* lawsuit, 37
  and *The Reason Why*, 46
  text of his essay, 209-223
  state's attorney—his appointment, 86-109
  and World's Columbian Exposition,
    41-42, 44
Barrett, W.H. (white Memphis grocer),
  27-28, 173-176, 199
Bentley, Dr. Charles E., 79, 83, 87
  and *Chicago Conservator*, 49
Bentley, Mrs. Charles, 79
Bills, Nelson, 201
Binga, Jesse, 92
Black Bourgeoisie (Frazier), 6
Black Chicago (Spear), 6
Black Metropolis (Drake and Cayton), 3, 6,
  86, 91
Blair, Congressman Henry William
  his anti-lynching resolution, 65
Blair Resolution, 65, 69
Blease, Governor, 277
Boone, Mrs. R.D.
  and World's Columbian Exposition, 42,
    213
Bowen, Louise
  and Wendell Phillips Settlement, 97
Branham, Charles, 6
Breckenridge, Sophonisba
  and Wendell Phillips Settlement, 97
Broad Ax
  criticisms of Frederick Douglass Center,
    96
  report on 3/3/13 suffrage parade, 102
Broderick, Francis
  quoted, 8-9
Brooks, Virginia, 104

Brown, Hallie Quinn
and World's Columbian Exposition, 43,
214-215
supports Francis Willard, 60
Brown, John, 183
Bruce, Blanche K., 22
Bundy, Dr. Leroy
and East St. Louis, Illinois riots, 120, 122
Burleigh, Harry T., 47
Butler, General Benjamin, 185

Cantrill, Mary Cecil
and World's Columbian Exposition, 43
Carey, A.J., 112
Cassells, T.F.
and Wells-Barnett's suit against railroad,
13
Caughey, John Walton
quoted on lynching, 25-26
Cayton, Horace
his book *Black Metropolis*, 3, 6, 86, 91
Chesapeake, Ohio and Southwestern Rail-
road
Wells-Barnett's suit against, 13-15
Chicago Conservator, 16
described, 49
Wells-Barnett joins staff, 48
Chicago Federation of Colored Women, 100
Chicago Federation of Women's Clubs, 104
Chicago Herald
quoted, 223
Chicago Inter-Ocean
hires Wells-Barnett, 49
its column *Ida B. Wells Abroad*, 54
quoted on lynching, 207
Chicago Political Equality League, 101, 129
Chicago Tribune, 5
quoted on Wells-Barnett's marriage, 86
their lynching statistics, 26, 33, 196,
239-240, 250-252
Chicago Urban League, 99-100, 130
Childs, B.J., 201
Cincinnati American Citizen, 51
Cleveland, Grover, 108
Conservator, 109-110
Coy, Edward
burning of, 181, 203
Crawford, Lloyd W., 4, 62
Crawford, William J.

and World's Columbian Exposition,
219-221
Crisis
its woman suffrage symposium (1912),
101-102
Curtis, Mrs. A.M.
and World's Columbian Exposition,
43-44, 218
Cutler, James
on lynching, 25, 26

Dancy, John C. (vice-president of Afro-
American Council), 74
Davis, Allan, 93-94
Davis, Elizabeth Lindsay
quoted, 90
Davis, George S.
and World's Columbian Exposition, 211
Davis, Sheriff Frank
his prisoners lynched, 114
reinstatement hearing, 115-117, 129
described by Wells-Barnett, 272-274
Davis, Dr. S.N., 221
Dawson, Frederick, 242
Delegal, John, 247
Democratic Party, 107
Deneen, Charles S., 86, 109, 113, 114, 125,
270
and Sheriff Davis reinstatement hearing,
116-117, 272-274
DePriest, Oscar, 105, 106, 119
Detroit Plaindealer
Wells-Barnett quoted in, 20
Diner, Steven, 97
Donnelly, Ignatius, 255
Douglas, Warren B., 126
Douglass, Frederick, 5, 5, 8
and rape myth, 32
A Red Record (Wells-Barnett)—his ideas
the basis for, 68-69
and *The Reason Why*, 41, 44-46
Southern Horrors (Wells-Barnett)—
involvement in publication of, 32-33
on southern mob and its victims, 56-57
Wells-Barnett requests letter of intro-
duction, 52-54
Wells-Barnett—encourages her to lecture
in England, 38
and Wells-Barnett/Willard controversy, 59

Willard, Francis—criticism of her interview, 56, 57
and World's Columbian Exposition, 44,
223
Colored American Day address, 47
Drake, St. Clair
his book *Black Metropolis*, 3, 6, 86, 91
Dreyfus, Captain Alfred, 243
Du Bois, W.E.B., 8-9, 101, 130
1899 Afro-American Council convention—quoted on, 77
1899 NACW meeting—quoted on, 77
and NAACP, 81-83
and Niagara Movement, 80-81
his book *The Souls of Black Folk*, 9, 79
and Wells-Barnett, 9
quoted on her death, 126
Duke, J.C., 30
Dunbar, Paul Laurence, 47
Duster, Alfreda (*see* Alfreda Barnett)

East St. Louis, Illinois
1917 riots there, 119-122
Edwards, Celestine, 52
The Ethnic Frontier (Holli and Jones), 6-7
Evening Star
Wells-Barnett edits, 15
Ewing, Quincy
quoted on blacks, 27

Farnham, G.N.
and World's Columbian Exposition, 220
Federation of Afro-American Women
endorsement of Wells-Barnett, 70
Fellowship Herald (Negro Fellowship League
publication)
described, 98-99
Fleming, J.L. (co-owner of *Free Speech*), 18,
22, 23, 29, 30, 179
quoted on Wells-Barnett's lecture tour, 51
Fortune, T. Thomas, 30, 63, 107
Afro-American Council
chair of executive committee, 74
and 1899 convention, 78
and the Afro-American League, 8, 20, 72
and Booker T. Washington, 79
on black immigration to Africa, 165
and Washington, Booker T., 75, 79
and Wells-Barnett, 19-20

first meeting with, 18
quoted on, 1, 2, 3, 18, 127
Franklin, John Hope
quoted, 1
Fraternity
Wells-Barnett article in, 57
Frazier, E. Franklin
his book *Black Bourgeoisie*, 6
his book *The Negro Family in the United
States*, 6
quoted, 7
quoted on black women, 2-3
Frederick Douglas Center, 94-96
Freedmen's Aid Society, 256
Free Speech
advises leaving Memphis, 176
contents of, 22-23
destruction of, 30, 177-180
Wells-Barnett describes its success, 172
Wells-Barnett purchases, 18-19

Gallinger, Senator, 264
Garrett, Edward (Isabelle Fyvie Mayo), 38
Garrison, William Lloyd, 183
General Federation of Women's Clubs, 89
denies Mary Church Terrell right to speak
at 1900 convention, 90
treatment of Josephine St. Pierre Ruffin
at 1900 convention, 90-91
Ginger, Ray, 92
Gosnell, Harold, 110
his book *Negro Politicians*, 6
Grady, Henry, 20
Graves, John Temple, 112
quoted defending lynching, 262
Green, Edward, 113
Green, Steve, 83, 128
charged with murder, 117-118
Greer, Judge
and Wells-Barnett's suit against railroad,
13-14
Griffin, Charles B., 105

Hall, Dr. George Cleveland, 100, 130
Halliday, John (leader of Cairo, Illinois
mob), 275
Hannah, Mark, 78
Harding, George F., 105
Harlan, Louis

on Booker T. Washington's Atlanta speech, 75,
quoted on Judge Robert H. Terrell's appointment, 79
Harrison, Carter H.
speaks at 1899 NACW meeting, 77
Harrison, President Benjamin
and World's Columbian Exposition, 41, 211, 217, 223
Haygood, Bishop Atticus G.
on lynching, 39-40
Hill, James, 11
Hill, T. Arnold (organizer of the Chicago Urban League), 100
Hirsch, Rabbi Emil G., 101
History of the Club Movement among Colored Women of the United States of America, A, 5
Holli, Melvin
his book *The Ethnic Frontier*, 6
Hose, Sam
burned alive, 240-241
Hoss, Reverend Dr. E.E.
on lynching, 39-40
House, Henry, 11
House, J.N., 201
Howard, Joan Imogene
and World's Columbian Exposition, 43, 214
Huntington, Collis P., 257
Hutton, Mary
her Ph.D. dissertation, 4

Ida B. Wells Abroad (Chicago Inter-Ocean column), 5
Ida B. Wells Club, 128
described, 90
founding of, 47-48
If Christ Came to Chicago (Stead), 47
Illinois Equal Suffrage Association, 101, 129
Imes, Reverend Benjamin A., 15, 36
Impey, Catherine
controversy with Isabelle Fyvie Mayo, 52
invites Wells-Barnett to speak in England, 37-38
Independent, 5
Indianapolis Freeman, 20/22
and *The Reason Why*, 44-45
quoted on Wells-Barnett and anti-lynching movement, 64-65

Indianapolis World, 16

Jacks, John W.
letter attacking Wells-Barnett, 69, 70
Jackson, R.R., 120
James, William, 114, 116
his lynching described, 271
Johnson, James Weldon, 9, 81, 122
Johnson, J.E.
and World's Columbian Exposition, 43, 218
Jones, John G.
and *Chicago Conservator*, 49
Jones, Peter d'A.
his book *The Ethnic Frontier*, 7
The Journal of Negro History
lack of articles on black women, 1-2

Kellogg, Charles Flint, 118
Knights of Labor meeting
Wells-Barnett article on, 15-16
Knights of the Golden Circle, 261
Knights of White Liners, 184
Knox, George, 44
Kraditor, Aileen
quoted, 102
Kreiling, Albert, 6
quoted, 34, 87-88, 110
Ku Klux Klan, 12, 184, 236, 237, 261, 268, 278

Langston, John M., 55
Lawson, Mrs. Victor
and Negro Fellowship League, 97, 99
League of Cook County Clubs, 90, 128
Lerner, Gerda
on black women's clubs, 90
Lewis, Will
lynching of, 182-183, 197
Liberia
and black immigration there, 167-168
Little Rock Sun, 18
Living Way
Wells-Barnett's articles in, 15
London Daily News
quoted, 60
Loudin, Frederick J.
and *The Reason Why*, 41

Lovejoy, Elijah, 184
Lowden, Frank O. (Illinois Governor), 119, 122
Lynch, Colonel William
and "lynch law," 195
Lyons, Maritcha
sponsors fund-raiser for Wells-Barnett, 32

McCadden, Mollie, 200
McCormick, Ruth, 125
McDowell, Calvin
lynching of, 27-28, 199
described by Wells-Barnett, 173-176
MacDowell, Mary, 93
McKinley, President William, 74
Wells-Barnett protests postmaster lynching to, 74
Macon Telegraph, 39
Majors, Monroe A.
quoted on Wells-Barnett, 2
Massa, Ann
on *The Reason Why*, 46-47
on World's Columbian Exposition, 42
Matthews, Victoria Earle
sponsors fund-raiser for Wells-Barnett, 32
Mayo, Isabelle Fyvie (Edward Garrett), 38
controversy with Catherine Impey, 52
Meier, August, 89
on lynching, 25
Memphis Appeal-Avalanche, 36, 39, 55
quoted, 203
Memphis Commercial
Wells Barnett considers suit against, 36-37
Memphis Commercial Appeal
on Wells-Barnett's second British tour, 51
Memphis Daily Commercial
on Wells-Barnett's anti-lynching campaign, 54-55
quoted, 177-178
Memphis lynchings (1892)
described by Wells-Barnett, 173-177
Midnight Raiders, 261
Miller, C.J.
burning of, 245
lynching of, 203-204, 207
Miller, Dean Kelly, 82
Mobile Register
on Wells-Barnett's second British tour, 51

Mob Rule in New Orleans (Wells-Barnett pamphlet), 5, 118
Montgomery, Isaiah
and 1899 Afro-American Council convention, 77-78
Montgomery Herald, 30
Moody, J.S., 201
Moody, Reverend Dwight L., 56
Moody-Sankey revival meeting
Wells-Barnett article on, 15-16
Moskowitz, Henry
and National Negro Conference, 81
Moss, Betty (wife of Thomas Moss), 176
photographed with Wells-Barnett, 31
Moss, Thomas
lynching of, 27-28, 199
described by Wells-Barnett, 173-176
quoted, 29, 175
Motts, Robert T., 112
Mundy, James A., 101
Murray, Pauli
on Wells-Barnett, 1-2
quoted, 3

NAACP, 8, 130
and Wells-Barnett, 81-84
founding of, 81-83
NACW (*see* National Association of Colored Women)
Nashville American
quoted, 185
National American Women's Suffrage Association
and 3/3/13 Washington suffrage parade, 102
National Association for the Advancement of Colored People (*see* NAACP)
National Association of Colored Women
1899 convention of, 75-77
formation of, 71-72
National Colored Press Association
1887 annual convention, 18
National Equal Rights League, 98
National Federation of Afro-American Women
formation of, 70-71
National League of Colored Women, 70, 71
National Negro Conference, 81
National Press Association, 23
National Urban League, 9

The Negro Family in the United States (Frazier), 6
Negro Fellowship League, 9
  founding and programs, 97-100
Negro Politicians (Gosnell), 6
Newby, I.A.
  quoted, 67
Newhouse, A., 201
New York Age, 18, 61
  Wells-Barnett joins, 30
New York Freeman, 16
  Wells-Barnett's articles in, 17
The New York News, 105
The New York Times, 5, 62
New York Voice
  Francis Willard interview, 57
Niagara Movement, 80-81
Nightingale, Reverend F. (co-owner of *Free Speech*), 18, 22, 23, 178, 179
Norris, I.F., 29
Northern, W.J. (Georgia governor), 61

O'Ferrall, Charles (Virginia governor), 62-63
Olson, Judge Harry
  appoints Wells-Barnett probation officer, 99, 119
  race for mayor, 105-106
Ovington, Mary White
  and National Negro Conference, 81
  quoted, 83

Palmer, Mrs. Potter
  and World's Columbian Exposition, 41, 42, 43
Park, Robert E., 100
Parker, Hale G.
  and World's Columbian Exposition, 41, 217
Penn, I. Garland, 5
  and *The Reason Why*, 46
Peterson, Jerome B. (co-editor of the *New York Age*), 30
Peterson, John
  lynching of, 203, 245-246
Pierce, Judge J.O.
  and Wells-Barnett's suit against railroad, 13-14
Pillsbury, A.E., 264
Plummer, Mrs. George W., 90, 94, 112

Price, J.C.
  and World's Columbian Exposition, 42

Ransom, Reverend Reverdy C.
  and 1899 Afro-American Council convention, 78
  his Chicago ministry, 93
  and kindergarten for blacks, 88-89
The Reason Why, 5, 41, 44-47
  text of two chapters, 189-223
A Red Record (Wells-Barnett), 5, 68-69
Republican Party, 36, 107
  Wells-Barnett on (1892), 186
Revels, Hiram Rhodes, 11
Rice, Colonel Edward
  and World's Columbian Exposition, 219-220, 221
Richmond Dispatch, 61
Ridley, Mrs. F.R., 70
Roberts, Adelbert
  defeats Wells-Barnett for state senate, 125, 126
Roosevelt, President Theodore
  appoints Robert H. Terrell to judgeship, 79
Ruffin, Josephine St. Pierre
  and 1899 NACW convention, 76
  treatment at 1900 convention of General Federation of Women's Clubs, 90-91
  and National Federation of Afro-American Women—formation of, 70-71
  and Women's Era Club, 69-70
Russell, Charles Edward
  and National Negro Conference, 81

Salzner, Henry, 116
  lynching of, 271-272
Shaw, Ed, 15
Shaw University, 12-13
Smith, Henry
  burning of, 181-182, 203
Smith, Lucy Wilmot, 2
Smith, T.L., 201
Society for the Recognition of the Brotherhood of Man, 52, 53
  founding of, 38-39
Somerset, Lady Henry
  and 1895 World WCTU convention, 60
  and Wells-Barnett/Willard controversy, 57

The Souls of Black Folk (Du Bois), 9, 79
Southern Horrors (Wells-Barnett), 5
  arguments described, 33-34
  publication of, 32
Southern Press Association, 23
Spear, Allan, 85, 87, 91
  his book *Black Chicago*, 6
Spingarn, Joel, 5, 9, 83, 119
  and Steve Green case, 118
Springfield, Illinois
  riots there (1908), 113-114
Squire, Belle, 104
Stead, W.T., 47
Stevens, Lou
  hanging of, 198
Steward, Henry
  murdered by mob, 27-28
Stewart, William
  lynching of, 199
  described by Wells-Barnett, 173-176
Still, William, 37
Stone, W.J (Missouri governor), 61
Strickland, Arvarh
  on Chicago Urban League, 100
Sumner, Charles, 184
Sumner, William Graham
  quoted on lynching, 25
Survey, 5

Taylor, C.H.J, 51
Taylor, Julius, 96
Terrell, Mary Church, 5, 82, 84, 98, 102
  1899 NACW convention—quoted on, 76-77
  excludes Wells-Barnett from, 71, 75-76
  General Federation of Women's Clubs 1900 convention—prevented from speaking, 90
  Harlan, Louis quoted on, 79
  NACW—elected president of, 71
  and National League of Colored Women, 70
Terrell, Robert H.
  appointed to judgeship, 79
Thompson, John W. (treasurer of Afro-American Council), 74
Thompson, Mayor, 123
Thompson, William Hale, 105, 106, 129
Tillman, Governor, 245
Tillman, Senator, 268

Topeka Weekly Call, 61
Tourgee, Judge Albion W., 5, 45, 54, 181, 203
  on anti-lynching campaign, 58-59
  quoted, 33
  Wells-Barnett consults, 36-37
Tourgee Club, 47
Trent, Mrs. Lettie A.
  and World's Columbian Exposition, 42, 213
Trotter, William Monroe, 8, 82, 83, 108
  speaks to Negro Fellowship League, 98
Tucker, David M., 28
Turner, Bishop Henry McNeal, 165
  and 1899 Afro-American Council convention, 78
  on black immigration to Africa, 167
  quoted, 55
  speaks at 1899 NACW meeting, 77
Turner, J. Thomas, 55
Turner, Nat, 183, 246

Union Signal (WCTU), 59

Vardaman, Governor, 258
Villard, Oswald Garrison, 9, 84
  and National Negro Conference, 81
  and Steve Green case, 118
  at 1909 national conference, 82
Virginia Lancet
  quoted, 195
The Voice of the Negro, 112

Waldran, A.C., 201
Walker, Eunice Rivers
  her MA thesis, 4
Walker, Lee
  lynching of described, 199-203
Walling, William English
  and National Negro Conference, 81
Walters, Bishop Alexander, 78
  and Afro-American Council, 74
  and Booker T. Washington, 79
Washington, Booker T., 7, 8, 130
  Afro-American Council—his domination of, 78-79
  and Fortune, T. Thomas, 79

NAACP founding conference—invited to, 81

Wells-Barnett attacks in print, 80
    text of article, 255-260

Wells-Barnett calls ideas erroneous, 74

Washington, Mrs. Booker T., 78
    first president of National Federation of Afro-American Women, 71

Washington, Margaret Murray, 102

Washington City Post, 39

Watchman
    Wells-Barnett article in, 15-16

WCTU
    and Willard/Wells-Barnett controversy, 56-61

Weems, Frank, 33

Wells, Jim (father of Wells-Barnett), 11, 12

Wells, Lizzie Warrenton (mother of Wells-Barnett), 11, 12

Wells-Barnett, Ida B.
    1899 Afro-American Council convention, 78
    Afro-American Council, 72-74
    Afro-American League, 20
    Alpha Suffrage Club, 101-105
    British lecture tour—first, 38-39
    second, *see* Chapter Five
    Colored American Day, 44
    Davis, Sheriff Frank—reinstatement hearing, 115-117, 129
    Douglass, Frederick—she asks for letter of introduction, 52-54
    Du Bois—her hostility toward, 83
    East St. Louis riots, 119-122
    Frederick Douglass Center, 94-96
    Free Speech, 18-19, 22
    Green, Steve case, 117-118
    Hoover, Herbert—campaigns for (1928), 124
    as Iola, 15, 16
    kindergarten for blacks, 88-89
    marriage to Ferdinand Barnett, 70, 85-86
    described, 108
    Memphis lynchings (1892), 28-29
    her description of, 173-177
    Mob Rule in New Orleans—her pamphlet, 118
    NAACP, 81-84
    NACW formation meeting, 71-72
    runs for presidency, 124
    excluded from 1899 meeting, 72, 75-76

Negro Fellowship League, 97-100

New York Age—joins staff, 30

postmaster lynching—protests to President McKinley, 74

railroad—suit against, 13-15

A Red Record—her pamphlet, 68-69

The Souls of Black Folk—her report on reception of, 79-80

Southern Horrors—her pamphlet, 32-34
    her state senate race, 125-126
    speech at 1909 national conference, 81
    suffrage parade—3/3/13, Washington, D.C., 102

Washington, Booker T.
    calls his ideas erroneous, 74
    she attacks in print, 80 [text of article, 255-260]

Willard, Francis—controversy with, 56-61

Wendell Phillips Settlement, 97

White, Congressman George, 246

White, Walter, 9

Willard, Frances
    Douglass, Mrs. Frederick—writes to, 60-61
    her offensive interview quoted, 56
    Wells-Barnett—her controversy with, 56-61

William Randolph Cowan, 105

Williams, A.M., 115

Williams, Dr. Daniel Hale, 49, 87, 130
    and World's Columbian Exposition, 42

Williams, Fannie Barrier, 47, 75, 79, 84, 93
    and 1899 NACW convention, 76
    background of, 44
    Chicago Women's Club—admitted to, 90
    and Frederick Douglass Center, 96
    and World's Columbian Exposition, 42, 44, 218
    women's club movement—quoted on, 89

Williams, S. Laing, 44, 79
    and lawsuit against *Memphis Commercial*, 37

Wilson, Woodrow, 108

Wolseley, Roland E.
    quoted, 2

Women's Christian Temperance Union (*see* WCTU)

Women's Era, 70

Women's Era Club, 69

Women's Loyal Union of New York and Brooklyn

    sponsors fund-raiser for Wells-Barnett, 32
Woodson, Carter G., 26
    his book *The Negro in Our History*, 1
Woodward, C. Vann
    on Southern racism, 67-68
Wooley, Celia Parker, 79, 83
    and Frederick Douglass Center, 94-96
World's Columbian Exposition (1893), 41-47
    blacks denied participation (F.L. Barnett describes), 209-223
    and *The Reason Why*, 193
World's Congress of Representative Women, 44
Wright, Edward H., 109, 119, 125, 129
    and Steve Green case, 118

Black Women in United States History: A Guide to the Series

Contents of the Series 3
Author Index 11
Subject Index 15

PUBLISHER'S NOTE

The sixteen volumes in this set contain 248 articles, in addition to five monographs. This *Guide to the Series* is designed to help the reader find *every* substantive discussion of a topic of interest in the articles. Included in the subject index are general topics such as education and family life, as well as individuals to whom articles are devoted. Geographical locations are included when they are an important part of the article. Professions are also included. Thus, one can look up Fannie Lou Hamer (three articles), Kansas (two articles), or nursing (four articles). The more than 200 authors represented in the index to authors are a who's who of contemporary scholarship.

For topics in the five monographs and for specific discussions in the articles, please see the comprehensive indexes for every title. The more than 10,000 entries in these indexes make this series a virtual encyclopedia of black women's history.

Contents of the Series

Vols. 1-4. **BLACK WOMEN IN AMERICAN HISTORY: FROM COLONIAL TIMES THROUGH THE NINETEENTH CENTURY,** Edited with a Preface by Darlene Clark Hine

1. Akers, Charles W. *'Our Modern Egyptians': Phillis Wheatley and the Whig Campaign Against Slavery in Revolutionary Boston.*
2. Alexander, Adele L. *How I Discovered My Grandmother...and the Truth About Black Women and the Suffrage Movement.*
3. Aptheker, Bettina. *Quest for Dignity: Black Women in the Professions, 1865-1900.*
4. Axelson, Diana E. *Women As Victims of Medical Experimentation: J. Marion Sims' Surgery on Slave Women, 1845-1850.*
5. Berkeley, Kathleen C. *'Colored Ladies Also Contributed': Black Women's Activities from Benevolence to Social Welfare, 1866-1896.*
6. Berlin, Ira, Steven F. Miller, and Leslie S. Rowland. *Afro-American Families in the Transition from Slavery to Freedom.*
7. Blackburn, George and Sherman L. Ricards. *The Mother-Headed Family Among Free Negroes In Charleston, South Carolina, 1850-1860.*
8. Bogin, Ruth. *Sarah Parker Remond: Black Abolitionist from Salem.*
9. Brooks, Evelyn. *The Feminist Theology of the Black Baptist Church, 1880-1900.*
10. Burnham, Dorothy. *The Life of the Afro-American Woman in Slavery.*
11. Bynum, Victoria. *On the Lowest Rung: Court Control Over Poor White and Free Black Women.*
12. Clinton, Catherine. *Caught in the Web of the Big House: Women and Slavery.*
13. Cody, Cheryll Ann. *Naming, Kinship, and Estate Dispersal: Notes on Slave Family Life on a South Carolina Plantation, 1786-1833.*
14. Cole, Johnnetta. *Militant Black Women in Early U.S. History.*
15. Conrad, Earl. *I Bring You General Tubman.*
16. Cunningham, Constance A. *The Sin of Omission: Black Women in Nineteenth Century American History.*
17. Davis, Angela. *Reflections on the Black Woman's Role in the Community of Slaves.*
18. de Graaf, Lawrence B. *Race, Sex and Region: Black Women in the American West, 1850-1920.*
19. Dodson, Jualynne. *Nineteenth-Century A.M.E. Preaching Women: Cutting Edge of Women's Inclusion in Church Polity.*
20. Dorsey, Carolyn A. *Despite Poor Health: Olivia Davidson Washington's Story.*
21. Dorsey, Carolyn A. *The Pre-Hampton Years of Olivia A. Davidson.*
22. Farnham, Christie. *Sapphire? The Issue of Dominance in the Slave Family, 1830-1865.*
23. Fish, Beverly. *Sojourner Truth: Crusader for Womens' Rights.*

Volumes 1-4, continued

24. Foster, Frances Smith. *Adding Color and Contour to Early American Self-Portraitures: Autobiographical Writings of Afro-American Women.*
25. Fox-Genovese, Elizabeth. *Strategies and Forms of Resistance: Focus on Slave Women in the United States.*
26. Fry, Gladys-Marie. *Harriet Powers: Portrait of a Black Quilter.*
27. Goldin, Claudia *Female Labor Force Participation: The Origins of Black and White Differences, 1870 and 1880.*
28. Goodson, Martia G. *Medical-Botanical Contributions of African Slave Women to American Medicine.*
29. Goodson, Martia G. *The Slave Narrative Collection: A Tool for Reconstructing Afro-American Women's History.*
30. Gregory, Chester W. *Black Women in Pre-Federal America.*
31. Griggs, A. C. *Lucy Craft Laney.*
32. Gundersen, Joan R. *The Double Bonds of Race and Sex: Black and White Women in a Colonial Virginia Parish.*
33. Gutman, Herbert G. *Marital and Sexual Norms among Slave Women.*
34. Gwin, Minrose C. *Green-eyed Monsters of the Slavocracy: Jealous Mistresses in Two Slave Narratives.*
35. Hanchett, Catherine M. *'What Sort of People and Families . . .' The Edmondson Sisters.*
36. Harris, William. *Work and the Family in Black Atlanta, 1880.*
37. Hartgrove, W. B. *The Story of Maria Louise Moore and Fannie M. Richards.*
38. Hartigan, Lynda R. *Edmonia Lewis.*
39. Hine, Darlene Clark. *Co-Laborers in the Work of the Lord: Nineteenth-Century Black Women Physicians.*
40. Hine, Darlene Clark. *Female Slave Resistance: The Economics of Sex.*
41. Horton, James Oliver. *Freedom's Yoke: Gender Conventions Among Antebellum Free Blacks.*
42. Jacobs, Sylvia M. *Three Afro-American Women Missionaries in Africa, 1882-1904.*
43. Johnson, Michael P. *Smothered Slave Infants: Were Slave Mothers at Fault?*
44. Jones, Jacqueline. *'My Mother Was Much of a Woman': Black Women, Work, and the Family Under Slavery.*
45. Kennan, Clara B. *The First Negro Teacher in Little Rock.*
46. Kulikoff, Alan. *Beginnings of the Afro-American Family.*
47. Lawson, Ellen N. *Sarah Woodson Early: 19th Century Black Nationalist 'Sister'.*
48. Lawson, Ellen N. and Merrell, Marlene. *Antebellum Black Coeds at Oberlin College.*
49. Leashore, Bogart R. *Black Female Workers: Live-in Domestics in Detroit, Michigan, 1860-1880.*
50. Lebsock, Suzanne. *Free Black Women and the Question of Matriarchy: Petersburg, Virginia, 1784-1820.*
51. Mabee, Carleton. *Sojourner Truth, Bold Prophet: Why Did She Never Learn to Read?*
52. Massa, Ann. *Black Women in the 'White City'.*
53. Matson, R. Lynn. *Phillis Wheatley—Soul Sister?*
54. Matthews, Jean. *Race, Sex and the Dimensions of Liberty in Antebellum America.*
55. Mills, Gary B. *Coincoin: An Eighteenth Century 'Liberated' Woman.*
56. Moses, Wilson Jeremiah. *Domestic Feminism Conservatism, Sex Roles, and Black Women's Clubs, 1893-1896.*
57. Newman, Debra L. *Black Women in the Era of the American Revolution in Pennsylvania.*
58. Obitko, Mary Ellen. *'Custodians of a House of Resistance': Black Women Respond to Slavery.*

Volumes 1-4, continued

59. Oden, Gloria C. *The Journal of Charlotte L. Forten: The Salem-Philadelphia Years (1854-1862) Reexamined.*
60. Parkhurst, Jessie W. *The Role of the Black Mammy in the Plantation Household.*
61. Perkins, Linda M. *Heed Life's Demands: The Educational Philosophy of Fanny Jackson Coppin.*
62. Perkins, Linda M. *The Black Female American Missionary Association Teacher in the South, 1861-1870.*
63. Perkins, Linda M. *The Impact of the 'Cult of True Womanhood' on the Education of Black Women.*
64. Perkins, Linda M. *Black Women and Racial 'Uplift' Prior to Emancipation.*
65. Pleck, Elizabeth H. *The Two-Parent Household: Black Family Structure in Late Nineteenth Century Boston.*
66. Porter, Dorothy B. *Sarah Parker Remond, Abolitionist and Physician.*
67. Quarles, Benjamin. *Harriet Tubman's Unlikely Leadership.*
68. Riley, Glenda. *American Daughters: Black Women in the West.*
69. Reiff, Janice L., Michael R. Dahlin, and Daniel Scott Smith. *Rural Push and Urban Pull: Work and Family Experiences of Older Black Women in Southern Cities, 1880-1900.*
70. Schafer, Judith K. *'Open and Notorious Concubinage': The Emancipation of Slave Mistresses by Will and the Supreme Court in Antebellum Louisiana.*
71. Sealander, Judith. *Antebellum Black Press Images of Women.*
72. Seraile, William. *Susan McKinney Steward: New York State's First African-American Woman Physician.*
73. Shammas, Carole. *Black Women's Work and the Evolution of Plantation Society in Virginia.*
74. Silverman, Jason H. *Mary Ann Shadd and the Search for Equality.*
75. Sloan, Patricia E. *Early Black Nursing Schools and Responses of Black Nurses to their Educational Programs.*
76. Soderlund, Jean R. *Black Women in Colonial Pennsylvania.*
77. Sterling, Dorothy. *To Build A Free Society: Nineteenth-Century Black Women.*
78. Sumler-Lewis, Janice. *The Forten-Purvis Women of Philadelphia and the American Anti-Slavery Crusade.*
79. Tate, Claudia. *Pauline Hopkins: Our Literary Foremother.*
80. Terborg-Penn, Rosalyn. *Black Women Freedom Fighters in Early 19th Century Maryland.*
81. Thompson, Priscilla. *Harriet Tubman, Thomas Garrett, and the Underground Railroad.*
82. Tucker, David M. *Miss Ida B. Wells and Memphis Lynching.*
83. Vacha, John E. *The Case of Sara Lucy Bagby: A Late Gesture.*
84. Wade-Gayles, Gloria. *Black Women Journalists in the South, 1880-1905: An Approach to the Study of Black Women's History.*
85. White, Deborah G. *The Lives of Slave Women.*

Vols. 5-8. BLACK WOMEN IN AMERICAN HISTORY: THE TWENTIETH CENTURY, Edited with a Preface by Darlene Clark Hine

1. *Votes for Women: A Symposium by Leading Thinkers of Colored America.*
2. Anderson, Karen T. *Last Hired, First Fired: Black Women Workers During World War II.*
3. Anderson, Kathie R. *Era Bell Thompson: A North Dakota Daughter.*
4. Blackwelder, Julia Kirk. *Quiet Suffering: Atlanta Women in the 1930s.*

Volumes 5-8, continued

5. Blackwelder, Julia Kirk. *Women in the Work Force: Atlanta, New Orleans, and San Antonio, 1930 to 1940.*
6. Brady, Marilyn Dell. *Kansas Federation of Colored Women's Clubs, 1900-1930.*
7. Brady, Marilyn Dell. *Organizing Afro-American Girls' Clubs in Kansas in the 1920's.*
8. Breen, William J. *Black Women and the Great War: Mobilization and Reform in the South.*
9. Brooks, Evelyn. *Religion, Politics, and Gender: The Leadership of Nannie Helen Burroughs.*
10. Brown, Elsa Barkley. *Womanist Consciousness: Maggie Lena Walker and the Independent Order of Saint Luke.*
11. Bryan, Violet H. *Frances Joseph-Gaudet: Black Philanthropist.*
12. Cantarow, Ellen and Susan Gushee O'Malley. *Ella Baker: Organizing for Civil Rights.*
13. Carby, Hazel V. *It Jus Be's Dat Way Sometime: The Sexual Politics of Women's Blues.*
14. Chateauvert, Melinda. *The Third Step: Anna Julia Cooper and Black Education in the District of Columbia, 1910-1960.*
15. Clark-Lewis, Elizabeth. *'This Work Had a End:' African-American Domestic Workers in Washington, D.C., 1910-1940.*
16. Coleman, Willi. *Black Women and Segregated Public Transportation: Ninety Years of Resistance.*
17. Ergood, Bruce. *The Female Protection and the Sun Light: Two Contemporary Negro Mutual Aid Societies.*
18. Farley, Ena L. *Caring and Sharing Since World War I: The League of Women for Community Service—A Black Volunteer Organization in Boston.*
19. Feinman, Clarice. *An Afro-American Experience: The Women in New York City's Jail.*
20. Ferguson, Earline Rae. *The Women's Improvement Club of Indianapolis: Black Women Pioneers in Tuberculosis Work, 1903-1938.*
21. Ford, Beverly O. *Case Studies of Black Female Heads of Households in the Welfare System: Socialization and Survival.*
22. Gilkes, Cheryl Townsend. *'Together and in Harness': Women's Traditions in the Sanctified Church.*
23. Gilkes, Cheryl Townsend. *Going Up for the Oppressed: The Career Mobility of Black Women Community Workers.*
24. Gilkes, Cheryl Townsend. *Successful Rebellious Professionals: The Black Woman's Professional Identity and Community Commitment.*
25. Gunn, Arthur C. *The Struggle of Virginia Proctor Powell Florence.*
26. Guzman, Jessie P. *The Social Contributions of the Negro Woman Since 1940.*
27. Harley, Sharon. *Beyond the Classroom: Organizational Lives of Black Female Educators in the District of Columbia, 1890-1930.*
28. Harley, Sharon. *Black Women in a Southern City: Washington, D.C., 1890-1920.*
29. Haynes, Elizabeth Ross. *Negroes in Domestic Service in the United States.*
30. Helmbold, Lois Rita. *Beyond the Family Economy: Black and White Working-Class Women during the Great Depression.*
31. Hine, Darlene Clark. *The Ethel Johns Report: Black Women in the Nursing Profession, 1925.*
32. Hine, Darlene Clark. *From Hospital to College: Black Nurse Leaders and the Rise of Collegiate Nursing Schools.*
33. Hine, Darlene Clark. *Mabel K. Staupers and the Integration of Black Nurses into the Armed Forces.*
34. Hine, Darlene Clark. *The Call That Never Came: Black Women Nurses and World War I, An Historical Note.*

Volumes 5-8, continued

35. Hine, Darlene Clark. *'They Shall Mount Up with Wings as Eagles': Historical Images of Black Nurses, 1890-1950.*
36. Hull, Gloria T. *Alice Dunbar-Nelson: Delaware Writer and Woman of Affairs.*
37. Hunter, Tera. *The Correct Thing: Charlotte Hawkins Brown and the Palmer Institute.*
38. Jacobs, Sylvia M. *'Say Africa When You Pray': The Activities of Early Black Baptist Women Missionaries Among Liberian Women and Children.*
39. Jacobs, Sylvia M. *Afro-American Women Missionaries Confront the African Way of Life.*
40. Jacobs, Sylvia M. *Their 'Special Mission': Afro-American Women as Missionaries to the Congo, 1894-1937.*
41. Janiewski, Dolores. *Seeking 'a New Day and a New Way': Black Women and Unions in the Southern Tobacco Industry.*
42. Janiewski, Dolores. *Sisters Under Their Skins: Southern Working Women, 1880-1950.*
43. Jones, Beverly W. *Race, Sex and Class:Black Female Tobacco Workers in Durham, North Carolina, 1920-1940, and the Development of Female Consciousness.*
44. Kendrick, Ruby M. *'They Also Serve': The National Association of Colored Women, Inc., 1895-1954.*
45. Lee, Don L. *The Achievement of Gwendolyn Brooks.*
46. Leffall, Dolores C. and Janet L. Sims. *Mary McLeod Bethune—The Educator; Also Including a Selected Annotated Bibliography.*
47. Lerner, Gerda. *Early Community Work of Black Club Women.*
48. Matthews, Mark D. *'Our Women and What They Think,' Amy Jacques Garvey and the Negro World.*
49. McDowell, Deborah E. *The Neglected Dimension of Jessie Redmon Fauset.*
50. McDowell, Margaret B. *The Black Woman As Artist and Critic: Four Versions.*
51. Nerverdon-Morton, Cynthia. *Self-Help Programs as Educative Activities of Black Women in the South, 1895-1925: Focus on Four Key Areas.*
52. Newman, Debra L. *Black Women Workers in the Twentieth Century.*
53. O'Dell, J. H. *Life in Mississippi: An Interview With Fannie Lou Hamer.*
54. Parks, Rosa. *Interview.*
55. Peebles-Wilkins, Wilma. *Black Women and American Social Welfare: The Life of Fredericka Douglass Sprague Perry.*
56. Pleck, Elizabeth H. *A Mother's Wages: Income Earning Among Married Italian and Black Women, 1896-1911.*
57. Porter, Dorothy B. *Maria Louise Baldwin, 1856-1922.*
58. Ross, B. Joyce. *Mary McLeod Bethune and the National Youth Adminstration: A Case Study of Power Relationships in the Black Cabinet of Franklin D. Roosevelt.*
59. Saunders, Deloris M. *Changes in the Status of Women During The Quarter Century (1955-1980).*
60. Seraile, William. *Henrietta Vinton Davis and the Garvey Movement.*
61. Smith, Elaine M. *Mary McLeod Bethune and the National Youth Administration.*
62. Smith, Sandra N. and Earle H. West. *Charlotte Hawkins Brown.*
63. Stetson, Erlene. *Black Feminism in Indiana, 1893-1933.*
64. Still, Judith Anne. *Carrie Still Shepperson: The Hollows of Her Footsteps.*
65. Terborg-Penn, Rosalyn. *Discontented Black Feminists: Prelude and Postscript to the Passage of the Nineteenth Amendment.*
66. Trigg, Eula S. *Washington, D.C. Chapter—Links, Incorporated: Friendship and Service.*
67. Tucker, Susan. *A Complex Bond: Southern Black Domestic Workers and Their White Employers.*

Volumes 5-8, continued

68. Woods, Sylvia. *You Have to Fight for Freedom.*
69. Woodson, Carter G. *The Negro Washerwoman: A Vanishing Figure.*
70. Yancy, Dorothy C. *Dorothy Bolden, Organizer of Domestic Workers: She Was Born Poor But She Would Not Bow Down.*

Vols. 9-10. BLACK WOMEN'S HISTORY: THEORY AND PRACTICE, Edited with a Preface by Darlene Clark Hine

1. Aldridge, Delores. *Black Women in the Economic Marketplace: A Battle Unfinished.*
2. Allen, Walter R. *Family Roles, Occupational Statuses, and Achievement Orientations Among Black Women in the United States.*
3. Allen, Walter R. *The Social and Economic Statuses of Black Women in the United States.*
4. Armitage, Susan, Theresa Banfield, and Sarah Jacobus. *Black Women and Their Communities in Colorado.*
5. Biola, Heather. *The Black Washerwoman in Southern Tradition.*
6. Bracey, John H., Jr. *Afro-American Women: A Brief Guide to Writings from Historical and Feminist Perspectives.*
7. Brown, Minnie Miller. *Black Women in American Agriculture.*
8. Collier-Thomas, Bettye. *The Impact of Black Women in Education: An Historical Overview.*
9. Dickson, Lynda F. *Toward a Broader Angle of Vision in Uncovering Women's History: Black Women's Clubs Revisited.*
10. Dill, Bonnie Thornton. *Race, Class, and Gender: Prospects for an All-Inclusive Sisterhood.*
11. Dill, Bonnie Thornton. *The Dialectics of Black Womanhood.*
12. Fox-Genovese, Elizabeth. *To Write My Self: The Autobiographies of Afro-American Women.*
13. Higginbotham, Evelyn Brooks. *Beyond the Sound of Silence: Afro-American Women in History.*
14. Hine, Darlene Clark. *An Angle of Vision: Black Women and the United States Constitution, 1787-1987.*
15. Hine, Darlene Clark. *To Be Gifted, Female, and Black.*
16. Hine, Darlene Clark. *Opportunity and Fulfillment: Sex, Race, and Class in Health Care Education.*
17. Hine, Darlene Clark. *Lifting the Veil, Shattering the Silence: Black Women's History in Slavery and Freedom.*
18. Jackson, Jacquelyne Johnson. *A Partial Bibliography on or Related to Black Women.*
19. Katz, Maude White. *The Negro Woman and the Law.*
20. Katz, Maude White. *She Who Would Be Free—Resistance.*
21. King, Deborah K. *Multiple Jeopardy, Multiple Consciousness: The Context of a Black Feminist Ideology.*
22. Ladner, Joyce A. *Racism and Tradition: Black Womanhood in Historical Perspective.*
23. Lewis, Diane K. *A Response to Inequality: Black Women, Racism, and Sexism.*
24. Marable, Manning. *Groundings with my Sisters: Patriarchy and the Exploitation of Black Women.*
25. Palmer, Phyllis Marynick. *White Women/Black Women: The Dualism of Female Identity and Experience in the United States.*
26. Patterson, Tiffany R. *Toward a Black Feminist Analysis: Recent Works by Black Women Scholars.*

Volumes 9-10, continued

27. Reagon, Bernice Johnson. *My Black Mothers and Sisters, or On Beginning A Cultural Autobiography.*
28. Reagon, Bernice Johnson. *African Diaspora Women: The Making of Cultural Workers.*
29. Rector, Theresa A. *Black Nuns as Educators.*
30. Render, Sylvia Lyons. *Afro-American Women: The Outstanding and the Obscure.*
31. Scales-Trent, Judy. *Black Women and the Constitution: Finding Our Place, Asserting Our Rights.*
32. Shockley, Ann Allen. *The Negro Woman in Retrospect: Blueprint for the Future.*
33. Smith, Eleanor. *Historical Relationships between Black and White Women.*
34. Snorgrass, J. William. *Pioneer Black Women Journalists from 1850s to the 1950s.*
35. Strong, Augusta. *Negro Women in Freedom's Battles.*
36. Terborg-Penn, Rosalyn. *Historical Treatment of Afro-Americans in the Woman's Movement, 1900-1920: A Bibliographical Essay.*
37. Terborg-Penn, Rosalyn. *Teaching the History of Black Women: A Bibliographical Essay.*
38. Thornbrough, Emma Lou. *The History of Black Women in Indiana.*
39. Walker, Juliet E. K. *The Afro-American Woman: Who Was She?*
40. Yellin, Jean Fagan. *Afro-American Women 1800-1910: A Selected Bibliography.*

Vol. 11. Daughters of Sorrow: Attitudes Toward Black Women, 1880-1920, by Beverly Guy-Sheftall

Vol. 12. Jane Edna Hunter: A Case Study of Black Leadership, 1910-1950, by Adrienne Lash Jones; Preface by Darlene Clark Hine

Vol. 13. Quest for Equality: The Life and Writings of Mary Eliza Church Terrell, 1863-1954, by Beverly Washington Jones
including Mary Church Terrell's selected essays:

1. *Announcement* [of NACW].
2. *First Presidential Address to the National Association of Colored Women.*
3. *The Duty of the National Association of Colored Women to the Race.*
4. *What Role is the Educated Negro Woman to Play in the Uplifting of Her Race?*
5. *Graduates and Former Students of Washington Colored High School.*
6. *Lynching from a Negro's Point of View.*
7. *The Progress of Colored Women.*
8. *The International Congress of Women.*
9. *Samuel Coleridge-Taylor.*
10. *Service Which Should Be Rendered The South.*
11. *The Mission of Meddlers.*
12. *Paul Laurence Dunbar.*
13. *Susan B. Anthony.*
14. *A Plea for the White South By A Colored Woman.*
15. *Peonage in United States: The Convict Lease System and Chain Gangs.*
16. *The Disbanding of the Colored Soldier.*
17. *What it Means to be Colored in the Capital of the United States.*
18. *A Sketch of Mingo Saunders.*
19. *An Interview with W.T. Stead on the Race Problem.*
20. *The Justice of Woman Suffrage.*
21. *Phyllis Wheatley, An African Genius.*
22. *The History of the Club Women's Movement.*
23. *Needed: Women Lawyers.*
24. *Sara W. Brown.*
25. *I Remember Frederick Douglass.*

Vol. 14. To Better Our World: Black Women in Organized Reform, 1890-1920, by Dorothy Salem

Vol. 15. Ida B. Wells-Barnett: An Exploratory Study of an American Black Woman, 1893-1930, by Mildred Thompson

including Ida B. Wells-Barnett's Selected Essays

1. *Afro-Americans and Africa.*
2. *Lynch Law in All Its Phases.*
3. *The Reason Why the Colored American is not in the World's Columbian Exposition.* Chapter IV. *Lynch Law*, by Ida B. Wells Chapter VI. *The Reason Why*, by F.L. Barnett
4. *Two Christmas Days: A Holiday Story.*
5. *Lynch Law in America.*
6. *The Negro's Case in Equity.*
7. *Lynching and the Excuse for It.*
8. *Booker T. Washington and His Critics.*
9. *Lynching, Our National Crime.*
10. *How Enfranchisement Stops Lynchings.*
11. *Our Country's Lynching Record.*

Vol. 16. Women in the Civil Rights Movement: Trailblazers and Torchbearers, 1941-1965

Edited by Vicki Crawford, Jacqueline A. Rouse, Barbara Woods; Associate Editors: Broadus Butler, Marymal Dryden, and Melissa Walker

1. Black, Allida. *A Reluctant but Persistent Warrior: Eleanor Roosevelt and the Early Civil Rights Movement*
2. Brock, Annette K. *Gloria Richardson and the Cambridge Movement*
3. Burks, Mary Fair. *Trailblazers: Women in the Montgomery Bus Boycott.*
4. Cochrane, Sharlene Voogd. *'And the Pressure Never Let Up': Black Women, White Women, and the Boston YWCA, 1918-1948.*
5. Crawford, Vicki. *Beyond the Human Self: Grassroots Activists in the Mississippi Civil Rights Movement.*
6. Grant, Jacquelyn. *Civil Rights Women: A Source for Doing Womanist Theology.*
7. Knotts, Alice G. *Methodist Women Integrate Schools and Housing, 1952-1959.*
8. Langston, Donna. *The Women of Highlander.*
9. Locke, Mamie E. *Is This America: Fannie Lou Hamer and the Mississippi Freedom Democratic Party.*
10. McFadden, Grace Jordan. *Septima Clark.*
11. Mueller, Carol. *Ella Baker and the Origins of 'Participatory Democracy.'*
12. Myrick-Harris, Clarissa. *Behind the Scenes: Doris Derby, Denise Nicholas, and the Free Southern Theater.*
13. Oldendorf, Sandra. *The South Carolina Sea Island Citizenship Schools.*
14. Payne, Charles. *Men Led, But Women Organized: Movement Participation of Women in the Mississippi Delta.*
15. Reagon, Bernice Johnson. *Women as Culture Carriers in the Civil Rights Movement: Fannie Lou Hamer.*
16. Standley, Anne. *The Role of Black Women in the Civil Rights Movement.*
17. Woods, Barbara. Modjeska Simkins and the South Carolina Conference of the NAACP.

Author Index

Boldface indicates volume numbers and roman
indicates article numbers within volumes.

Akers, Charles W., 1-4:1
Aldridge, Delores, 9-10:1
Alexander, Adele L., 1-4:2
Allen, Walter R., 9-10:2, 3
Anderson, Karen T., 5-8:2
Anderson, Kathie R., 5-8:3
Aptheker, Bettina, 1-4:3
Armitage, Susan, 9-10:4
Axelson, Diana E., 1-4:4

Banfield, Theresa, 9-10:4
Berkeley, Kathleen C., 1-4:5
Berlin,Ira, 1-4:6
Biola, Heather, 9-10:5
Black, Allida, 16:1
Blackburn, George, 1-4:7
Blackwelder, Julia Kirk, 5-8:4, 5
Bogin, Ruth, 1-4:8
Bracey, John H., Jr., 9-10:6
Brady, Marilyn Dell, 5-8:6, 7
Breen, William J., 5-8:8
Brock, Annette K., 16:2
Brooks, Evelyn, 1-4:9, 5-8:9
Brown, Elsa Barkley, 5-8:10
Brown, Minnie Miller, 9-10:7
Bryan, Violet H., 5-8:11
Burks, Mary Fair, 16:3
Burnham, Dorothy, 1-4:10
Butler, Broadus (ed.), 16
Bynum, Victoria, 1-4:11

Cantarow, Ellen, 5-8:12
Carby, Hazel V., 5-8:13
Chateauvert, Melinda, 5-8:14
Clark-Lewis, Elizabeth, 5-8:15
Clinton, Catherine, 1-4:12
Cochrane, Sharlene Voogd, 16:4
Cody, Cheryll Ann, 1-4:13
Cole, Johnnetta, 1-4:14
Coleman, Willi, 5-8:16

Collier-Thomas, Bettye, 9-10:8
Conrad, Earl, 1-4:15
Crawford, Vicki, 16:5
Crawford, Vicki (ed.), 16
Cunningham, Constance A., 1-4:16

Dahlin, Michael R., 1-4:69
Davis, Angela, 1-4:17
de Graaf, Lawrence B., 1-4:18
Dickson, Lynda F., 9-10:9
Dill, Bonnie Thornton, 9-10:10, 11
Dodson, Jualynne, 1-4:19
Dorsey, Carolyn A., 1-4:20, 21
Dryden, Marymal (ed.), 16

Ergood, Bruce, 5-8:17

Farley, Ena L., 5-8:18
Farnham, Christie, 1-4:22
Feinman, Clarice, 5-8:19
Ferguson, Earline Rae, 5-8:20
Fish, Beverly, 1-4:23
Ford, Beverly O., 5-8:21
Foster, Frances Smith, 1-4:24
Fox-Genovese, Elizabeth, 1-4:25, 9-10:12
Fry, Gladys-Marie, 1-4:26

Gilkes, Cheryl Townsend, 5-8:22, 23, 24
Goldin, Claudia, 1-4:27
Goodson, Martia G., 1-4:28, 29
Grant, Jacquelyn, 16:6
Gregory, Chester W., 1-4:30
Griggs, A. C., 1-4:31
Gundersen, Joan R., 1-4:32
Gunn, Arthur C., 5-8:25
Gutman, Herbert G., 1-4:33
Guzman, Jessie P., 5-8:26
Gwin, Minrose C., 1-4:34

Hanchett, Catherine M., 1-4:35

Harley, Sharon, **5-8**:27, 28
Harris, William, **1-4**:36
Hartgrove, W. B., **1-4**:37
Hartigan, Lynda R., **1-4**:38
Haynes, Elizabeth Ross, **5-8**:29
Helmbold, Lois Rita, **5-8**:30
Higginbotham, Evelyn Brooks, **9-10**:13
Hine, Darlene Clark, **1-4**:39, 40; **5-8**:31, 32, 33, 34, 35; **9-10**:14, 15, 16, 17
Horton, James Oliver, **1-4**:41
Hull, Gloria T., **5-8**:36
Hunter, Tera, **5-8**:37

Jackson, Jacquelyne Johnson, **9-10**:18
Jacobs, Sylvia M., **1-4**:42; **5-8**:38, 39, 40
Jacobus, Sarah, **9-10**:4
Janiewski, Dolores, **5-8**:41, 42
Johnson, Michael P., **1-4**:43
Jones, Beverly W., **5-8**:43
Jones, Jacqueline, **1-4**:44

Katz, Maude White, **9-10**:19, 20
Kendrick, Ruby M., **5-8**:44
Kennan, Clara B., **1-4**:45
King, Deborah K., **9-10**:21
Knotts, Alice G., **16**:7
Kulikoff, Alan, **1-4**:46

Ladner, Joyce A., **9-10**:22
Langston, Donna, **16**:8
Lawson, Ellen N., **1-4**:47, 48
Leashore, Bogart R., **1-4**:49
Lebsock, Suzanne, **1-4**:50
Lee, Don L., **5-8**:45
Leffall, Dolores C., **5-8**:46
Lerner, Gerda, **5-8**:47
Lewis, Diane K., **9-10**:23
Locke, Mamie, **16**:9

Mabee, Carleton, **1-4**:51
Marable, Manning, **9-10**:24
Massa, Ann, **1-4**:52
Matson, R. Lynn, **1-4**:53
Matthews, Jean, **1-4**:54
Matthews, Mark D., **5-8**:48
McDowell, Deborah E., **5-8**:49
McDowell, Margaret B., **5-8**:50
McFadden, Grace Jordan, **16**:10
Merrell, Marlene, **1-4**:48
Miller, Steven F., **1-4**:6
Mills, Gary B., **1-4**:55

Moses, Wilson Jeremiah, **1-4**:56
Mueller, Carol, **16**:11
Myrick-Harris, Clarissa, **16**:12

Nerverdon-Morton, Cynthia, **5-8**:51
Newman, Debra L., **1-4**:57; **5-8**:52

O'Dell, J. H., **5-8**:53
O'Malley, Susan Gushee, **5-8**:12
Obitko, Mary Ellen, **1-4**:58
Oden, Gloria C., **1-4**:59
Oldendorf, Sandra, **16**:13

Palmer, Phyllis Marynick, **9-10**:25
Parkhurst, Jessie W., **1-4**:60
Parks, Rosa, **5-8**:54
Patterson, Tiffany R., **9-10**:26
Payne, Charles, **16**:14
Peebles-Wilkins, Wilma, **5-8**:55
Perkins, Linda M., **1-4**:61, 62, 63, 64
Pleck, Elizabeth H., **1-4**:65; **5-8**:56
Porter, Dorothy B., **1-4**:66; **5-8**:57

Quarles, Benjamin, **1-4**:67

Reagon, Bernice Johnson, **9-10**:27, 28; **16**:15
Rector, Theresa A., **9-10**:29
Reiff, Janice L., **1-4**:69
Render, Sylvia Lyons, **9-10**:30
Ricards, Sherman L., **1-4**:7
Riley, Glenda, **1-4**:68
Ross, B. Joyce, **5-8**:58
Rouse, Jacqueline A. (ed.), **16**
Rowland, Leslie S., **1-4**:6

Saunders, Deloris M., **5-8**:59
Scales-Trent, Judy, **9-10**:31
Schafer, Judith K., **1-4**:70
Sealander, Judith, **1-4**:71
Seraile, William, **1-4**:72; **5-8**:60
Shammas, Carole, **1-4**:73
Shockley, Ann Allen, **9-10**:32
Silverman, Jason H., **1-4**:74
Sims, Janet L., **5-8**:46
Sloan, Patricia E., **1-4**:75
Smith, Daniel Scott, **1-4**:69
Smith, Elaine M., **5-8**:61
Smith, Eleanor, **9-10**:33
Smith, Sandra N., **5-8**:62
Snorgrass, J. William, **9-10**:34

Soderlund, Jean R., 1-4:76
Standley, Anne, 16:16
Sterling, Dorothy, 1-4:77
Stetson, Erlene, 5-8:63
Still, Judith Anne, 5-8:64
Strong, Augusta, 9-10:35
Sumler-Lewis, Janice, 1-4:78
Tate, Claudia, 1-4:79
Terborg-Penn, Rosalyn, 1-4:80; 5-8:65;
    9-10:36, 37
Terrell, Mary Church, 13
Thompson, Priscilla, 1-4:81
Thornbrough, Emma Lou, 9-10:38
Trigg, Eula S., 5-8:66
Tucker, David M., 1-4:82
Tucker, Susan, 5-8:67

Vacha, John E., 1-4:83

Wade-Gayles, Gloria, 1-4:84
Walker, Juliet E. K., 9-10:39
Walker, Melissa (ed.), 16
Wells-Barnett, Ida B., 15
West, Earle H., 5-8:62
White, Deborah G., 1-4:85
Woods, Barbara, 16:17
Woods, Barbara (ed.), 16
Woods, Sylvia, 5-8:68
Woodson, Carter G., 5-8:69

Yancy, Dorothy C., 5-8:70
Yellin, Jean Fagan, 9-10:40

Subject Index

Boldface indicates volume numbers and roman indicates article numbers within volumes.

Africa, **1-4**:42; **5-8**:38, 39, 40; **15**:1
agriculture—black women in, **9-10**:7
AME Church, **1-4**:19
American Missionary Association, **1-4**:62
Anthony, Susan B., **13**:13
anti-lynching movement, **1-4**:82, **13**:6, **15**:2, 3, 5, 7, 9, 10, 11
anti-slavery movement, **1-4**:1, 8, 78, 82; **15**:2, 3, 5, 7, 9, 10, 11
armed forces, **5-8**:33; **13**:16, 18
artists, **1-4**:38; **9-10**:15
Atlanta, **1-4**:36; **5-8**:4, 5
autobiography, **1-4**:24, 34; **9-10**:12

Bagby, Sara Lucy, **1-4**:83
Baker, Ella, **5-8**:12; **16**:11
Baldwin, Maria Louise, **5-8**:57
Baptist church, **1-4**:9
Bethune, Mary McLeod, **5-8**:46, 58, 61
bibliography, **9-10**:6, 18, 26, 36, 37, 40
Black Mammy role, **1-4**:60
Black Feminist ideology, **9-10**:21
Blackwell, Unita, **16**:5
blues (women's), **5-8**:13
Bolden, Dorothy, **5-8**:70
Boston, **1-4**:1, 65; **16**:4
Brooks, Gwendolyn, **5-8**:45
Brown, Sara W., **13**:24
Brown, Charlotte Hawkins, **5-8**:37, 62
Brownsville affair, **13**:16, **13**:18
Burks, Mary Fair, **16**:3
Burroughs, Nannie Helen, **5-8**:9

Cambridge, Maryland, **16**:2
Charleston, South Carolina, **1-4**:7
citizenship schools, **16**:8; **16**:13
civil rights movement, **5-8**:12, 53, 54; **16**
Clark, Septima, **16**:8, **16**:10, **16**:13
Coincoin, **1-4**:55

Coleridge-Taylor, Samuel, **13**:9
colonial period, **1-4**:30, 32, 46, 57, 76
Colorado, **9-10**:4
community workers, **5-8**:23, 24, 55
Constitution (United States), **9-10**:14, 31
convict lease system, **13**:15
Cooper, Anna Julia, **5-8**:14
Coppin, Fanny Jackson, **1-4**:61
Cult of True Womanhood, **1-4**:63

Davidson, Olivia A., **1-4**:20, 21
Davis, Henrietta Vinton, **5-8**:60
Depression (the), **5-8**:4, 30
Derby, Doris, **16**:12
Devine, Annie Bell Robinson, **16**:5
domestic workers, **1-4**:49; **5-8**:15, 29, 67
Douglass, Anna Murray, **9-10**:30
Douglass, Frederick, **13**:25
Dunbar, Paul Laurence, **13**:12
Dunbar-Nelson, Alice, **5-8**:36

Early, Sarah Woodson, **1-4**:47
Edmondson, Mary and Emily, **1-4**:35
education, **1-4**:31, 45, 48, 61, 62, 63, 64, 75; **5-8**:14, 27, 37, 46, 57, 62, 64; **9-10**:8, 16, 29, 37
employment, **1-4**:27, 36, 49, 69, 73; **5-8**:2, 4, 5, 15, 23, 29, 30, 41, 42, 43, 52, 56, 68, 67, 70; **9-10**:1, 2, 3
Ethel Johns Report, **5-8**:31

family life, **1-4**:6, 7, 13, 17, 22, 65, 36, 44, 46, 50, 69; **5-8**:21, 30, 56; **9-10**:2, 3, 11, 22
Fauset, Jessie Redmon, **5-8**:49
Female Protection Society, **5-8**:17
Fischer, Ruth Anna, **9-10**:30
Florence, Virginia Proctor Powell, **5-8**:25
Forten, Charlotte L., **1-4**:59

Forten-Purvis women, 1-4:78
Free Southern Theater, 16:12
Fugitive Slave Law, 1-4:83

Garrett, Thomas, 1-4:81
Garvey, Amy Jacques, 5-8:48
Garvey, Marcus, 5-8:60
gender conventions, 1-4:41
girls' clubs, 5-8:7

Hamer, Fannie Lou, 5-8:53; 16:9, 15
Highlander Folk School, 16:8; 16:13
history (black women in), 9-10:13, 17, 37, 39
Hopkins, Pauline, 1-4:79
Horton, Zilphia, 16:8
Hudson, Winson, 16:5
Hunt, Adella, 1-4:2
Hunter, Jane Edna, 12

Independent Order of Saint Luke, 5-8:10
Indiana, 5-8:63; 9-10:38
Indianapolis, Indiana, 5-8:20
infanticide, 1-4:43
International Congress of Women (1904), 13:8

Johns, Ethel, 5-8:31
Joseph-Gaudet, Frances, 5-8:11
journalists, 1-4:84; 5-8:3; 9-10:34

Kansas, 5-8:6, 7

Laney, Lucy Craft, 1-4:31
lawyers, 1-4:3; 13:23
League of Women for Community Service, 5-8:18
legal system, 1-4:11, 70; 9-10:14, 19, 31; 13:15; 13:23, 15:6
Lewis, Edmonia, 1-4:38
librarians, 5-8:25
Links, 5-8:66
literature, 1-4:24, 34, 53, 79; 5-8:36, 49, 45, 50; 9-10:12, 15
Little Rock, Arkansas, 1-4:45
Lorde, Audre, 5-8:50
Louisiana, 1-4:70
lynching (see anti-lynching movement)

mammy role, 1-4:60
Maryland, 1-4:80; 16:2

medical schools, 9-10:16
medical experimentation, 1-4:4
Memphis, Tennessee, 1-4:82
Methodist church, 16:7
missionaries, 1-4:42; 5-8:38, 39, 40
Mississippi Freedom Democratic Party, 16:9
Mississippi, 16:5, 14
Montgomery bus boycott, 5-8:54; 16:3
Moore, Maria Louise, 1-4:37
Morrison, Toni, 5-8:50
mutual aid societies, 5-8:17,

NAACP, 16:17
National Association of Colored Women, 5-8:44; 13:1, 2, 3, 22
National Youth Administration, 5-8:58, 61
New York City, 5-8:19
New Orleans, 5-8:5
newspapers—treatment of black women, 1-4:71
Nicholas, Denise, 16:12
nuns (black), 9-10:29
nursing, 1-4:3, 75; 5-8:31, 32, 33, 34, 35
nursing schools, 1-4:75; 5-8:31, 32; 9-10:16

Oberlin College, 1-4:48

Parks, Rosa, 5-8:54; 16:3
patriarchy, 9-10:24
Pennsylvania, 1-4:57, 76
Perry, Fredericka Douglass Sprague, 5-8:55
physicians, 1-4:3, 39, 72
Powers, Hariett, 1-4:26
prisoners, 5-8:19
Purvis-Forten women, 1-4:78

quilting, 1-4:26

racism, 9-10:23
Reagon, Bernice Johnson, 9-10:27
religion, 1-4:9, 19, 42; 5-8:9, 22, 38, 39, 40; 16:6, 7
Remond, Sarah Parker, 1-4:8, 66
Richards, Fannie M., 1-4:37
Richardson, Gloria, 16:2
Robinson, Bernice, 16:8, 16:13
Robinson, Jo Ann, 16:3
Roosevelt, Eleanor, 16:1

San Antonio, 5-8:5
Saunders, Mingo, 13:18

segregated transportation protests, **5-8**:16
self-help programs, **5-8**:51
sexism, **9-10**:23
Shadd, Mary Ann, 74
Shepperson, Carrie Still, **5-8**:64
Simkins, Modjeska, **16**:17
sisterhood, **9-10**:10
slave medicine, **1-4**:28
Slave Narrative Collection, **1-4**:29
slavery, **1-4**:4, 10, 12, 13, 14, 17, 25, 22, 30, 32, 33, 34, 40, 43, 44, 46, 58, 73, 85
social welfare, **1-4**:5
South (the), **13**:10, 14
Staupers, Mabel K., **5-8**:33
Stead, W.T., **13**:19
Stephens, Charlotte Andrews, **1-4**:45
Steward, Susan McKinney, **1-4**:72
suffrage, **5-8**:1, 65; **9-10**:36; **13**:20
Sun Light Society, **5-8**:17

Terrell, Mary Church, **9-10**:30; **13**
theology, **16**:6
Thompson, Era Bell, **5-8**:3
Truth, Sojourner, **1-4**:23, 51
tuberculosis work, **5-8**:20
Tubman, Harriet, **1-4**:15, 67, 81

underground railroad, **1-4**:81
union organizing, **5-8**:68, 70
Universal Negro Improvement Association, **5-8**:48, 60

Virginia, **1-4**:73

Walker, Alice, **5-8**:50
Walker, Maggie Lena, **5-8**:10
Walker, Margaret, **5-8**:50
washerwoman, **5-8**:69; **9-10**:5
Washington, Booker T., **15**:8
Washington, D.C., **5-8**:15, 27, 28, 66; **13**:17
Washington (D.C.) Colored High School, **13**:5
Washington, Olivia Davidson, **1-4**:20, 21
welfare system, **5-8**:21
Wells-Barnett, Ida B., **1-4**:82; **15**
West—black women in, **1-4**:18, 68
Wheatley, Phillis, **1-4**:1, 53; **13**:21
white women, **9-10**:25, 33

women's clubs, **1-4**:56; **5-8**:6, 7, 13, 20, 44, 47; **9-10**:9; **13**:1, 2, 3, 22
women's suffrage, **5-8**:1, 65; **9-10**:36; **13**:20
Woods, Sylvia, **5-8**:68
World War I, **5-8**:8, 34
World War II, **5-8**:2
World's Columbian Exposition, **1-4**:52; **15**:3

YWCA, **16**:4